CHINA CLIPPER

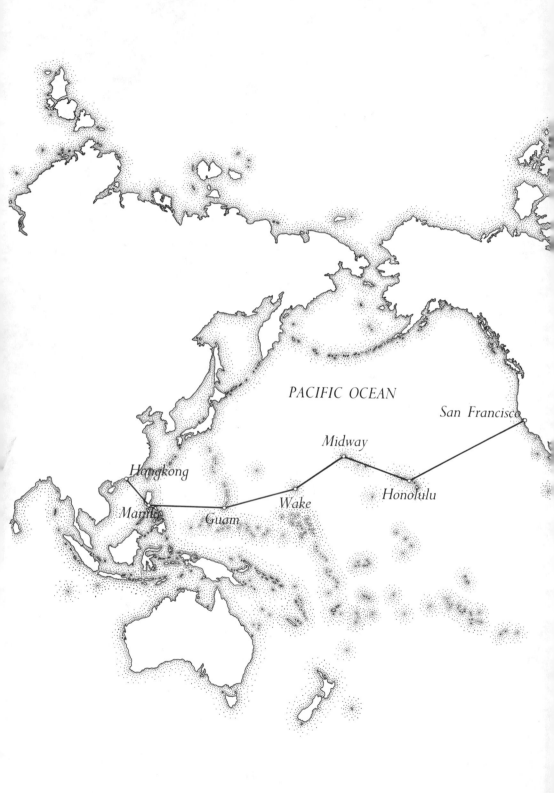

PACIFIC OCEAN

San Francisco

Midway

Honolulu

Hongkong

Manila
Guam
Wake

CHINA CLIPPER

The Age of
the Great Flying Boats

Robert L. Gandt

NAVAL INSTITUTE PRESS • Annapolis, Maryland

© 1991
by the United States Naval Institute
Annapolis, Maryland

LIBRARY OF CONGRESS CATALOGING-IN-PUBLICATION DATA

Gandt, Robert L.
    China clipper : the age of the great flying boats / by Robert
Gandt.
        p.   cm.
    Includes bibliographical references and index.
    ISBN 0-87021-209-5
    1. Seaplanes—History.   I. Title.
    TL684.2.G36   1991
629.133'347—dc20   91-15386

Printed in the United States of America on acid-free paper ⊗

04 03 02 01 00 99   11 10 9 8 7 6 5

All line drawings by J. P. Wood. Frontispiece map by William Clipson.

To Ruth Gandt
with love

Contents

Preface   *ix*

1.   Musick   *1*

2.   Curtiss and Company   *4*

3.   Extended Range   *11*

4.   Boats for Hire   *18*

5.   Trippe   *23*

6.   NYRBA   *29*

7.   Sikorsky   *39*

8.   Teutonic Ambitions   *46*

9.   The Latins   *52*

10.   The Flying Forest   *60*

11.   The Next Step   *67*

12.   Pacific   *72*

13.   Wings of Empire   *82*

14.   The French Flair   *86*

15.   Martin   94

16.   *China Clipper*   99

17.   Orient Express   *106*

18.   Losses   *112*

19.   The Right Vehicle   *119*

20.   Boats of the Reich   *124*

21.   American Export Airlines   *128*

22.   Boeing   *134*

23.   War Day   *142*

24.   In Service   *152*

25.   Requiem for the Big Boats   *159*

26.   Dinosaurs and Might-Have-Beens   *167*

       Appendix A. Line Drawings   *173*

       Appendix B. Charts   *188*

       Notes   *191*

       Sources   *205*

       Index   *209*

Preface

Why the Flying Boat?

By the third decade of powered flight, when aeronautical technology had evolved to the contemplation of over-ocean travel, not one major civil airport yet possessed a long, flat, paved surface sufficient to accommodate the weight of an oceangoing transport airplane. Nor was any airline or sponsoring government inclined to construct such a surface. A more expedient option seemed available—the two-thirds of the planet that happened to be already flat, unobstructed, and, incidentally, covered with water.

Thus arrived the age of the great flying boats. It lasted sixteen years, commencing with the news of the Dornier Do X project and ending with the postwar scuttling of the Boeing boats. This brief episode occurred at a crossroads in history. It was a time when the ancient rites of the sea were joined, for just a moment, with the infant craft of flight.

From the beginning, its days were numbered. Even the unlikely name—*flying boat*—was an anachronism. The hybrid craft was regarded just as its name implied—a *boat* that happened to be capable of flight.

It was never a wholly satisfactory scheme. "Neither grand pianos nor airplanes belong in sea water," quipped the critics, with justification. For airplanes, the ocean was a place of peril. Salt water ate like acid into metal components. Flotsam and submerged objects ruptured fragile duralumin hulls. Ice floes lurked like mine fields in northern waters. Giant swells turned sheltered harbors into heaving, mountainous seascapes. Boarding docks and motor launches were required to embark and deplane passengers, often in tossing seas.

These harsh realities are often blurred in latterday recountings. Histories of the flying boat, like those of the airship and steam locomotive, tend to conjure up nostalgia. Mystique substitutes for fact. Which aircraft

was the most "romantic?" The most famous? Appeared in the most
headlines? Engaged in the most spectacular flights? Carried the most
eminent passengers? Which was the fairest of them all?

Aeronautical history ought to interweave with *function*. As a prereq-
uisite to understanding, we must ask unromantic questions: What was
the aircraft's weight? Tare? Wing loading? Power-to-weight? Load-to-
tare? Range with a revenue payload? Without? When and where did it
fly?

But there is more. The pure "fact book" disregards the subtle historical
nuances of an era. In aviation history, machines are inextricably bound
to the lives of the men who construct them, fly them, deploy them,
destroy them. The account is punctuated by human pride, greed, courage,
soaring ambition, egregious folly. Soulless machines become imbued with
the passions of their flesh-and-blood builders.

People thus count for as much as machines. From the record of the
great flying boats, we ought to ask: By whom was this airplane built?
Why? By whom flown? What was it designed to do? Did it do it well?
If not, why not?

Why the flying boat?

The feel and flavor of the flying boat era were eloquently conveyed
to me during the past decade by three pioneer captains, Marius Lodeesen,
Horace Brock, and William Masland, all now deceased. Further valuable
insight was contributed by old boat captains Fran Wallace, Jim O'Neal,
Harry Beyer, Bob Ford, Al Terwilleger, Thomas Roberts, and Ken Ray-
mond, all veterans of Pan American.

Navigator/instructor E. F. "Blackie" Blackburn contributed his knowledge of celestial navigation as practiced on the flying boats.

Mr. Sergei Sikorsky kindly reviewed the text concerning his father,
Igor Sikorsky, and made available the archives of United Technologies
Corporation, which are managed by Ms. Anne Milbrooke.

The considerable resources of Pan American World Airways were
indispensable in the research for this book. For this kind assistance I
am indebted to Pan Am's Vice Preident for Corporate Communications,
Jeff Kriendler, and librarian Li Wa Chiu. Valuable materials were also
contributed by the Martin Marietta Corporation, Dornier GmbH, Lufthansa, British Airways, and the Boeing Company.

Old friend and colleague, Captain J. P. Wood, produced the excellent
line drawings and the appended graphics.

Of particular assistance with French flying boat data was Stephane Nicolaou of the Musée de l'Air et de l'Espace at Le Bourget Airport. Materials and advice about the German boats were generously given by historian Fred Gutschow of Munich, Germany. Mr. R. E. G. Davies, Curator of Air Transport at the Smithsonian Institution's National Air and Space Museum, lent frequent help and provided the recently unearthed story of the Martin M-156. A special acknowledgment is owed Dr. R. K. Smith, author and historian, for his forthright critique throughout the production of this work.

CHINA CLIPPER

Musick

Ed Musick had never wanted to be a hero. It was hard to understand, looking at him, why he had been chosen for the role. He possessed none of Lindbergh's youthful charisma. He was a slender, soft-spoken man, neither handsome nor articulate, forty-one years of age. He spoke infrequently, and then with a sparsity of description.

Musick was a pilot, which was all he had ever aspired to be. But the events of the past year had changed everything. To his own astonishment, Ed Musick had become the most famous airline pilot in the world.

It was the afternoon of 22 November 1935. The departure ceremony was scheduled for two-forty-five. The band played a Sousa march while the guest speakers mounted the platform. Behind the reviewing stand waited the great ship, her massive wings forming the backdrop for the scene. A gigantic flag was stretched across the grass, guarded by 170 boy scouts.

In the lobby of the seaplane base, Musick saw the map that someone had stapled to the wall. It was a chart of the Pacific Ocean. The inner blue expanse of the chart was mostly empty, containing only a pattern of widely scattered dots connected by a penciled line. Musick could read the names of the dots: *Hawaii*, *Midway*, *Wake*, *Guam*.

The Pacific had never been crossed by a commercial airliner. Only eleven days ago, Musick had taken delivery of the flying boat at the Glenn L. Martin factory in Middle River, Maryland. Now he was supposed to fly the new ship westward, across the widest part of the world's widest ocean. If all went well, he would fly her all the way to Asia.

There were so-called experts who said it shouldn't be done. Such an undertaking, they said, was too dangerous, at least for a commercial airline. Such stunts should be left to the military. The Pacific was too wide, too unpredictable, too filled with unknowns. The craft of aerial navigation was still too primitive, and the new radio direction finders had not yet been proven. The new flying boat, they pointed out, had never actually flown across an ocean, not even as far as Hawaii. Musick had heard all this. He quietly went ahead with his job.

Bombs and rockets were bursting overhead. Sirens wailed from boats in the bay. It was said that a hundred thousand people were lining the shores of San Francisco Bay to watch the departure. A circuslike script had been written by the airline's publicity department. There would be speeches and a ceremonial loading of mail bags, and then Musick's sailing orders would be delivered by his boss, Juan Trippe. The entire event was being broadcast by CBS and NBC and transmitted live on seven foreign networks.

Musick wore the all-black, double-breasted uniform of the Pan American pilot. There were no stripes to denote his rank. Without the white, navy-style cap and the gold wings, he might have been taken for an undertaker. People seldom noticed when Musick came into a room.

It was only when he entered the cockpit that Ed Musick seemed to grow in size. He would settle himself into the left seat, his brown eyes flicking over every gauge, instrument, knob, and lever. "Meticulous Musick" he was called. He believed in precision in everything from the knot in his tie to the tiniest details of an ocean flight.

He had a ritual. With thumb and forefinger he would straighten the creases in his trousers. He would adjust and readjust his seat until his hands reached the yoke at precisely the right angle. With a handkerchief he would clean the face of each instrument. His fingers would glide to each lever and knob, turning, setting, making fine adjustments. Not until everything was to Musick's satisfaction would he give the command, in his soft voice, "Start number one."[1]

Free of her moorings, the great ship glided out into San Francisco Bay. The four Pratt and Whitney R-1830 power plants growled in a low rumble. Behind the flying boat trailed a wake, sparkling in the autumn sunshine.

She was the largest airliner ever constructed in America. Her sleek lines were a radical departure from the wire-bound, strut-braced machines of her day. Until she was built, no transport aircraft yet existed that could carry both a payload and the vast store of fuel required to reach the distant bases of the Pacific.

"Captain Musick," said a voice on the radio, "you have your sailing orders. Cast off and depart for Manila in accordance therewith."

The band played "The Star Spangled Banner." Twenty-two aerial bombs exploded over San Francisco Bay. Ships' whistles blew, and fire hoses streamed geysers of water.

Ed Musick eased the four throttles forward. The thunder of the Pratt and Whitney engines echoed from the buildings on the shore.

The giant ship surged ahead. She was aimed between the spans of the unfinished Bay Bridge. As she swept past, onlookers read the name emblazoned on her bow: *China Clipper*.[2]

Curtiss and Company

There was something typically American about them. They were dreamers and tinkerers and adventurers—and prodigious achievers. They sprang from the same soil that produced Edison and Ford and Sperry.

It was more than coincidence that a nation like the United States would produce a Wilbur Wright and his brother, Orville. And it was inevitable that the brothers would be followed by a man like Glenn Hammond Curtiss.

Like the Wrights, Curtiss began as a builder of bicycles. His fascination with things mechanical led him into experiments with gasoline engines and then, adapting them to his cycles, the manufacture of the fastest motorcycles in the world. Typical of Curtiss, he rode the machines himself. At the Florida Speed Carnival in 1907, he set a speed record of 136.3 miles per hour over a measured mile, a record that stood for twenty years.[1]

In 1907 Curtiss became one of five members of a group called the Aerial Experiment Association. Headed by the famous inventor Dr. Alexander Graham Bell, this group dedicated itself, according to its charter, "... to get into the air by the construction of a practical aerodrome* driven by its own motive power and carrying a man."[2]

The work of the AEA was both historically significant and controversial. Since 1903 the Wright brothers had held a clear lead in the development of powered flight. But their obsessive secrecy and deter-

---

*Bell and the AEA favored "aerodrome" to label their flying machines. Not until "aerodrome" had entered usage as the name for a flying facility did the AEA reluctantly accept the more popular "aeroplane." By the end of WW I "aeroplane" was supplanted by "airplane."

mination to maintain exclusive rights to their inventions led ultimately to bitter and withering court battles with their rivals. Prominent among these were the members of the AEA and, particularly, Glenn Curtiss.[3]

Curtiss's contribution to the AEA was that of practicality. Lacking the formal education of his colleagues, Curtiss preferred to sketch his ideas on shop walls, measure by thumb, derive his solutions by trial and error. An innovator rather than a theoretical engineer, he was a man most comfortable in the workshop.

The AEA produced a series of aircraft, beginning with gliders. Their third aircraft, the *June Bug*, was designed by Curtiss. With this machine, at his hometown of Hammondsport, New York, Curtiss won a trophy sponsored by *Scientific American* magazine offered for the first officially observed aeroplane flight of a distance of one kilometer or greater.

Curtiss had begun to think about a seaplane. In a letter for the *AEA Bulletin* on 19 August 1908, he wrote:

> The scheme of starting a flying machine from, and landing on, the water has been on my mind for some time. It has many advantages, and I believe can be worked out. Even if a most suitable device for launching and landing on land is secured, a water craft will still be indispensable for war purposes, and if the exhibition field is to be considered, would, I believe, present greater possibilities in this line than a machine which works on land.[4]

Outfitting the *June Bug* with floats and renaming it the *Loon*, Curtiss experimented that winter on Lake Keuka, near his home at Hammondsport. The *Loon* would not fly. Additional horsepower did not help. The *Loon* could not free itself from the water.

This was Glenn Curtiss's first encounter with the matter of "unsticking" a waterborne aircraft from a smooth body of water. Before he could solve the problem, the *Loon* ruptured one of its floats and sank into the freezing water of Lake Keuka.

To a Frenchman, Henri Fabre, fell the distinction of making the first flight of an aircraft from the water. Fabre, who was the scion of a wealthy shipping family, had already produced one non-flying aircraft. In 1910 he completed construction of a machine he called *Hydravion*. *Hydravion*'s design owed much to the Wrights: It was a biplane with a forward-mounted elevator, using a system of wing warping for roll control.

On 28 March 1910, after a previous unsuccessful attempt, he flew *Hydravion* from the water at La Mède, near Marseille, and traveled 1,640 feet before returning to the water.[5]

Fabre's experiments were generally successful, although the fragile *Hydravion* had severe limitations and never became a truly practical seaplane.

With a successor to the *June Bug* named the *Golden Flier*, Glenn Curtiss had set the earliest aviation records during the Rheims aviation meet in France in 1909, establishing himself as the premier American aviator. With this machine, he resumed extensive testing of float configurations.

"Unsticking"—the vexing matter of water suction around the pontoons—still eluded him. Fleeing the bitter cold of upstate New York, Curtiss established a winter headquarters and flying school on North Island, an isolated sandy island near San Diego. Here he experimented with over fifty various float combinations.

The navy, meanwhile, concluded that they could no longer afford to ignore these events. To Curtiss's flying camp on North Island they sent an officer, Lieutenant T. G. Ellyson, to receive instruction.

"Spuds" Ellyson was a submariner by training. He possessed an engineer's analytical mind and a zeal for flying.* It was the team of Ellyson and Curtiss that launched the navy into the age of aviation.

By 1911, Ellyson and Curtiss had devised a float arrangement consisting of a pair of wide, planing "sea wing" pontoons, installed in tandem. Curtiss managed to fly this contraption from the surface of San Diego Bay. He then tinkered for the next several weeks with the design, refining it to a single, twelve-foot-long, flat-bottomed float with small cylindrical outrigger floats installed at the wingtips.

In a demonstration for the navy, he flew from North Island to the USS *Pennsylvania*, anchored in San Diego Bay. Landing alongside the battleship, Curtiss and his airplane were hoisted aboard by crane. After he had paid his respects to the captain, Curtiss had himself and his machine lowered back to the water. He took off and flew home to North Island.

This performance, as well as the successful deck launch and recovery of another Curtiss machine flown by Eugene Ely, was sufficient proof of the airplane's potential. In May of 1911, the U.S. Navy placed orders

---

*When the designation of aviators became formalized, Ellyson was designated Naval Aviator No. 1.

for two Curtiss airplanes, designated A-1 and A-2. The age of naval aviation had begun.

A week after his flight to the *Pennsylvania*, Curtiss fitted retractable wheels to the floats of his hydroaeroplane. With this configuration he demonstrated a water takeoff followed by a landing on the beach at Coronado, near San Diego. Named *Triad* because of its land, sea, and air capabilities, Curtiss's machine entered the records as the world's first amphibious airplane as well as the first aircraft equipped with retractable landing gear. That year, 1911, Curtiss was awarded the Collier Trophy for his work with the hydroaeroplane.

In January 1912 Curtiss enlarged the float of his seaplane to incorporate the cockpit into the hull. This two-seat, flat-bottomed machine, though underpowered and, like *Triad*, hampered by the "water suction" problem, thus became the first true flying boat.

The "unsticking" problem that bedeviled every builder of floatplanes was solved in typical Curtiss fashion. Back in Hammondsport in early 1912, Curtiss and Naval Constructor Holden Richardson were experimenting with the flat-bottomed flying boat on Lake Keuka. While Curtiss followed the machine about the lake studying the action of the hull on the water, he hit upon an idea. Returning to the shop, he instructed his foreman to attach two wedge-shaped blocks to the bottom of the hull. On the next flight, the flying boat lifted easily from the water. Curtiss had invented the "step," a feature that would be employed in every flying boat built from that day on.[6]

The new aircraft, called the F-boat, achieved spectacular success. Eventually powered by the new Curtiss OXX eight-cylinder, 100-horsepower engine mounted between the wings, the aircraft had a modernistic tail assembly constructed integrally with the hull. F-boats were sold to the U.S. Navy and to the army and were built under license in Britain by the S. E. Saunders firm. The F-boat also attracted civilian buyers, mainly wealthy sportsmen undaunted by the $6,000-plus price.

In 1912 Glenn Curtiss received his second successive Collier Trophy. Through his energies, the flying boat had become a practical flying machine. By late 1913 at least ten American and European builders, including the Wright brothers and a newcomer named Glenn L. Martin, were producing flying boats. It was time for the flying boat to graduate from a sporting vehicle to a vessel of commerce.

* * *

In 1913 the *London Daily Mail* stimulated Glenn Curtiss's Yankee businessman's imagination with the offer of a prize—10,000 pounds sterling (then $50,000) for the first flight across the Atlantic Ocean. The offer stipulated that the flight must be "from any point in the U.S., Canada or Newfoundland, to any point in Great Britain or Ireland, in seventy-two consecutive hours."

The Atlantic! It had been only a decade since the events at Kitty Hawk, scarcely three years since *Hydravion*'s first wobbling ascents. Flying boats and floatplanes were still capable of little more than leapfrogging from lake to pond.

That same year the American department store tycoon, Rod Wanamaker, agreed to finance the building of a Curtiss flying boat that would capture the prize.

The implications of an aircraft that could span oceans caught the attention of the U.S. Navy. After a study of Curtiss's plans, the navy detailed two officers, Lieutenant John Towers and Lieutenant (j.g.) Patrick Bellinger, to the Curtiss plant in Hammondsport.*

Wanamaker had wanted Curtiss to be the pilot of the Atlantic flight. Curtiss declined, saying that in his opinion Lieutenant Towers was the best choice for the mission. The Navy Department, however, had other plans for Towers. Their handful of qualified aviators had to be available in the event of an expected conflict in Mexico. At Wanamaker's suggestion, a British aviator, John Cyril Porte, was recruited for the Atlantic flight.

Porte was a former Royal Navy officer who had worked in England with Curtiss's licensee, White and Thompson. Medically retired from the Royal Navy in 1911, Porte had learned to fly in France and was an early devotee of the flying boat. He became caught up in the adventure of Curtiss's project, which was then called the "Transatlantic Flyer."[7] Porte's copilot was to be George Hallett, a skilled aviator and Curtiss Company mechanic.

The design of the Transatlantic Flyer evolved from a single-engine, tractor-driven machine to an aircraft of massive proportions. Given the name *America*, the flying boat's final configuration was a biplane with a streamlined hull-fuselage, powered by two Curtiss OX-5 100-horsepower engines mounted between the wings. *America*'s upper wing spanned seventy-two feet and the lower forty-six feet. Her hull was thirty-eight feet long.

*Towers was Naval Aviator No. 3. Bellinger became No. 8.

By the time of the christening at Lake Keuka on 21 June 1914, *America* was a celebrity. During flight tests, though she performed gracefully, the flying boat could not lift as much load from the water as would be required to cross the Atlantic. Further experiments were conducted, including the addition of a third engine. Several hulls were tested. A finned hull beam was installed which, combined with the power of the third engine, allowed *America* to lift some 6,203 pounds from the water— the greatest load then ever taken into the air.

Porte planned to launch the oceanic flight during the summer of 1914. His route would be a nonstop track from Trepassey Bay, Newfoundland, directly to the Bay of Horta in the Azores. Though *America*'s instrumentation was primitive by later standards, she was equipped with engine and flight instruments and provisions for celestial navigation, including a device donated by Lawrence Sperry for measuring drift. A wireless apparatus had been offered, but Curtiss decided to dispense with radio because of its weight. *America*, the world's most advanced aircraft, would carry for primary communications a cage of carrier pigeons.[8]

Curtiss's design changes on the hull and engine configuration caused postponements. Weather further delayed the departure. Finally in midsummer *America* and her sister ship, which would serve as a backup, were crated and shipped from Hammondsport to St. John's, Newfoundland. Porte announced that they would take off in early August.

On 3 August 1914, Germany declared war on France. The following day Great Britain declared war on Germany. John Porte left to rejoin the Royal Navy. There would be no transatlantic flight.

America and her sister ship finally made an Atlantic crossing—beneath tarpaulins on the deck of a freighter. As a squadron commander in England, John Porte had persuaded his superiors in the Royal Navy to acquire the aircraft for maritime patrol. It was designated the H-4. Sixty-two models of the *America* were shipped to the Royal Navy.

Dubbed the "Small America," the H-4 was replaced in 1916 by the larger H-12, called the "Large America." With engines of either 275 horsepower or 375 horsepower, the H-12 had an endurance of over six hours and could carry a four-man crew, four machine guns, and 400 pounds of bombs. Just prior to the end of the war, an even larger version appeared, designated the H-16.

Another successful flying boat that appeared near the war's end was the HS series, built for both the U.S. Navy and the Royal Navy. Smaller in scale than the "Large America," the HS mounted a single Liberty twelve-cylinder, 400-horsepower engine and was designed to meet a requirement for a flying boat that could be stowed aboard a seaplane carrier.

Even Curtiss's little F-boat went to war. Versions were employed as reconnaissance aircraft, and some 150 updated models were delivered to the U.S. Navy as flying boat trainers. In 1916 the U.S. Coast Guard received its first F-boat, thus beginning the era of Coast Guard aviation.

John Porte was posted to the Seaplane Experimental Establishment at Felixstowe, on the east coast of Britain. There he became a key figure in the development of the Curtiss designs. Porte's redesigned hull and the addition of Rolls-Royce engines resulted in a series of British-produced Curtiss derivatives called the Felixstowe flying boats.

The distinction of becoming the first U.S.–built aircraft to destroy an enemy aircraft fell to a Curtiss boat. On 14 May 1917, an RAF H-12 attacked the German Zeppelin L-22, riddling the airship with machine-gun fire. The Zeppelin crashed into the North Sea. In another action in June 1918, three Felixstowe flying boats and an H-12 engaged twelve German Brandenburg seaplanes. In the melee, the H-12 and one Felixstowe were downed. They had accounted for six German aircraft.[9]

Curtiss's civilian Transatlantic Flyer had metamorphosed into a weapon of war. But with its destructive power, the flying boat had acquired range and a lifting capability that was undreamed of when Curtiss built the *America* in 1914.

The Atlantic, like an unclaimed trophy, waited to be crossed.

3

Extended Range

Almost from the inception of manned flight, the notion of crossing the great gulf by air had titillated the imaginations of airmen. But by man's second decade of flight, flying the Atlantic still amounted to nothing more than a risky adventure.

The risks were enormous, both in lives and material. Such risks required subsidy. Glenn Curtiss, a bona fide adventurer, was also a consummate capitalist who understood subsidy. He had undertaken the *America* venture with Rod Wanamaker's money and the *Daily Mail* prize as his profit.

And then in the fifth year of the Great War, the notion of flying over the Atlantic gained a new, noncapitalistic impetus. German U-boats had turned the ocean into a killing ground. In 1917, 2,600 vessels had been lost to a U-boat fleet of only 127.[1] The submarine had evolved as a weapon of war just as dramatically as the airplane.

Despite the strides made in range and endurance, maritime patrol aircraft were still not an effective deterrent to the U-boat menace. The British concentrated their aerial antisubmarine forces around seaplane tenders and aircraft carriers, tethering their warplanes to their mother ships. The strategy had netted only minimal success. The ships and aircraft served mainly as daytime, fair-weather convoy escorts.

And then the United States entered the war. Rear Admiral David W. Taylor, chief of the navy's Bureau of Construction and Repair, wrote in a memorandum: "It seems to me the submarine menace can be abated, even if not destroyed, from the air. The ideal solution would be big flying boats . . . able to fly across the Atlantic to avoid difficulties of delivery."[2]

In the summer of 1917 Taylor issued an official requirement for a new class of flying boat. This would be a flying boat that not only could remain on station for extended periods, but was specifically designed to be ferried across the ocean.

A contract was struck with Glenn Curtiss. The new Curtiss design received the designation *NC—N* for navy, *C* for Curtiss.

The prototype, *NC-1*, made her maiden flight on 4 October 1918 at Rockaway Beach, New York. With a 126-foot wingspan and an empty weight of 12,956 pounds, the huge craft drew the attention of the world. Her flight tests had barely begun, though, when history erased her mission. On 11 November 1918, the Great War ended.

In the tumult of the next months, the plans for the NC boats went on the shelf. But in offices of the chief of naval operations aviation section, a lone voice continued to propose a mission for the NC boats. Commander John Towers, Naval Aviator Number 3 and original choice as one of the pilots on Curtiss's transatlantic venture, was the senior aviator in the navy. Towers was proposing that the NC boats become the first aircraft in history to fly the Atlantic.

In the climate of demilitarization, the idea might have been regarded as extravagant and ill-timed. But the navy—and the country—were changing. Fresh from a short but victorious foray into the Great War, the United States was brimming with patriotic fervor and a zeal to demonstrate American know-how. Though aviation had come of age during the war, the United States had yielded its early lead to the Europeans, who for four frenetic years spent their energies and national treasuries on instruments of war.

There was glory to be won. The distinction of flying a nation's flag from America to Europe would be a symbolic victory, amounting to far more than a bid for the *Daily Mail* prize money, still unclaimed since 1914. The Atlantic race was a contest of national prestige.

In the spring of 1919, NC Seaplane Division One was commissioned. Assigned as commanding officer of the unit was, appropriately, John Towers. Towers recruited his crews from the best talent of 1919 naval aviation.

In command of *NC-1* was Lieutenant Commander Patrick N. L. Bellinger, Naval Aviator Number 8. Assigned as pilot of the *NC-1* was Lieutenant Commander Marc A. Mitscher. The names of both officers would figure prominently in future naval history.

Commanding *NC-4* was Lieutenant Commander Albert C. Read. Read was a calm and competent officer, a naval aviator since 1915. His pilot was Lieutenant (j.g.) Walter Hinton, a skilled young aviator who would make history as a pioneer ocean pilot. The copilot was Lieutenant Elmer Stone, the Coast Guard's first designated aviator.

NC-3 was commanded by Towers himself, who chose as his pilot Lieutenant Commander Holden C. "Dick" Richardson, a brilliant engineer who had participated almost from the beginning in the evolution of the oceangoing flying boat. Like most of the airmen assigned to the NC Division, Richardson was a Curtiss-trained aviator.

NC-2, originally configured as a three-engined aircraft, would not make the flight. Following a hangar fire and several engine and cockpit configuration changes, she was cannibalized to outfit her sister ships. The final versions of the NC boats were powered by four 400-horsepower Liberty engines, the two center engines mounted in tandem. This pusher-puller installation eliminated much of the power asymmetry problem in the event of an engine loss in the yaw-critical aircraft. The cockpits were relocated from the center nacelle to the more practical forward fuselage station.

The aircraft commanders served as the navigators, an early naval practice that emphasized the role navigation was expected to play in the transatlantic endeavor. In addition to the pilot and navigator, each aircraft carried a relief pilot, a radio officer, an engineering officer and a mechanic.

Shortly before dusk on Friday, 16 May 1919, all three NC boats thundered across the choppy surface of Trepassey Bay and became airborne. In a loose formation they turned eastward and droned into the gathering darkness, bound for the Azores.

The Atlantic proved to be a formidable foe. Oceanic weather reporting and forecasting were a nonexistent craft in 1919. Celestial navigation, using the bubble sextant developed by a young naval officer named Richard E. Byrd, depended on a clear view of the stars and smooth air. The NC navigators depended heavily—too heavily, it turned out—on their chain of ocean-based naval vessels. The ships were supposed to emit smoke, fire star shells, train searchlights, and provide meteorological data and radio direction finding. But this method required close contact between the aircraft and their surface guardians. The primitive airborne radios had a range of only about fifteen miles.

A full moon glinted over the Atlantic. On two occasions the lumbering flying boats nearly collided in the misty gloom as the navy airmen peered downward for signs of their oceanic checkpoints. NC-4, the fastest of the boats, gradually outdistanced her sister ships and disappeared from view.

And then came the dawn. Gone were the moon and the smooth air. Gone, too, were the readily identifiable lights of the ocean stations. Fog blanketed the sea. Rain squalls battered the flying boats, and the air turned the planes into bucking, heaving monsters. In the open cockpits, the cold-soaked pilots battled to keep the unstable flying boats straight and level.

Peering into the murk from the NC-3, John Towers spotted a ship that he judged to be the USS Maddox on station 15. Using the new fix, he adjusted his course accordingly. The fix turned out to be erroneous. From then onward NC-3 was off track.

Meanwhile Pat Bellinger, in NC-1, was having troubles of his own. There had been no time to rig properly the new flying surfaces pirated from the NC-2. Now his aircraft was flying poorly. In the turbulent air the strength of two pilots was required on the controls to keep the wallowing airplane upright. With no visual reference in the turbulent clouds, the pilots were having extreme difficulty maintaining level flight.

Finally forced down to 75 feet above the waves, flying in fog, Bellinger worried about running into the 7,600-foot-high volcanic island of Pico. He made the decision to attempt a water landing and then shut down the engines in order to obtain a fix with the radio direction finder. In the heaving seas, the NC-1 slammed into a trough and lost the lower portion of her tail assembly.

For five hours Bellinger's seasick crew bailed water and transmitted S.O.S. signals. Finally the Greek ship Ionia steamed out of the murk, rescued the fliers and attempted to take the damaged flying boat in tow. In the tossing sea, however, the tow cable snapped. Soon thereafter the NC-1 was lost to the Atlantic.

John Towers, after fifteen hours' flying in the NC-3, had no knowledge of the fate of NC-1. Realizing that he was now lost, and unable to obtain any further surface sightings, he reached the same decision as Bellinger. He would land on the sea and determine his position with the radio direction finder.

But the heaving Atlantic treated NC-3 no gentler than it had the NC-1. Glancing off the crest of a huge swell, the fragile craft skipped once more, then plunged into a trough. As she shuddered to a halt, Towers already knew the worst. The hull was ruptured. The controls were gone. The center engine mount was irreparably damaged. NC-3 would fly no more.

They were only 45 miles from Flores, but considerably off the track where ships would be searching. They could hear the destroyers chattering on the radio, but they could not break in. Towers's immediate problem was to save his aircraft. The NC-3 was sinking under the weight of the water collecting in her wings. Emergency patchwork was accomplished. For nearly two days NC-3 sailed the Atlantic, tail first, crew members stationed on each wing to keep the precarious craft balanced. On 19 May 1919, the battered aircraft and her weary crew reached Ponta Delgada. John Towers ordered the engines started. The distress signal was lowered and the Stars and Stripes hoisted. Under her own power, NC-3 taxied into the harbor unassisted.

Only NC-4 remained in the game. Dubbed the Lame Duck for her lateness in joining the others at Trepassey, she had outdistanced her sister ships during the night. From the navigator's station in the nose of the aircraft, Albert Read checked off each ocean station precisely on schedule. Then came the dawn, and the Lame Duck, like the others, flew into fog and squalls and severe turbulence. In the gray murk, Read missed station 17. Walter Hinton, at the controls of NC-4, wrestled to maintain control of the wallowing aircraft. Finally Read ordered him to climb above the overcast and, with neither the ocean stations nor celestial navigation available for guidance, continued toward the Azores by dead reckoning.

At 0930 Azores time, through a gap in the cloud cover, Read spotted the dark color of land—the cliffs of the island of Flores. Hinton spiraled the flying boat down through the overcast. Cruising low on the water, the Lame Duck flew toward the island of Faial and the harbor of Horta. Fifteen hours and eighteen minutes after her departure from North America, NC-4 came to rest in the Azores.[3]

For Read and his crew, the rest of the trip was routine. After a lengthy delay for weather, they continued to Ponta Delgada, then across the eight-hundred-mile span of ocean to Lisbon, Portugal. Beneath them, as before, was a lifeline of some fourteen navy ocean stations. Three days later they were airborne again, stopping at Figueira and Ferrol. They followed their "bridge of boats" onward to England. Amid wild acclaim, salutes, sirens, and official greetings, *NC-4* arrived in Plymouth. The *Lame Duck* and her crew of U.S. Navy airmen had won the distinction of being the first to conquer the Atlantic by air.

In Newfoundland, two teams of British flyers were poised for their own transatlantic attempts. Harry Hawker and his navigator, Mackenzie Grieve, and Freddie Raynham with his fellow Briton, C.W.P. Morgan, received the report that the navy boat had safely landed in the Azores. Although the news subtracted from the historical significance of the British efforts, the navy's feat was not a nonstop flight to European soil. The *Daily Mail* prize money was still up for grabs.

Hawker and Grieve took off in their single-engine Sopwith and proceeded out to sea. An hour later, Raynham and Morgan strapped into their Martinsyde biplane and roared down their makeshift Newfoundland runway, bound for Europe.

Neither made it. The heavily loaded Martinsyde *Raymor*, caught by a gust, collapsed its landing gear and crashed on takeoff. Meanwhile, Hawker and Grieve, in their Sopwith *Atlantic*, reached mid-ocean before their engine lost its coolant and forced them to ditch in the ocean alongside a Danish freighter. Despite their bad luck, both British crews managed to survive their crashes.

Early in June the team of John Alcock and Arthur Whitten Brown took off from Newfoundland in their twin-engined Vickers Vimy bomber. Sixteen hours and twelve minutes later, after a nose-down landing in an Irish bog, they became the first to cross the Atlantic in a single flight.

So what did it all mean? Who had, in fact, been first to cross the Atlantic? Patriotic fervor prevailed on both sides of the Atlantic. In the New World, jingoistic American newspapers left no doubt that Albert Read and the crew of the *NC-4* were indeed "first across." Harry Hawker, on the opposite shore, bespoke the British view: "I am more gratified than I can say that British air supremacy has been maintained by British aviation and a British machine has made the first successful crossing."

What, in fact, had been proved by the NC adventure? The planned use of the "bridge of boats" obviated much of the need for self-contained navigational means. The over-dependence on the lifeline of destroyers led, in part, to the undoing of the *NC-1* and *NC-3* who, when contact was lost with their surface guardians, chose open-sea landings in order to verify their positions. Little practical use came of the weighty radio gear installed in the NCs.

There were the inevitable cries of indignation at the outlay of material and money. These were the same arguments raised half a century later during the Apollo missions to the moon. Why, asked the skeptics, should a nation's treasury be expended on an exploit—transatlantic flight or lunar exploration—that produces no tangible military or economic reward?

But priceless lessons *were* learned. *NC-1* and *NC-3* survived their downings at sea—an overwhelming argument for the practicality of flying boats. The requirement for specialized airborne celestial navigation techniques, including the use of Byrd's bubble sextant, was established. The infant craft of meteorology, particularly in the oceanic regions, came into its own.

The flying boat, it had been proved, could cross an ocean. In the case of the NC boats, the flight was a government-sponsored endeavor. But it raised questions: Was there a commercial future in such an enterprise? Would passengers *pay* to fly across bodies of water? Could money be made with flying boats?

4

Boats for Hire

On New Year's Day, 1914, the mayor of St. Petersburg, Florida, A. C. Pheil, settled himself into the passenger seat of a two-place Benoist Airboat. While the mayor waved to the cheering crowd, the wooden-hulled flying boat skipped across the bay and clattered off in the direction of Tampa, Florida, where it landed twenty-three minutes later in the Hillsboro River. Mr. Pheil had become the first airline passenger in history. His pilot, Tony Jannus, was one of the pioneer seaplane airmen of the day.[1]

The St. Petersburg–Tampa Airboat Line flew between the two cities twice daily, charging five dollars for a ticket. Though the Benoist could carry only one passenger, the airline soon acquired a larger model with double the capacity—two passengers. The boats were products of the Benoist Aircraft Company of St. Louis, Missouri. Similar in appearance to the Curtiss F-boat, the wood and fabric biplane was powered by a seventy-five horsepower Roberts engine connected by chain drive to a single propeller that was mounted behind the cockpit and between the wings. It had a top speed of about seventy miles per hour. Each of the airline's two aircraft cost $4,150, a hefty investment in equipment for 1914.

The St. Petersburg–Tampa Airboat Line lasted only three months. The trickle of revenue failed to match expenses, a condition endemic to the airline business for years to come. The little airline had operated its flying boats with great regularity, covering some 11,000 miles and carrying over 1,200 passengers.[2]

* * *

18

Until 1926, the only significant airline passenger service in the New World was provided by flying boats. On the inland routes of continental America, the slow-flying war-surplus land planes had nothing to offer that could beat the nearly-as-fast passenger trains with their Pullman accommodations. Only on the fair-weather, over-water routes did the airplane—and particularly the flying boat—have a distinct advantage over surface transport.

The end of World War I was followed by two events that shaped the course of commercial aviation. The first was Prohibition, imposed in 1919, casting its dry pall over America. The second was the sudden availability of war-surplus aircraft, including flying boats, suitable for conversion to passenger transports. Thus was provided both the need and the means for affluent pleasure-seekers to be flown beyond United States borders, to Cuba or the Bahamas, for their fun and spirits.

Two types of war-surplus flying boats were favored for passenger operations. The first to become available was the Curtiss HS-2L, developed from the HS-1 built in 1917. More than a thousand of these boats had seen U.S. Navy patrol service. The HS-2L was a wooden aircraft, powered by a single 350-horsepower Liberty engine driving a four-bladed pusher propeller. Fully loaded, she weighed a maximum of 6,223 pounds and could fly at a top speed of eighty miles per hour. Her range of 375 miles was sufficient to reach any of the Bahamian islands or Cuba from Florida.

The largest of the surplus boats, the F-5L, had a mixed ancestry. The F series of flying boats was developed at the Seaplane Experimental Station in Felixstowe from the original Curtiss design. The last of the series, the F.5, fitted with Liberty engines, was manufactured in the United States at the Naval Aircraft Factory in Philadelphia and at the Curtiss factory on Long Island. When the F-5Ls became available after the war, several were acquired by the American Plane and Motor Company in New Jersey and modified for passenger transport. These became known as the Aeromarine 75 or Curtiss 75.

A large flying boat for her day, the Aeromarine 75 had broad wings, the upper overhanging the lower, spanning 103 feet, 9 inches. She had a maximum takeoff weight of 14,348 pounds and could fly a still-air distance of 830 miles. Her crew of two sat in an open cockpit, between the wings. Two enclosed cabins accommodated up to twelve passengers.[3]

Two small flying boat operators, Aero Limited and West Indies Airways, both flying from Florida to Nassau and Havana, amalgamated in

1919 to form Aeromarine West Indies Airways. Their assets were, in turn, taken over by Aeromarine Airways, an airline founded by Inglis M. Uppercu, who had been a manufacturer of navy seaplanes during World War I.

Aeromarine commenced a passenger service in November 1919 from Key West to Havana, flying the Aeromarine 75 flying boats. The fare for the 105-mile trip was fifty dollars, an exorbitant sum in 1919, particularly compared to the nineteen-dollar ticket aboard a steamer. The flight took one-and-a-half to two hours, depending on the wind.[4]

Aeromarine adopted an ingenious system to match the seasonal ebb and flow of their passenger traffic. Beginning in May 1921, they moved their flying boats north and began service between New York and Atlantic City. In June the airline flew between Detroit and Cleveland, cruising straight across Lake Erie, operating six days a week. In the autumn, with the return of cool temperatures and a renewal of thirst and tourism, the airline resumed flights from Florida to the Caribbean.

Aeromarine was a pioneering airline, both in its use of flying boats and its approach to the economics of the business. On 1 November 1919, Aeromarine became the first United States airline to receive a foreign airmail contract. Between the mail subsidy and the seasonal deployment of their flying boat fleet, the airline managed to stay afloat.

Both the single-engine HS-2Ls and the Aeromarine 75s were, for their day, comfortable passenger aircraft. In their advertising brochures, Aeromarine declared:

> "Passengers wear their ordinary clothes. No leather garments, goggles or other paraphernalia are necessary in Aeromarine Cruisers!"

In another brochure, passengers' questions were asked and then answered:

Q: "Can passengers carry baggage?"
A: "Yes—thirty pounds. Your heavy baggage follows the same night by steamer."

Q: "Is this really an event to look forward to?"
A: "Yes, no advance in transportation on this hemisphere has been so eventful. Once by flying boat from Key West to Havana you will say 'Never again by steamer.' "[5]

Aeromarine continued its operation, expanding in size, until 1924. Suddenly its economic underpinning was yanked away. Without warning, mail subsidies were withdrawn by both the United States and Cuba. The airline flew its last scheduled trip, Miami to Nassau, on 1 May 1924.

Excepting the brief life of the St. Petersburg–Tampa Airboat Line, Aeromarine was America's first scheduled passenger airline and the first to make commercial use of the flying boat. It had accounted well for itself, carrying over 30,000 passengers and undetermined tons of mail and cargo. It had proven the viability of the flying boat as an instrument of air commerce. It had served as a test bed for future airlines and a training ground for flying boat pilots. One of Aeromarine's pilots, a former naval aviator named Ed Musick, would become the most famous airline pilot of his time.

Across the Atlantic, the former belligerents were assembling fleets of seagoing aircraft. The colonial powers, including a beaten but still vital Germany, viewed seaplanes and flying boats as the logical commercial vehicles to link them to their Asian, African, and South American subsidiaries.

About to be fettered by the Versailles Treaty, the German aircraft industry was continuing the development and production of commercial aircraft via licensees in Italy, Sweden, Denmark, and even in Soviet Russia. An airline called Deutsche Luft Reederei commenced operations only two months after the 1918 armistice. Flying converted A. E. G. JII military biplanes, the airline served a route between Berlin and Weimar.[6] Early in the 1920s, German-owned airlines made their appearance in South America. The firms of Junkers and Dornier turned their energies toward the production of flying boats and float-equipped transport aircraft.

In July 1920, the Belgian airline SNETA began an adventurous operation in equatorial Africa using the Levy-Lepen R flying boat. Called the Ligne Aérienne du Roi Albert (LARA), this Congo River airline flew from Kinshasha to N'Gombe and then, the following year, expanded its route system inland to Lisala and Stanleyville. The Levy-Lepen, originally built for the French Navy in 1917, accommodated only two passengers in addition to the pilot. The little flying boat was powered by a Renault 300-horsepower engine, driving a pusher propeller. With a loaded weight of 5,401 pounds, the Levy-Lepen had a speed of ninety miles per hour.

Among the airline's many problems was the irksome necessity, because of the heat and humidity, to re-attach the fabric to the structure of the aircraft after each flight. When the company went out of business in

1922, it had flown some 77,000 miles. Though it had hauled 4,400 pounds of mail, the airline had managed to accommodate only ninety-five passengers.[7]

With an eye on the Atlantic, in 1919 the Italian firm Caproni conceived the idea of an enormous flying boat designed to cross the ocean with one hundred passengers plus a crew of eight. The bizarre aircraft, the Caproni Ca 60 Transaero, had a fuselage like the hull of a ship. She was equipped with no fewer than nine wings mounted in triplane stacks on the front, mid, and aft sections of the fuselage. Within the forest of wings, wires, braces, and struts were eight Liberty engines arranged in a mixture of pusher and puller installations. Two lateral pontoons for stability on the water were installed at mid-fuselage.

The Ca 60 Transaero had a brief life. During her maiden flight on 4 March 1921, she rose to an altitude of sixty feet above Lake Maggiore. From that lofty height she abruptly nose-dived into the water and broke up. The project was abandoned.[8]

As a commercial vehicle, the flying boat still had not proved itself. Nor had it yet been demonstrated either in Europe or America that a commercial overwater airline could turn a profit and sustain itself. An enterprise as uncertain as the airline business appealed in the 1920s only to a few men. These were, for the most part, visionaries and entrepreneurs with the energy and optimism of youth. One such man was a young former naval aviator named Juan Trippe.

5

Trippe

Juan Terry Trippe was part visionary, part Yankee businessman, part conniving schemer. He and the flying boat came of age at the same time. More than anyone else, it was Trippe who made the flying boat an instrument of international commerce.

Aviation had been Trippe's abiding passion since the day in 1909 when his father had taken him to an air race. He had just turned ten years old. The Wright Brothers were engaged in a grim competition with their arch rival, Glenn Curtiss, whom they had accused of stealing their patented "wing warping" design for aeroplane roll control.

In the strong autumn winds, Curtiss could stay airborne no longer than forty-five seconds. The day belonged to Wilbur Wright, who made three separate flights, soaring around the Statue of Liberty, climbing high enough for millions of New Yorkers to see him.[1]

From that day forward, Trippe was obsessed. When the United States entered World War I during his freshman year at Yale, Trippe and most of his teammates on the football squad quit college and volunteered for military service. Despite his less-than-perfect vision, he finagled his way into navy flight training. He made his first solo in a Jenny biplane over Long Island. After flying boat training at Hampton Roads, Virginia, he volunteered for night flying training at Pensacola, Florida. At Pensacola, on 17 June 1918, he was commissioned an ensign and designated Naval Aviator Number 1806. On his way to New York to embark for Europe, he heard that the war had ended.

Back at Yale, Trippe played football, rowed, played golf, studied business, and began to cultivate the connections that would further his later career. He helped re-form the Yale Aero Club, and participated in intercollegiate flying competitions.

Trippe became a contributor, and eventually an editor, for Yale's illustrated magazine, the *Graphic*. In May 1919, as the U.S. Navy was readying the NC boats for their transatlantic attempt, Trippe contributed his viewpoint:

> If our big sea plane is the first to get across, and needless to say, all Americans hope she will be, her pilots will have doubly distinguished themselves, for they will have been not only the first to fly across the Atlantic Ocean but also the first to demonstrate that a flight across the Atlantic Ocean is a perfectly safe and sane commercial proposition and not a gigantic gamble in which the prospective transatlantic pilot or passenger has big odds against his safe arrival in the U.S.[2]

In the spring of 1921 Trippe graduated from his three-year curriculum at Yale with a degree and little money. Aviation, his chosen profession, had little to offer. He chose a traditional course, one that befitted a Yale man and his father's son. He accepted a job as bond salesman in the Wall Street firm of Lee, Higginson & Co.

After two stifling years, Trippe declared his independence. Disregarding the counsel of family and associates, he announced that he would pursue a career in the aviation business. Invoking the Yale connection, he made the rounds of former classmates. He produced letterheads for his business-to-be, using as an address 50 Vanderbilt Avenue, which happened to be the Yale Club. He sold stock in the new corporation, which he called Long Island Airways. He exercised his prerogative as principal shareholder and elected himself president and general manager.

At an auction in Philadelphia, Trippe paid $500 each for seven navy surplus Aeromarine floatplanes, designated type 49-B. These were single-engine aircraft that normally accommodated a pilot and one passenger. By replacing the Aeromarine's 90-horsepower Curtiss OX-5 with a 220-horsepower Hispano-Suiza engine, Trippe modified the floatplane to carry *two* passengers. Early in the game he had learned a fundamental premise of the airline business: *Increase capacity by whatever means, and you multiply revenues.*[3]

For two years Long Island Airways provided a platform for Trippe's theories. From the former naval air station at Rockaway Beach in Queens, Trippe sent his Aeromarines on round trips to the Long Island summer places of the rich. He sold excursions to Atlantic City. He chartered his aircraft to destinations as far south as Honduras and northward to Canada. He swept floors and carried bags. He sometimes flew the airplanes. He kept the books, and he learned the vagaries of payrolls, airline schedules, and the management of temperamental pilots.

When the airline folded in 1924, Trippe seemed hardly dismayed. He had learned what he needed to know and was ready for bigger things.

Of one future condition, Trippe was certain: The airlines, like the railroads, would sooner or later be regulated. Regulation meant government control. In the case of the airlines, that meant authority to operate over specific routes. The U.S. Post Office, in the form of mail subsidies, would provide both the incentive and the license for airlines to profit and expand.

The Air Mail Act of 1925, called the Kelly Act, attracted applications from hundreds of speculators and entrepreneurs. Through a consulting business formed by Trippe, a corporation called Eastern Air Transport was created on paper. The corporation was then persuaded to merge with another, better financed company called Colonial Air Transport. On behalf of the new airline Trippe went to Washington to enter a bid for a proposed new airmail route. On 7 October 1925, the contract airmail route from Boston to New York, via Hartford (CAM 1), was awarded to Colonial Air Transport.

Trippe became a vice president of Colonial with the duty of managing the operation. His salary, when the airline became operational, was $7,500 per year.[4] He hired employees, rented facilities, and placed orders for the new trimotored airplanes manufactured by Fokker and Ford. He recruited investors and directors like John Hambleton, war hero and son of a wealthy banker, Cornelius "Sonny" Whitney, aviation enthusiast and heir to a banking fortune, and William A. Rockefeller, who had been a member of the Yale aviation unit.

During a publicity flight to Cuba with a new Fokker trimotor, Trippe managed to obtain an appointment with the new Cuban president, Gerardo Machado. Trippe was able to persuade Machado to grant him exclusive landing rights at Camp Colombia, the army airport in Havana. When Trippe came home with the Machado letter in his pocket, he had, though he didn't yet realize it, the key to his future.

Inevitably, Trippe's style rankled the conservative directors of the company. To the older men, Trippe's schemes were brash and ill-conceived. After extensive boardroom lobbying, a majority of the share-holders voted against Trippe's bid to extend Colonial's routes into the Chicago–New York market.[5]

Trippe cleaned out his desk. It was the spring of 1927. He was jobless, but Trippe had reason for optimism. He still had his connections. He still had the Machado letter granting him landing rights in Havana. And the news was good. The Atlantic Ocean had just been crossed in a single flight by another young man named Charles Lindbergh.

With his two allies from Colonial, Sonny Whitney and John Hambleton, Trippe formed another airline. Whitney and his wealthy family had access to vast sources of investment capital. Hambleton had the connections—and requisite charm—to recruit powerful support on Wall Street. Trippe, who possessed few personal assets, brought with him his insider's knowledge of the airline business.

On 2 June 1927 they incorporated Aviation Corporation of America. Backing them was a powerful group of investors, including William H. Vanderbilt, Sherman Fairchild, Grover Loening, and William Rockefeller. This group contributed the initial capital of $200,000.[6] Trippe was in charge of operations. Whitney and Hambleton were directors. The airline's first goal was the soon-to-be-awarded foreign airmail route from Key West to Havana.

Two other companies were in competition for the same route. One was the dream child of a group of military pilots that included Army Air Corps Major Henry H. "Hap" Arnold and Major Carl Spaatz. Arnold had raised an alarm in Washington about a German-operated airline in Central and South America called SCADTA (Sociedad Colombo-Alemana de Transportes). The specter of an unfriendly foreign power operating an airline in the Americas, particularly near the Canal Zone, had inspired Arnold and his backers to form their own airline. The new company was called Pan American Airways.

It was the intention of Arnold and Spaatz to resign from the service. But in 1925 the Billy Mitchell controversy rocked the army. Both Arnold and Spaatz felt obliged to remain in the army and continue Mitchell's work.* The project was taken up by a former naval aviator, John K. Montgomery, who had been associated with SCADTA and was well

---

*"Hap" Arnold rose to command the American Army Air Forces in World War II. Carl Spaatz ranked directly beneath him.

connected on Wall Street. In March 1927 he and his group incorporated
Pan American Airways, Inc. The new company commenced a vigorous
campaign for the Key West–Havana foreign airmail authority.

Another consortium, headed by thirty-nine-year-old financier Richard
F. Hoyt, chairman of Wright Aeronautical Corporation, also applied for
the Havana route. This group, Atlantic, Gulf and Caribbean Air Lines,
was the resurrection of a defunct airline, Florida Airways, founded by
war ace Eddie Rickenbacker.

At the urging of Second Assistant Postmaster General W. Irving
Glover, the three groups were persuaded to merge. On 19 July 1927,
the U.S. Post Office awarded FAM 4, the airmail route from Key West
to Havana, to Pan American Airways.

Harmony did not prevail among the merged groups. Montgomery,
who represented the original creators of the airline, assumed he would
take charge. But Richard Hoyt, craftier in the game of stock manipu-
lation, executed a series of moves intended to narrow the field. He
created a holding company, Atlantic, Gulf Caribbean Airways, Inc., with
which he bought Pan American Airways. He then sold 52 percent of
the holding company's stock to the Trippe-Hambleton-Whitney group,
the Aviation Corporation of America. Montgomery found himself odd
man out.

In the new corporation, Hoyt became chairman of the board. Trippe
assumed the duties of president and general manager of the airline
subsidiary, Pan American. Hambleton was named a vice president. Both
he and Whitney became directors.

Montgomery and his group packed their briefcases and went off to
organize yet another airline.

Pan American had a route and an airmail contract. They would soon
have airplanes, four new trimotored Fokker VIIs, which Trippe had
ordered while still at Colonial Air Transport. They had the vital landing
rights in Havana, thanks to Trippe's Machado letter.

One significant problem remained. The airmail contract contained a
deadline, 19 October 1927, for the new service to commence. There
was still no runway at Key West that could accommodate the big Fokker
land planes.

For weeks frantic construction had been under way at an unused
military airfield in Key West. As the days ticked by, the rains came and
washed away each newly laid patch of gravel. If Pan Am did not fly by

the nineteenth, they would lose not only the contract but would forfeit the $25,000 bond posted with the application. Pan American would be finished before it left the ground.

Trippe's request for an extension was denied. Pan American would fly on the nineteenth or lose the mail contract. With two days remaining, one of the new Fokkers arrived in Miami, poised for the flight to Key West. The runway was nearly ready. Then an overnight tropical deluge converted the field back to a sodden, brackish swamp.

Just as the matter seemed hopeless, an unlikely hero appeared. His name was Cy Caldwell. He belonged to the generation of itinerant aviators in the twenties—barnstormers, rumrunners, fly-for-hire adventurers. On this occasion, one day before the expiration of Pan American's contract, Cy Caldwell had in his custody an item of inestimable value—a Fairchild FC-2 floatplane, which he was ferrying to the Dominican Republic by way of Miami.

Would Caldwell consider diverting his airplane to Key West, and then flying to Havana? After a round of deal-making by telephone, Caldwell agreed to fly Pan American's mail for a fee of $175. The next morning seven bags of mail containing some 30,000 letters were loaded aboard the Fairchild, which bore the name *La Niña*.

Caldwell took off, and one hour and twenty minutes later he landed *La Niña* in Havana harbor. The date was 19 October 1927.[7]

The airline was in business. Pan American's route system would snake its way southward, through the republics of Latin America. Along the way, it would collide with an equally ambitious airline, guided by a man with the same vision as Juan Trippe.

6

NYRBA

In 1928, an airline that connected the rich South American seaports of Rio, Montevideo, and Buenos Aires to the markets of New York amounted to nothing more than a dream. Such an airline would fly the longest air route in the world—7,800 miles of jungled coastline and open sea, coping with a polyglot of customs and governments. It was a route that could be served only by flying boats.

The New York, Rio and Buenos Aires Line existed only in the imagination of a pugnacious young man named Ralph O'Neill. O'Neill, in the summer of 1928, occupied a hospital bed in Minas, Uruguay, recovering from his most recent crash. During an attempted record flight from Rio to Buenos Aires, he had smashed his Boeing F2B fighter into the side of a mountain during a night landing.

The sprawling, tumultuous continent of South America suited the talents of a man like O'Neill. While working there, he had conceived a bold idea: he would found an airline, a north-south route along the fertile east coast, all the way to New York.

To many people, Ralph O'Neill seemed arrogant, loud of mouth, and quick of temper. He was a good-looking, muscular young man who didn't mind taking risks. As a pilot in World War I, he had become the fourth American ace in history, winning three distinguished service crosses with a croix de guerre. For five years after the armistice, he had trained the Mexican Air Force before going to South America as the chief salesman for the Boeing Airplane Company.

All he needed was money. In July 1928, still bandaged from his crash, Ralph O'Neill boarded a steamer for New York.

O'Neill had done his homework. He arrived on Wall Street with detailed reports on the economic, political, and operational aspects of his proposed airline.

Sixteen countries, including Chile, would be served. The route was composed of seven dawn-to-dusk segments, each of about a thousand miles, with individual legs averaging no more than 250 miles. A chain of harbors spaced at suitable intervals linked the ports of call. Weather, his greatest adversary, would be avoided by means of weather reporting stations and radio facilities along the entire route. For nervous investors, O'Neill produced statistics predicting that the airline could repay its backers within two years after an initial six-month shake down.

At first, O'Neill found doors slamming in his face. New York, he discovered, was the headquarters of Pan American. Juan Trippe and his wealthy backers had their own ambitions in South America. O'Neill was the outsider.

But then he met Jim Rand, the maverick president of Remington Rand, who decided to invest half a million dollars in O'Neill's airline. Another ally was Admiral William Moffett, chief of the navy's Bureau of Aeronautics. Moffett was a visionary officer who often bucked the military's proprietary attitude towards aviation. He believed in the future of air commerce and thought O'Neill's ideas had merit.

O'Neill needed airplanes, and Moffett had one in mind. "Reuben Fleet's Consolidated Aircraft recently won a design competition for a new flying boat," he told O'Neill. "We'll be testing it at Anacostia within nine months. It's a big boat. One-hundred-foot wingspread with bracing to outrigger pontoons and a hull sixty-two feet long. Of course, we haven't flown it yet, but you ought to keep it in mind."[1]

There was another new airplane that Moffett particularly liked. It was the S-38 amphibian, built by Russian immigrant Igor Sikorsky, for which the navy already held options. Moffett thought that such an airplane, if O'Neill could contrive to acquire it, would function admirably in the rugged environment of South America.[2]

Thereafter, things quickly fell in place. Major Reuben Fleet, president of Consolidated Aircraft, came on board, promising to deliver six commercial versions of the Admiral flying boat and thereby becoming a major stockholder in the new airline. Fleet's flying boat, called the Commodore in its civilian colors, would be the largest and most luxurious commercial aircraft in existence.

Rand lined up more investors. Stock was sold, and within a few months the airline was capitalized in the amount of some six million dollars. The airline took a name: The New York, Rio & Buenos Aires Line. It was a grand label, intended to connote railroad comfort and reliability. It implied, too, special ties with the three greatest cities on the Atlantic.

The government of Argentina responded favorably to O'Neill's application for a mail contract, and it seemed likely that similar contracts could be expected from Chile, Uruguay, and Brazil. But a condition of the crucial Argentine contract was that the new airline, NYRBA, be in regular operation—with fines for each day of delay—within twelve months.

O'Neill needed flying boats. The Commodore boats were slow in coming, with many development snags to be smoothed out. NYRBA had ordered six Sikorsky S-38s as interim aircraft, but the U.S. Navy was already first on the delivery list with their own order of six aircraft. Pan American was next with an order for two. The small and underfinanced Sikorsky plant could deliver the amphibians at a rate of only one every four weeks.

O'Neill's benefactor, Admiral Moffett, again came to his aid. The Bureau of Aeronautics, at Moffett's direction, would postpone acceptance of their S-38s and exchange delivery slots with NYRBA.

And what about pilots? O'Neill's second most pressing need, after he had airplanes, was the men to fly them. Moffett made available to O'Neill a roster of the most experienced navy flying boat pilots. O'Neill was "free to try to wean them from the Navy." This O'Neill intended to do by offering them a salary double that of their navy pay.[3]

NYRBA's inaugural flight departed Norfolk, Virginia, on 11 June 1929, bound for Rio. Christened the *Washington*, the new S-38 was loaded with seven passengers including a mechanic and a 600-pound radio bolted to the cabin floor. The pilot-in-command on this special occasion was NYRBA's president, Ralph O'Neill.

The trip was a series of near-disasters. Even with normal loads, the S-38 sprayed vast amounts of water back over itself during takeoff. The *Washington*, burdened with a load it had never been designed to carry, plowed through the water like a trawler. Each takeoff along the route required multiple attempts before the sluggish craft could free itself from the water. Water sloshed over the fuselage, through the cabin, and upward into the engines. The deluge diminished the engines' power and chewed into the propeller blades.

As they flew southward over the Caribbean and across South America, it became necessary after each stop to file down the pitted propeller blades. O'Neill was finally forced to reduce the *Washington*'s weight, off-loading the mechanic, removing the overweight and water-soaked radio, and eventually even detaching the Sikorsky's retractable landing gear. By the time the bedraggled S-38 at last reached Rio, it had been transformed to a pure seaplane.[4]

But the trailblazing flight, despite its problems, put NYRBA in the airline business. Six weeks later service commenced between Buenos Aires and Montevideo. Shortly thereafter a twice-weekly service was begun with Ford trimotors, flying the overland segment from Buenos Aires, across the Andes, to Santiago, Chile.

Ralph O'Neill was building his airline from south to north. For the next year he would devote his energies to South America, eight thousand miles from the airline's headquarters in New York. It would turn out to be his worst mistake.

The Commodore outclassed any commercial land or seaplane of 1929. Her enormous wings—a 100-foot span with a chord of 12 feet—were capable of supporting 10 tons in the air. Beneath the wings, mounted between the hull and the outboard pontoons, were the two 550-horse-power Hornet engines.

The Commodore's cabin set a new standard in airborne comfort. On either side of the center aisle, under a high-domed ceiling, were the four Pullman-like compartments. The richly upholstered seats faced each other and were equipped with padded armrests and reading lights. Large, silk-curtained windows afforded a spectacular view outside. In the after compartment were a spacious lounge and adjoining lavatories. A separate compartment for mail was installed in the forward fuselage.

The Commodore had begun her life as an experimental navy flying boat. She had taken the name Admiral, in honor of Admiral William Moffett, Chief of the Bureau of Aeronautics, and received the designation XPY-1. Built by the Consolidated Aircraft Company, she was Reuben Fleet's entry in a navy design competition for a giant flying boat with the range to fly from mainland America to Hawaii.

The XPY-1 made her maiden flight from the Anacostia River in

Washington, D.C., on 22 January 1929. "The big plane," reported the *New York Times*, "roared down the river on a ten-mile wind. . .lifted easily after a 650-foot run and climbed quickly. Two Navy Corsairs, one with photographers, swooped after it in formation."

Among those on board was Captain Holden Richardson, whose flying boat experience went back to the early days with Glenn Curtiss and the famous NC boats. After the first flight, Richardson bestowed his approval on the new aircraft. It was "very stable," he said. "It felt good to have something solid under foot."

Also on board for the flight was Assistant Secretary for Aeronautics Edward Warner, who spoke of how the navy's sponsorship of such designs might contribute to the progress of commercial flying boat development.[5]

Warner's words were prophetic. In an ironic twist of free enterprise, the Bureau of Aeronautics decided to open the Admiral flying boat production contract to bids from qualified companies. The contract to produce the Consolidated-designed flying boat then went to the Glenn L. Martin Company. Reuben Fleet was outraged. "We had to bid so as to recoup our investment in development of the first ship. Glenn L. Martin had bid against us and the Navy had to give him the contract because with no engineering cost he was able to bid a half million dollars under Consolidated."[6]

Glenn Martin then produced his own version of Consolidated's design, which became the navy P3M-1. Reuben Fleet found himself stuck with a new flying boat and all its development costs—and no customer. Later he would say that Martin "underbid us a half million and lost a million on the job."[7]

Then appeared the bumptious Ralph O'Neill. And in the background remained the formidable presence of Admiral Moffett, still quietly orchestrating the conversion of the XPY-1 to a commercial configuration for O'Neill's airline. Thus Reuben Fleet became a shareholder in NYRBA, and his Admiral flying boat, in civilian colors, became the elegant Commodore.

The christening of the Commodore was scheduled for 2 October 1929. O'Neill planned to greet Mrs. Herbert Hoover, wife of the president of the United States, who would arrive at Anacostia by motorcade. He intended to escort her to the stand where, after O'Neill made a short speech, the first lady was to swing a beribboned bottle of fizz water (Prohibition was still the law of the land), christening the *Buenos Aires* and bestowing the presidential blessing on O'Neill's airline. It would be Ralph O'Neill's long-awaited moment of triumph.

Mrs. Hoover's motorcade arrived on schedule. Behind a phalanx of secret service men she was escorted to the dais. Her guards pushed the crowd back. "Clear the way—everybody!"

The order included O'Neill. With the rest of the crowd, he found himself shunted aside. He watched while the first lady's party proceeded to the stand, escorted by the White House chief of protocol, the Argentine ambassador and his wife, and—to Ralph O'Neill's horror—*Juan Trippe*. In disbelief O'Neill stared as Trippe took his place on the christening stand next to the wife of the president. Newsmen, photographers, and spectators closed in around them and the ceremony began.

While O'Neill seethed in a rage at the back of the crowd, Juan Trippe delivered his own speech. Pan American Airways, he announced, would soon establish its own route to Buenos Aires. Pan Am's Central American routes would extend to all of South America.

The nation's first lady then christened the new flying boat. Juan Trippe beamed his approval. No one seemed to notice the *NYRBALINE* on the Commodore's hull.[8]

Trippe had won another round. More than ever it became a grudge fight between NYRBA and Pan Am. Ralph O'Neill needed no further convincing that his enemy was Juan Trippe. And beyond a doubt, the enemy wielded huge clout in the centers of power—New York and Washington, D.C.

NYRBA's code name for Pan American became "Coyote." In intercompany communications, the activities of "Coyote" were treated like the movements of hostile forces.

NYRBA needed mail contracts—U.S. mail. But the U.S. Post Office, O'Neill learned, was the domain of Pan American. The assistant postmaster general, Washington Irving Glover, had remained in office during the transition from the Coolidge to the Hoover administrations. Glover was a Pan American ally and routinely blocked any intrusion by Pan Am's competitors in the South American market. Among Juan Trippe's Washington allies, NYRBA was sarcastically referred to as "near beer."[9]

O'Neill's only mail contracts were with the South American governments. He had agreements from Argentina, Chile, Brazil, and Uruguay for NYRBA to carry mail *to* the United States. The contract with Argentina required that the mail from Buenos Aires reach Miami in seven days.

O'Neill commenced the new service on the night of 19 February 1930 under a full moon. The success of this first flight was vital to the future of NYRBA. The Argentine press had made much of the proposed new link with the U.S., and the U.S. Post Office was announcing plans to extend existing U.S. mail contracts to the South American routes. If NYRBA were to prevail in its war with Pan American, the first flight had to succeed.

O'Neill spared nothing. To ensure success, he planned to fly the *Rio de Janeiro*, a big new Commodore, as the lead aircraft, followed by a Sikorsky S-38 back up. O'Neill would personally fly the entire route, changing crews at each division port.

The inaugural mail flight was a journey of incredible mishaps. At Porto Alegre, the first stop, the Commodore struck a buoy on takeoff, damaging her hull and rupturing an oil line. O'Neill had the mail—and himself—transferred to the S-38 and continued northward.

The Sikorsky, flown by William Grooch, an ex-navy pilot, arrived in Santos after nightfall in the midst of a violent thunderstorm. Landing on the blackened, storm-tossed ocean, the S-38 struck the waves with such force that her hull was ruptured. Grooch and O'Neill managed to lower the wheels and beach the amphibian before she sank.

O'Neill would not give up. By telephone he ordered another Sikorsky, held in reserve in Rio, to fly to Santos and pick him up. A few hours later, he received the news that the Sikorsky, instead of being en route, was being held by the Rio harbor police as a result of an injunction brought against NYRBA by a Brazilian airline.

O'Neill ordered yet another Sikorsky, this one in Bahia, to fly to Rio. He ordered the crew to land on the far side of the harbor to avoid the police. He then hired a taxi and, with his precious mail sacks, drove all night to Rio to join the waiting S-38. At dawn, pursued by a police speed boat, O'Neill took off from Rio.

At Vitória there was more mail. And, incredibly, another crash. This time the S-38, piloted by Clarence Woods, struck a seawall on takeoff, crumpling the hull. Ralph O'Neill climbed from his third crash in two days, delivered a tongue-lashing to everyone in sight, then ordered another airplane flown in.

The inaugural mail flight was badly behind schedule. Never reluctant to take risks, O'Neill decided to fly north, directly over the jungle instead of along the coastal bulge of Brazil. The route would cut precious hours off the total flight time but risk a forced landing in the impenetrable jungles of the Amazon.

There were no more crashes. On 25 February 1930, after six days en route, O'Neill reached Miami aboard the Commodore *Cuba*. He had delivered the mail well within the seven-day time limit specified in his contract with the Argentine government.

Storms, accidents, and police had not been O'Neill's only adversaries. Along the route northward he had encountered newly appointed NYRBA executives, hired by headquarters without his knowledge. He heard disquieting stories that within NYRBA's board of directors was a movement to replace him as president.

O'Neill remained in character. As he met each new executive, he fired him on the spot. In Miami he learned that twenty new land plane pilots had been hired without his knowledge. One at a time he summoned the pilots to his room. He fired each one.

O'Neill's list of enemies grew longer. While he had been concentrating his energies—and NYRBA's assets—on the development of the South American route system, he had ignored events in New York and Washington.

It took money to run an airline. The Great Depression had rolled over Wall Street like a tidal wave. Although NYRBA was now operating the most efficient, longest, and safest airline in the world, it was losing $400,000 a month. The company had been capitalized, through stock sales, in the amount of $6 million. By mid-1930 its cash balance was down to $16,000.

The backers of NYRBA were being nudged by both the Post Office and the State Department toward a merger with Pan American. Repeatedly the Post Office had excluded NYRBA from the lucrative foreign airmail contracts. Postmaster General Walter Brown's position was that competitive bidding in South America was "of doubtful value" and was not in the best interests of the United States. "There would be," he said, "very little real substantial bidding by men of experience able to carry on an industry of this kind. . ."

What Brown meant was that the foreign airmail contracts in South America were reserved for Pan American.

In the wings waited Juan Trippe. Trippe's strategy was simple: He would let NYRBA spend itself into oblivion. Without mail contracts and without the backing of the State Department, NYRBA could not continue.

By mid-1930 NYRBA's backers, frightened by their losses and intimidated by Pan American's influence in government, were being pressured to accept Trippe's offer of a buy-out.

At a final board meeting, Ralph O'Neill listened while the terms of the takeover were read. Then he stood and made a last impassioned speech. "To demonstrate the rooking we are getting," he said, "I would like to bring all our planes to Washington and anchor them on the Potomac. In other words, to display publicly the greatest and most modern fleet of transport airplanes in the world—all being sacrificed to the whims or interest of a shameless bureaucrat."[10]

The board listened impassively. O'Neill could no longer sway them. NYRBA's directors had no stomach for further fighting with Pan American or the government. The board voted, and the New York, Rio and Buenos Aires Line passed into history.

The unmaking of NYRBA put Pan American solidly in the airline business. The Commodore flying boat, ideally suited for the harbors of the South American coast, was the "right" airliner.

For Reuben Fleet, the NYRBA–Pan American war had a happy ending. "We sold fourteen Commodores," he reported, "ten Fleetsters [single-engine, high-wing land planes], and ten Fleet trainers and made a profit of $208,000 for our company on the deal. And, of course, we got back all our development cost on the original XPY-1 Admiral flying boat.

"Above all else we established that in fifteen months we could produce fourteen flying boats modified for commercial service. Martin took twenty-seven months to produce their nine copies of the Admiral for the Navy. That taught the Navy a good lesson which they never, never forgot—don't alienate the original designer from his design by giving it to someone else."

The Commodore lived a full and productive life. In his 1934 Report to Stockholders, Fleet wrote, "Consolidated Commodores have flown more than five million miles of scheduled passenger and mail flying in the service of Pan American; to our knowledge no passenger or person has ever been hurt in a Commodore in the five years they have been the backbone of that great American company's service from Miami to Buenos Aires."[11]

The stately Commodores continued in Pan American service and that of its subsidiaries, Panair do Brazil and China National Airline Corporation, until the end of World War II. In 1945 Pan American sold its last Commodore to Bahama Airways, Ltd. Twenty years after its first flight, the old boat still carried passengers on scheduled flights.

7

Sikorsky

In 1913, factual knowledge about the science of flight still lay obscured in a haze of pseudoscientific myth. One such notion of the day was the "ostrich" theory. Proponents of this idea insisted that it was nature's will to inhibit the flight of objects, whether birds or airplanes, that exceeded a certain dimension. Birds the size of gulls and hawks, for example, could fly with ease and agility and even carry a load. But when a bird reached the size of an ostrich, the rules changed. The creature was incapable of flight. This same immutable logic, declared the experts, should apply equally to airplanes.

Thus, when Igor Sikorsky's four-engine airplane, the *Grand*, neared completion in 1913, crowds gathered at the factory in Petrograd. The *Grand* was a clear example of a man-made ostrich. No aircraft of that size had ever flown. Her wings spanned ninety-two feet. Her gross weight amounted to 9,000 pounds. She was powered by four one-hundred-horsepower, water-cooled, four-cylinder Argus engines installed in two tandem mounts close to the aircraft centerline. The *Grand*, in the judgment of the ostrich theorists, was a presumptuous attempt to defy the will of nature.

In addition to her great size, the *Grand* incorporated features that, for 1913, seemed drawn from Jules Verne. The closed pilots' cabin, unique for its day, had dual seats, dual controls and a full panel of instruments. A door in front allowed access to an open balcony in the nose of the aircraft. The passenger cabin was luxuriously decorated with seats, sofa, table, a washroom, and cabinets.

The *Grand* flew. As a test platform, she proved the feasibility of the multi-engined configuration. The *Grand* not only earned for Sikorsky the acclaim of the aviation world, she lay to rest forever the "ostrich" theory.[1]

Igor Sikorsky, designer and engineer, was also a mystic. He placed much faith in dreams, and he believed in the power of intuition, which he called the "mysterious faculty." Technological advances, he believed, were mostly wrought by men whose imagination could transcend time and perceive facts, natural laws, and future events that were not yet known.[2]

When he was an eleven-year-old boy in Russia, Sikorsky had a dream so vivid that he would remember each detail for the rest of his life. In his dream he was walking along a narrow passageway. On either side of the passageway were elegant walnut doors that opened to staterooms. Overhead glowed a spherical light that cast a pleasant blue illumination. Beneath his feet, under the plush carpet, he could feel a slight but steady vibration, which he already knew came from the engines of a giant flying ship. When he reached the end of the passageway, he opened the door to a luxurious lounge. Before he could enter, he awoke from his dream.

The year was 1900. The first successful powered flight still lay three years in the future. When the boy spoke of his dream, he was told by adults that flying ships existed only in children's fantasies. In any case, they said, such things were amusing but quite impossible.

Years passed. In the autumn of 1931, Pan American Airways took delivery of the S-40 four-engine flying boat, christened the *American Clipper*. The designer and builder of the huge craft was invited, with members of Pan Am's board of directors, for a flight over New York. He had not seen the S-40's cabin since it was completed and furnished to Pan Am's specifications.

It was an evening of special beauty. The air was gossamer smooth. In the soft glow of the setting sun, the giant flying boat seemed suspended in an ethereal vacuum.

Igor Sikorsky was walking through the front cabin toward the forward lounge when the steward suddenly switched on the cabin lights. Sikorsky froze, taken aback at what he saw.

There were the walnut doors. Above his head glowed the bluish electric light. The carpeted passageway led to the lounge. Beneath his feet, under the plush flooring, he felt the satisfying rumble of the flying boat's four engines. It all seemed familiar to him.

It was just as he had seen in his dream thirty years before.[3]

* * *

Igor I. Sikorsky was born 25 May 1889 in Kiev, in southwest Russia. Both his parents had studied medicine, and his father was a professor of psychology at St. Vladimir University in Kiev.

After three years at the Naval Academy in Petrograd, Sikorsky entered the Polytechnic Institute of Kiev in the fall of 1907. To pursue his interest in the new science of aviation, he interrupted his studies and went to Paris, then the international forum for all things aeronautical.

When he returned to Russia, Sikorsky took with him an Anzani 25-horsepower engine and commenced work on his first manned flying machine, a helicopter of his own design. The primitive helicopter did not fly, nor did his next machine, a pusher biplane that he designated the S-1.

With the S-2, powered by the 25-horsepower Anzani from the flightless helicopter, Sikorsky achieved his first true powered flight. Though he had never flown before, the young builder assumed the duties of chief test pilot. When the airplane and its test pilot had each accrued a total of eight minutes flying time, the S-2 inadvertently stalled above a swamp and crashed. Uninjured and scarcely perturbed, Sikorsky disentangled himself from the wreckage and commenced plans for an improved model.

Other experimental airplanes followed. More mishaps occurred, all survivable. In 1911 Sikorsky's S-6 set a world speed record (113 kilometers per hour, about 70 miles per hour) for a plane with a pilot and two passengers. That same year he received a contract with the Russian Baltic Railroad Car Factory to construct airplanes of his own design.

And then on 13 May 1913, the *Grand* flew, acquiring for the twenty-four-year-old Sikorsky international attention. With the test data obtained from the *Grand*, he began construction of an even larger, more sophisticated four-engine transport.

The *Ilia Mourmetz* took her name from the hero of a popular tenth-century Russian legend. While the *Grand* had disproved the "ostrich" idea and shown the possibilities of multi-engine aircraft, the *Ilia Mourmetz* made them a matter of record. On 11 February 1914, she took off with sixteen persons on board, establishing the first of several new world records.

The *Ilia Mourmetz* had a wing span of 102 feet, a wing area of 1,700 square feet, and a gross weight of over 10,000 pounds (a kitelike wing loading of 5.8 pounds per square foot of wing area). The first model used the same power plants as the *Grand*—four Argus engines of 100

horsepower each. The second model, identical in size, was fitted with
two inboard engines of 140 horsepower, and the outboards of 125
horsepower each, producing an improvement in performance. With a
power-to-weight ratio of twenty pounds per horsepower, the *Ilia Mourmetz* was hardly a rocket, but for her day she gave an impressive performance.

In July 1914, at the request of the Russian Navy, Sikorsky conducted
experiments with a floatplane configuration of the *Ilia Mourmetz*. Despite
his lack of experience with waterborne aircraft, relying, perhaps, on his
"mysterious faculty" of intuition, Sikorsky produced a set of wooden,
flat-bottomed, shock-mounted floats. The primitive floats, unsophisti-
cated by the standards of Glenn Curtiss, worked surprisingly well. The
Ilia Mourmetz became the world's largest seaplane.

When the great powers of Europe lunged into World War I, Sikorsky
found himself designing bombers for his beleaguered country. These
were upgraded versions of the *Ilia Mourmetz*, and although equipped
with the same four engines and similar wing area, were nearly twenty
miles an hour faster and capable of an altitude of 10,000 feet with a
full bomb load.

Sikorsky's bombers accounted well for themselves. Altogether some
seventy-five models were delivered, half of which saw active combat.
The bombers flew a total of about four hundred raids with a loss of
only one aircraft. Faster and more powerful versions were in the works
when, in the spring of 1917, the life of Czarist Russia came to an end.
In the Bolshevik revolution that convulsed Russia, Igor Sikorsky, like
thousands of his countrymen, became a refugee.

He was a jobless immigrant, nearly thirty years old, when he stepped
ashore in New York on 30 March 1919. Quickly he learned what every
designer and builder of airplanes in America was discovering. Aviation,
in the postwar world, was a moribund enterprise. There was a glut of
flyers and flying machines. Sikorsky was forced to support himself by
teaching mathematics to other immigrants, living in a six-dollar-a-month
single room on New York's East Side. In the evenings he delivered
lectures on aviation and astronomy. The glory days of the *Ilia Mourmetz*
seemed gone forever.

But among the growing Russian colony in New York, Sikorsky's name
still carried considerable weight. By the spring of 1923, he was able to
raise enough funds through a stock subscription to found the Sikorsky

Aero Engineering Corporation. A principal supporter, stockholder, and vice president of the corporation was the famous Russian pianist and composer, Sergei Rachmaninoff.[4]

The first Sikorsky aircraft built in the United States was designated the S-29A (the A appended as a salute to the builder's adopted country). Money was always insufficient. Sikorsky's "factory" was a makeshift shop on Long Island, near Roosevelt Field. Tools and components came from hardware stores and junk yards. The power plants were sickly war-surplus Liberty engines. The tires were worn and prone to blowing out while the aircraft stood parked.

On its initial test flight in May 1924, with eight optimistic Russians on board, the S-29A's engines lost power and the aircraft crashed on a nearby golf course. There were no injuries, but the new airplane—as well as the builders' morale—suffered grievous damage.

Sikorsky's backers dug deeper in their pockets. The S-29A was revived and went on to live a productive life. Despite the continuing hard times, the small company stayed in business, producing several small training airplanes and a trimotored long-range aircraft designated the S-35. This sleek machine possessed a range and load-carrying capability unequaled by any other airplane of her day. Selected by the French ace, René Fonck, for his 1926 attempt to fly the Atlantic, the S-35 might have become the most famous airplane in the world. Instead, the venture ended in disaster when the heavily loaded aircraft's gear collapsed on takeoff. In the flaming crash at the end of the runway, the S-35 was destroyed. Two of Fonck's four crewmen lost their lives.[5]

New aircraft orders were few. The S-35 debacle had left the company demoralized and nearly bankrupt. Its successor, the S-37, was a twin-engined, long-range aircraft with which Fonck was to have another try at the Atlantic. Lindbergh's stunning triumph in May 1927 ended the transatlantic race.

For a while Sikorsky had hopes of marketing the S-37 as a commercial transport. One of his potential customers was the manager of Colonial Air Transport, an affable young man named Juan Trippe. After a ride in the new aircraft, with Sikorsky at the controls, Trippe decided the big airplane was unsuitable for Colonial.[6]

A twin-engine amphibian, designated the S-34, was completed in 1926. This experimental design had numerous flaws, and during a test flight the aircraft developed engine troubles and crashed. But the project provided invaluable test data for a new lineage of Sikorsky aircraft. In

1927 came the S-36, a further refinement of Sikorsky's twin-engined amphibian concept. Several of these were produced and sold, including one model to the U.S. Navy.

During the early months of 1928 the Sikorsky company produced a ten-seat amphibian, the S-38. This air-land-sea craft, powered by two 400-horsepower Pratt and Whitney Wasp engines, became an immediate success. It possessed performance unlike any other waterborne aircraft of the day, climbing at 1,000 feet per minute with a full load, cruising at 100 miles per hour, with a maximum speed of 130 miles per hour. The amphibian could stay comfortably airborne on one engine, a powerful selling point in 1928.

The first order, placed by the U.S. Navy, was deferred in favor of the new airline, NYRBA. The next series of S-38s went to Pan American, serving as the workhorse for the airline's push into the Southern Hemisphere.

The S-38 resembled a prehistoric flying reptile, with its long, bill-like prow of a nose and a chopped-off, blunt, aft fuselage. Its high, upper wing, built of wood and covered with fabric, spanned seventy-one feet eight inches. The two Wasp engines were suspended beneath the upper wing. The thirty-six-foot one-inch lower sesquiplane was, like the hull, covered in aluminum to withstand the pressures of water handling. The tail surfaces were appended by twin booms to the upper wing and supported by a strut connected to the aft fuselage.

The rugged little machine made history. In 1929 an S-38 was flown by Charles Lindbergh to inaugurate service between the United States and the Panama Canal. Another S-38 appeared prominently in motion pictures, painted in zebra stripes, as the jungle vehicle of the African explorers, Osa and Martin Johnson. The government of Chile ordered an S-38 to provide transportation for an official visit of the Prince of Wales. Many models of the S-38 were delivered to private sportsmen and adventurers. At least ten airlines ordered the S-38, including Pan Am, Pan American–Grace Airways, Inter-Island Airways, Curtiss-Wright Flying Service, Colonial Western Airways, Canadian Colonial Airways, and NYRBA. Both the army and the navy ordered substantial numbers of the S-38.[7]

For the hard-pressed Sikorsky company, the S-38 was the breakthrough. The first series of ten aircraft sold out immediately. The next series went into production and was also sold out. The Sikorsky company found itself, in the midst of a numbing depression, with more business than it could handle.

The company was reorganized as the Sikorsky Aviation Corporation, capitalized at $5 million, and moved to a sprawling new factory complex in Stratford, Connecticut. In place of the original makeshift, war-surplus and secondhand equipment, the corporate headquarters was outfitted with new machinery, research laboratories, drafting rooms, offices, and a wind tunnel. The site adjoined deep-water facilities for the testing of the new generation of Sikorsky seagoing airplanes. In 1929 the Sikorsky Corporation became a subsidiary, and then a division, of the United Aircraft Corporation.

On 20 December 1929, Sikorsky was approached by Juan Trippe, who now headed Pan American. He wanted an oceangoing craft with four engines, amphibious capability, and a size, range, and load-carrying capacity unmatched by any airplane in the world. Could Sikorsky construct such a flying boat?

Igor Sikorsky's "mysterious faculty" was already at work. He would build Trippe's flying boat. It would be superior, at least in performance, to the giant flying boat, the Dornier Do X, that had startled the world that summer with its first flight in Germany.

Teutonic Ambitions

All the pent-up frustrations of postwar Germany crystallized in the immense form of the Do X. Teutonic in scale and spirit, she was the largest airplane in the world. The Do X had been built to be a transatlantic airliner, but her very enormity outreached the technology of the day. The appearance of the German-built Do X delivered a signal to the rest of the world. The race had begun for a transatlantic airplane.

Claude Dornier, designer of the Do X, began his career in 1910 with the German airship company Luftschiffbau Zeppelin. When the firm established a subsidiary in 1914 for the construction of metal flying boats, thirty-year-old Dornier was put in charge.

In August of that year, Germany went to war. For the next four years Dornier designed a succession of metal-clad flying boats for the military. One of these, a twin-engined craft designated the Gs I, was nearly completed when the armistice was signed. Dornier modified the flying boat as a civil transport, equipping it with an open cockpit and a six-seat cabin in the bow.

The Gs 1 first flew in July 1919. She was intended to enter service with Ad Astra Aero (a forerunner of Swissair). The innovative flying boat featured a broad-beamed hull fitted with *Flossenstümmel* (sponsons, or sea wings), which were to become a Dornier trademark. Her single, square-tipped, untapered wings were mounted above the hull. Two tandem-mounted 260-horsepower Maybach engines were installed above the center section.

The Gs I might have left her mark in history. In performance she outclassed any comparable aircraft possessed at the time by the allied

46

countries. Instead, the unthinkable happened. The victorious allies, in their fervor to disarm their former antagonists, committed the stupidity of destroying the Gs I in 1920 and sinking her to the bottom of the North Sea.[1]

In the early twenties Dornier produced a series of single-engine flying boats given the collective name, Delphin (Dolphin). These peculiar-appearing aircraft were of steel and duralumin construction with the single water-cooled engine mounted high above the nose and, in its initial version, an open cockpit located abaft the engine. An enclosed cabin for five or six passengers lay directly behind the cockpit. The final variant of this design, the Delphin III, appeared in 1927 and had an enclosed cockpit beneath the engine and a cabin accommodating twelve to thirteen passengers.

And then in 1922 appeared the aircraft that established Claude Dornier as one of the world's foremost designers of seagoing aircraft. The Do J Wal (Whale) was an outgrowth of the unfortunate Gs I. The Wal was an all-metal monoplane with an untapered wing mounted on struts above a streamlined fuselage. Showing her Dornier heritage, she featured the familiar sea wings—air-foil-shaped sponsons at water level instead of outrigger floats—and tandem-mounted, pusher-puller engines atop the center section.

By the terms of the postwar restrictions imposed on Germany, Dornier was forbidden to build the Wal in his own country. Thus, from 1923 the Wal was produced in Italy by Construzioni Meccaniche Aeronautiche SA (CMASA) and later by the Piaggio Company. In all, a total of 117 Wals were built in Italy. The aircraft was eventually constructed by factories in Spain, the Netherlands, Japan, and finally again in Germany after the ban had expired. For fourteen years the successful Wal continued in production, appearing in some twenty versions and powered by a variety of engines, including the 300-horsepower Hispano-Suiza, the 360-horsepower Rolls-Royce Eagle, the 450-horsepower Napier Lion engine, and eventually twelve-cylinder BMW VI engines of 600 horsepower each. Her maximum gross weight swelled from about 8,000 pounds to over 22,000 pounds.

Like the sturdy Sikorsky S-38, the Wal found employment around the world. The Italian airlines SANA and Aero Espresso used Wals throughout their Mediterranean networks. The German airline, Aero Lloyd, flew Wals on their Scandinavian service, and the enterprising Deutsche Luft Hansa, founded in 1926, began operating the Wal on their Baltic routes. The German-owned SCADTA of Colombia purchased Wals, as did Syndicato Condor in Brazil and Nihon Koku Yuso Kaisha in Japan.

Wals served several pioneering and exploration efforts. The Norwegian explorer, Roald Amundsen, used two Italian-built Wals in his 1925 attempt to reach the North Pole. One of his two flying boats, renamed the *Amundsen Wal*, later gained fame as the aircraft flown by Wolfgang von Gronau in 1930 from Germany, via Iceland and Greenland, to America. An Italian, Count Locatelli, and a Briton, Captain Frank Courtney, each made transatlantic attempts with the Wal.[2] In 1926 Major Franco, brother of the Spanish dictator-to-be, made the first successful east-to-west flight over the South Atlantic, flying to Buenos Aires from Palos de Magues, Spain, in a Wal.

By 1932 it had become possible for Dornier to resume constructing aircraft within Germany. At the Dornier facility in Friedrichshafen, two Wal derivatives were developed, the so-called eight-ton Wal and the ten-ton Wal. These models went into the South Atlantic service of DLH, and in May 1933 a Wal christened *Monsun* (Monsoon) made a proving flight from Bathurst, on the west coast of Africa, to Natal on the eastern shore of South America. Two ships, the *Westfalen* and the *Schwabenland*, were equipped to catapult and retrieve the Wals. By this means over 300 crossings of the Atlantic were accomplished by the doughty Wals.[3]

In September 1926 appeared the Super Wal. Though similar in appearance to its predecessor, the Do R4 Super Wal II had a maximum weight of 22,046 pounds, twenty feet more wing span than the original Wal, and was configured both as a twin-engined aircraft and as a four-engined flying boat with two pairs of tandem engines. The Super Wal had fore-and-aft cabins, an enclosed cockpit (as did the ten-ton Wal and all subsequent models) and could accommodate as many as twenty-nine passengers.

DLH put the Super Wal into service on its northern Europe routes. Several others were flown by the Italian airline SANA, and two four-engined Super Wals, powered by Pratt and Whitney Hornet engines, flew for Stout D & C Air Lines on a Great Lakes service in 1929.[4]

The success of the Wal series emboldened Claude Dornier to undertake his most ambitious project. Dornier wanted an aircraft that could cross the oceans. From his drawing boards came the design for the world's largest aircraft, a flying boat powered by no fewer than *twelve* engines and a long-range capacity for seventy passengers.

Do X*, built at Dornier's Swiss factory at Altenrhein, first flew on 25 July 1929. In October of that year the Do X astonished the world by taking off from the Bodensee with a human cargo of 169 persons—150 passengers, ten crew, and nine stowaways.

The Do X, despite her great size, possessed classic Dornier features, including the familiar *Flossenstummel* (sea wings), a broad, untapered main wing, and a long, slender, Wal-like fuselage with a two-step hull. She was driven by twelve air-cooled Siemens-built Jupiter Bristol engines of 525 horsepower each, mounted in six Dornier-style tandem nacelles. Each nacelle sat atop a streamlined turret through which a mechanic, via a passageway in the thick main wing, could reach the engine in flight. A narrow secondary wing, atop the main wing, connected each of the nacelles. Each engine drove a fixed-pitch, four-bladed wooden propeller. Her deep hull contained three decks and was divided into cabins that could accommodate sixty-six passengers on long flights or over a hundred on shorter segments. With her wing span of over 157 feet and maximum weight of 114,640 pounds, she easily outsized any airplane in the world.

From the beginning, though, the giant Do X was plagued with problems, largely because of the number and inadequacy of her power plants. Early in the Do X's career Dornier decided to replace the inefficient Jupiters with 600-horsepower Curtiss Conqueror water-cooled engines. At the same time, the unneeded secondary wing was eliminated. With the new engines, the Do X's advertised maximum weight was increased to 123,469 pounds versus an empty weight of 65,036 pounds. Despite this apparent load-carrying capacity—a load-to-tare of 48:52—the Do X stowed scarcely enough fuel to fly a thousand miles. Because of her rear-engine cooling troubles, she had a service ceiling of only 1,540 feet (500 meters).

On 2 November 1939, amid great fanfare, the Do X departed Friedrichshafen on a grand tour of Europe and the Americas. Bad luck dogged the giant flying boat throughout the journey. She suffered fire damage in Lisbon. She damaged her hull during a takeoff in the Canary Islands. In Brazil her captain was relieved of command because of his objection to giving "joy rides." After wintering in New York, the Do X recrossed the Atlantic, via Newfoundland and the Azores, but ran short of fuel approaching Lisbon and water-taxied the last six miles up the Tagus

*The *X* stood for "experiment" rather than "ten."

River. What was intended to be a triumphal procession of German technology turned into a trail of broken parts, aborted schedules, and wounded Teutonic egos.

By the time the grand tour was finished, so was the Do X. She was flown briefly by DLH, and then passed to the Deutsche Versuchsanstalt fur Luftfahrt (DVL)—the German aviation research and testing institute. Two more versions of the Do X were constructed for Italy, powered by 550-horsepower Fiat water-cooled engines. These aircraft, however, never entered commercial service and were retired as experimental vehicles.[5]

Claude Dornier's behemoth, an amalgam of good and bad ideas, had foundered largely on the inadequacy of her power plants. She entered history as a bold but failed flying boat experiment.

Meanwhile, another German builder, Adolf Rohrbach, was designing flying boats intended for DLH's seagoing operations. In 1922 Rohrbach established the Rohrbach-Metall-Aeroplane Co A/S in Copenhagen. There he began producing a series of seaplanes, the Ro I, II, III, and IV, which were squarish, flat-surfaced aircraft, all similar in shape and design but graduated in size and power plant. Rohrbach's hull-bottom design employed a deep V with a concave contour up to the chines at water level. This feature provided exceptional hydrodynamic lift and at the same time caused the water to spray back and downwards, reducing the spray pattern. Another unusual feature in the Ro III was conventional sailing gear—it had two masts on the hull and sails that could be raised to sail the vessel into port or be used in event of an open-sea landing.

In 1927 appeared a series of Rohrbach boats intended for DLH's transatlantic service. The first of these, the Rocco, accommodated up to ten passengers and was powered by two 650-horsepower water-cooled Rolls-Royce Condor engines mounted on struts above the wing. Each engine turned a wooden four-bladed propeller. Though the Rocco operated briefly in 1928 on DLH's Germany–Scandinavia service, the aircraft did not enjoy great success.

A follow-on flying boat, the Romar, first flew in August 1928. Like its smaller predecessor, the Romar was a high-winged monoplane with a marked dihedral, single fin and rudder, and large floats mounted under the wing and close to the hull. Her slab-sided hull was covered with duralumin and enclosed two cabins seating a total of twelve passengers.

Three BMW 500-horsepower water-cooled engines were fitted atop the wing, each driving a four-bladed wooden propeller.

Two versions of this aircraft were built, and then came a third powered by 750-horsepower BMW VIuz engines and accommodating as many as sixteen passengers. By contemporary standards the Romar was a sizeable flying boat, larger than any of the Dornier aircraft excepting the Do X. Her wings spanned 121 feet and supported a maximum gross weight of 40,785 pounds. With a cruising speed of 110 miles per hour, the Romar's operating range was said to be 1,242 miles.[6]

The Rohrbach flying boats, though innovative in design and ambitious in purpose, were overshadowed by the more successful Dornier designs. They proved to be unsuitable for the long transatlantic operations and from 1929 were relegated to DLH's Baltic services.

The ambitious Germans were extending their wings. German flyers and flying boats were operating in European waters, across the South Atlantic, and into Latin America. In Colombia, an airline called SCADTA (Sociedad Colombo-Alemana de Transportes Aéreos) was founded by German nationals and directed by an Austrian named Peter Paul von Bauer.

It was inevitable that a German-speaking airline, operating in the heart of the Americas, would draw the attention of a suspicious United States—and its flag carrier, Pan American Airways.

The Latins

With fourteen Commodore flying boats and eight S-38s acquired from NYRBA, Pan American gobbled up its competitors. Each new, lesser-financed and under-represented airline that opened routes in Central and South America became fair game for Pan American.

The presence of the German-owned SCADTA, operating in the region of the Panama Canal, not only caused alarm in Washington, it alerted Juan Trippe to a new takeover opportunity. In a clandestine series of negotiations, Pan American contrived to buy out the controlling interest in SCADTA. Though SCADTA continued to operate for another ten years, the facts of its true ownership remained a secret. Pan American was thus allowed to continue its expansion unopposed into South America.[1]

Another airline enterprise, West Indian Aerial Express, was begun by a barnstorming pilot named Basil Rowe in mid-1927. It had been WIAX's Fairchild FC-2, *La Niña*, flown by Cy Caldwell, that saved the day for Juan Trippe, flying Pan American's first official mail flight from Key West to Havana on 19 October 1927. Rowe and Caldwell would live to regret their samaritan act.

As WIAX developed its route system across the Caribbean, flying between San Juan, Santo Domingo, Port-au-Prince, and the Virgin Islands, they found themselves in a bidding competition for FAM 6 (Foreign Air Mail Route Six). Because of their already-established route network and demonstrated expertise, Basil Rowe had no doubt that WIAX would receive the contract. "The only other bidder," he recalled, "was the air line which I had helped to midwife with the now-lost

Fairchild. [The FC-2 floatplane, La Niña, with which Cy Caldwell flew Pan Am's first flight, was destroyed in a severe hurricane that struck San Juan in September 1928.] When the bids were opened, they were both identical, but our competitor was awarded the contract for flying the mail over the routes I had pioneered. We realized too late that while we had been developing an air line in the West Indies, our competitors had been busy on the much more important job of developing a lobby in Washington."

It was a familiar pattern. Trippe had won again, not in the steamy backwaters of the Caribbean where the airplanes were flown and the mail delivered, but in the hospitable lobbies of Washington. The *coup de grace* for WIAX came on 22 December 1928. WIAX and all its assets were absorbed by Pan American.[2]

When the U.S. Post Office advertised on 2 January 1929 for bids on FAM 8, from Brownsville, Texas, to Mexico City, via Tampico, Pan American again entered a bid at the top rate of $2.00 per mile. Again, Pan American won the contract. This time Trippe went after an American-founded airline called Compañía Mexicana de Aviación (C.M.A.), whose origins dated back to 1921. C.M.A.'s Fairchild FC-2s and Ford Trimotors were, by 1929, serving routes between Mexico City, Tampico, Tuxpan, and Yucatan.

On 23 January 1929, with the freshly awarded contract for FAM 8 in his hand, Juan Trippe bought out all the stock of C.M.A. from its founder, George Rihl. Since the purchase was by an exchange of stock, another principal C.M.A. stockholder, Sherman Fairchild, who had already acquired a large block of stock from the WIAX buy-out, was able to add to his already substantial holdings in Pan American.

With the acquisition of C.M.A., Pan American gained an uncontested network of Central American air routes and, via this new gateway, access to South America. The shortest and most desirable route to Buenos Aires, however, was down the west coast of the continent. A major obstacle along this route was the W. R. Grace Corporation, an American trading company with powerful political connections in the South American republics. Grace was in the shipping business, as well as banking and warehouses, and had no intention of allowing an upstart airline on its turf.

Trippe's tactic was to establish local, token airlines in both Peru and Chile. With this toehold, and with his Central American routes and exclusive U.S. foreign airmail contracts, he effectively managed to thwart

Grace's ambitions in the airline business. The two parties commenced negotiations and, on 21 February 1929, agreed to form a new airline, Pan American–Grace Airways. In March, Panagra, as the company was soon called, was duly awarded FAM 9. The new airline's mail contract gave them authority over the entire 4,500-mile route from Cristobal, Panama, down the western shore of South America, across the Andes to Montevideo and, as Trippe had hoped, to the crown jewel of South America, Buenos Aires.[3]

Now the Pan American network—and that of its affiliates—encircled all of Central and South America. Little of this spectacular growth could be attributed to individual route development by Pan American. By acquisition, by annexation, by overwhelming economic pressure backed by benevolent government support, Pan American established its hegemony in Latin America. The fifteen land planes acquired from C. M. A. brought Pan American's fleet to ninety-seven aircraft, with another seventeen in Panagra colors. By the end of 1930 Pan American had the largest route system of any airline in the Western Hemisphere.[4]

In 1927 Trippe hired a small, bald-headed Dutchman named Andre Priester. In his homeland Priester had worked at KLM under the much-respected Dr. Albert Plesman. In 1925, chafing under the slowness of promotion in the Netherlands, he and his wife came to America. His countryman, Tony Fokker, found him a position with a short-lived airline operated by Philadelphia Rapid Transit. When that came to an end, he made ends meet by working in Detroit at the Ford factory. And then came a telegram from Juan Trippe.

During the next few years, Andre Priester would place his indelible stamp on the life and times of Pan American Airways. The little Dutchman imbued the airline with a tradition of conservative, hard-nosed, by-the-book, meticulously planned operations.

Priester was assigned the duties of chief engineer, but his role swelled to embrace all of Pan American's flight operations. He made himself directly responsible for the design specifications and acquisition of new aircraft. He hired and fired air and ground staff. He reported directly to Trippe, who rarely interfered with Priester's activities.

Whereas Trippe, the patrician and aloof head of the airline, was seldom seen by the rank and file, Priester was highly visible. He would appear everywhere, inspecting, snooping, running a finger along a surface, searching out untidiness.

It was Priester who introduced to the barnstorming, anything-goes, fly-for-the-hell-of-it airline business a new principle: *standardization*. He wrote manuals and procedures and checklists. He dictated that there would be one and only one standard way—the Pan American way—to fly, dispatch, and maintain their airplanes.

Pilots, being individualists, resisted such autocratic ways. They joked about Priester's bald-headed, gnome-like appearance. They mimicked his thick, nearly indecipherable accent.

Priester personally hired his pilots. One airman, Bill Masland, remembered going to Priester's office on the fifty-eighth floor of the Chrysler Building in New York. "I could make out little of the man behind the desk: a dark outline and a pair of unblinking yellow eyes, no more. I waited for him to speak. He uttered not a word. So, after an interval of silence, I launched into my carefully prepared presentation. . ."

That was Priester's style. He would listen in icy silence while the young man squirmed. "I vant that you should talk," he would eventually tell the applicants. If he liked what he heard, he would hire them.

Pilot applicants were required to have not only a commercial pilot's license, but an aircraft and engine mechanic's license, and a second-class radiotelegraph operator's license. New pilots found themselves assigned for several months to the shops as apprentice mechanics before being allowed into Pan American's cockpits.

Priester issued to his crews a document headed "Safety First." "Always bear in mind the comfort of your passengers," the manual directed. "Handle your aircraft and regulate your flight as to accomplish maximum comfort for them and to inspire their confidence in yourself, your aircraft and in air transportation."

"Bumby [*sic*] air is psychologically disturbing to passengers and should be avoided whenever practicable." The manual gave specific instructions about how to do this:

a. by flying above clouds when they are sufficiently broken to permit glimpses of land and water.
b. by not flying in clouds.
c. by flying at high altitudes when smooth air can be found.
d. by flying over the water when air is rough over land, provided a too great deviation from the regular course, or too great increase of time required for the flight does not result.

We give rain squalls and local disturbances a wide berth when practicable.[5]

Priester had a love-hate relationship with his pilots. In his office he kept a picture of every crew member on the roster. Whenever an incident involved a pilot, Priester could associate a face with the name. He sent Christmas cards to each one, usually with a subtle company message. One year, Horace Brock received such a card. "Rather obscurely on the card could be found two little numbers, perhaps .87 in the upper right-hand corner and .55 in the upper left. For the many pilots with some aeronautical training, the meanings were obvious. The upper right referred to propeller efficiency, and the upper left to specific fuel consumption, efficiencies not yet attainable."[6]

Priester's zeal for perfection approached a religious attitude. He forbade smoking and drinking on Pan American aircraft, even for the passengers. He would fire a pilot for smoking in public, or a mechanic for possessing a dirty tool box.

With his dictatorial style, he was the quintessential airline boss. He was a man passionately devoted to duty, and he demanded a similar devotion from his people. He saw himself as father, mentor, disciplinarian, director. He was the counterpart of France's legendary airline chief, Didier Daurat, whom Antoine de Saint-Exupéry portrayed as the tough, uncompromising Rivière in his novel, *Night Flight*. "Love the men under your orders," said Rivière, perhaps speaking for Andre Priester, "—but do not let them know it."[7]

In Juan Trippe's view of his airline as the "chosen instrument," Pan American was to be an airborne maritime service. It flew the American flag and represented American interests around the globe. Its spirit and traditions would be naval and nautical. Its seagoing aircraft were to be called clippers, after the fast, full-rigged sailing vessels of the nineteenth century. Speed was measured in knots. Periods of airborne duty were called watches. The men who commanded Pan American's clippers were given the title of captain. Copilots were first officers. Instead of the typical flyers' attire of riding breeches, leather jacket, and silk scarf, Pan American pilots wore black, naval-style uniforms and white officer's caps. A discipline and protocol worthy of the merchant marine was established. For those airmen who would eventually command the great ocean-crossing clippers that Trippe and Priester had in mind, an even loftier title was created: Master of Ocean Flying Boats.

In 1928 Priester recruited to Pan American a young radio technician named Hugo Leuteritz. Leuteritz, who at the time was under contract to RCA to develop an aerial transmitter, was given the task of devising an airborne navigation system for Pan American's aircraft. Aerial navigation in 1928 amounted to no more than guesswork. Pilots depended exclusively on surface references for finding their way, and when visual contact with the earth was lost, so was the hapless aviator.

Leuteritz's interest in aerial navigation became a personal matter. One day in 1928, during a flight between Havana and Key West aboard one of Pan American's two Fokker F-7s, he was experimenting with an airborne radio. The pilot of the Fokker became lost, missed his Florida landfall and was forced to ditch the land plane in the Gulf of Mexico. The aircraft and one passenger sank at sea. Leuteritz received a fractured pelvis and shoulder. Upon emerging from the hospital, he said to Priester, "We better do something about navigation."[8]

Trippe's greatest recruiting coup came in 1929. A year and a half earlier, a young American flyer had electrified the world with his single-handed conquest of the Atlantic. Since then Charles Lindbergh had been deluged with offers to appear in motion pictures, endorse an assortment of commercial products, and tour the lecture circuit. He declined them all. Lindbergh's abiding interest was the advancement of aviation.

Pan American lost no time in making overtures to Lindbergh. Already the Lone Eagle had signed a contract with Clement Keys of Transcontinental Air Transport (which ultimately became the modern TWA), becoming chairman of TAT's technical committee. The domestic routes he surveyed and organized became advertised as the "Lindbergh Line."

During the summer of 1928 Lindbergh made a number of visits to Trippe's office in New York to discuss Pan American's plans for an international American airline. Lindbergh was intrigued by Trippe's ideas, by the route and facility development the airline had in mind, and, particularly, by the futuristic airplanes scheduled to fly in Pan American colors. In January of 1929, Lindbergh signed a four-year contract as technical advisor to Pan American. His compensation would be $10,000 per year, plus options on ten thousand shares of Pan American stock at $15 per share, and another ten thousand shares at $30 per share. His duties included the surveying of new routes, flight-testing new machines, and contributing to the development of new aircraft.

Lindbergh's true value to Pan American was incalculable. No hero of the twentieth century had received the adulation that was showered on Lindbergh. Still in his twenties, he was regarded as an oracle in all matters related to aviation. The publicity that automatically attended his movements exceeded anything that could have been generated by a public relations department.

On his 27th birthday, 4 February 1929, Lindbergh took off in an S-38, inaugurating FAM 5, Pan American's new airmail route from Miami to Cristóbal, in the Canal Zone. The historic flight would include stops in Havana, Belize, and Managua, Nicaragua. Copilot for the journey was Pan American vice president John Hambleton, Trippe's old friend and a Pan American cofounder.[9]

Like all Lindbergh's public appearances, the flight attracted huge crowds. Trippe came along as far as Havana. He told the assembly at the airport that the flight was "but a forerunner of air mail and passenger service that will go to Valparaiso [Chile] by April first."

In Belize Lindbergh renewed his warm relationship with the people of the British colony—he had landed there in the *Spirit of St. Louis* in December 1927 during his goodwill tour of the Caribbean. A crowd of two thousand people turned out to cheer when Lindbergh landed the Sikorsky at Gatun Lake in the Canal Zone. Airmail had come to Panama from the United States, a distance of nearly two thousand miles in twenty-one hours and twenty-seven minutes flying time.[10]

Lindbergh's next mission attracted even more attention. In September of 1929, acting as Pan American's technical adviser, he inaugurated FAM 6, the new airmail route from Miami to Paramaribo, Dutch Guiana. That spring he had married Anne Morrow, daughter of the U.S. ambassador to Mexico. On the new trailblazing airmail flight, Lindbergh was accompanied by his twenty-three-year-old bride and by Juan and Betty Trippe. The trip extended into a 7,000-mile, three-week junket through Latin America.

The press treated the journey like a royal procession. The expedition departed Miami amid circuslike fanfare, speeches, and a deluge of roses. Lindbergh, who had once been a full-time airmail pilot, wore a dark business suit. He carried his flying helmet rolled up in his hand.

They flew the workhorse of the Pan American fleet, the reliable S-38 amphibian. In addition to the two couples, the crew was augmented by a copilot and a radio operator.

It was a hectic routine. Officially, the journey was an airmail flight. A schedule had to be kept. The air was often turbulent, the facilities usually primitive. In many ports of call the natives had never before seen an airplane. Waiting at every stop were adoring crowds eager for a glimpse of Lindbergh and anxious to inspect his shy young wife. There were government officials intent on delivering speeches. Admirers reached out to clasp the flyer's hand. Dictators wanted to bask in the warm publicity that attended his arrival.

For Trippe, each of the Latin republics was a marketplace. Pan American needed routes and facilities and concessions. While Lindbergh rode at the head of the processions and confronted the hungry press, Trippe put in long days in conferences with government officials.

En route to Venezuela, Lindbergh reverted briefly to the airshowman he had once been. In order to take aerial photographs with an unobstructed view, he turned the controls over to the copilot and crawled forward into the bow of the amphibian. In full view of his horrified passengers, he climbed up through the hatch, onto the bow of the aircraft, into the slipstream. At 1,500 feet above the jungle, without a parachute, he crawled out on the bow of the S-38 and positioned himself where he could shoot his pictures. With the wind nearly tearing the clothes off his lanky frame, he crawled back by the same route. He climbed into the cabin and resumed flying the airplane.

At Barranquilla, Colombia, a giant crowd had swarmed over the airfield, making it impossible to land. Darkness was falling, and the S-38 was nearly out of fuel. Lindbergh tossed notes asking the police to clear the crowd. The crowd remained. Lindbergh climbed the S-38 to seek another landing spot. At that moment, both engines sputtered, then fell silent.

The occupants of the cabin kept their silence while Lindbergh calmly glided the S-38 away from the airfield. He had spotted a lagoon about two miles away, and he dead-sticked the S-38 toward the narrow channel. Smoothly, Lindbergh skimmed the hull of the amphibian onto the lagoon. As the S-38 rocked to a stop in the darkening water, the tension broke. Laughter erupted inside the cabin.

They were picked up by natives in dugout canoes who took them to shore. They then transferred to an automobile where they were taken, late but unruffled, to yet another a gaudy reception. An illuminated sign greeted them: WELCOME LINDY.

The Flying Forest

S he was the largest airplane ever constructed in the United States. On 19 November 1931, when she took off from Miami for her inaugural journey to the Canal Zone, the age of the great flying boats had officially begun.

The Sikorsky S-40 was the culmination of a design effort that began in early 1930. Igor Sikorsky had signed a contract with Pan American to build two giant, four-engined, oceangoing aircraft. A third ship would be optioned. Each would cost $125,000. The S-40 would be the first airplane ever to be built to a particular airline's specifications.

That winter Sikorsky made numerous trips down from his Stratford plant to Juan Trippe's little three-room New York office at 100 West Forty-second Street. There, around a long table, he huddled with Trippe, Lindbergh, and Priester over the drawings of the new flying boat.

European conservatism often clashed with American impatience. Lindbergh wanted the S-40 to reflect the newest aeronautical technology—clean lines, a sleek airframe, cantilevered wings, fully cowled engines mounted integrally into the wings. He was disappointed when he first saw the S-40's maze of struts, braces, flying wires, and outriggers. She resembled nothing so much as an overgrown S-38, still featuring the boat hull slung beneath the wing, tail surfaces appended by twin booms to the wing and supported by braces from the stubby aft fuselage. Lindbergh could not resist calling the new amphibian a "flying forest."

Sikorsky held his ground. In his view, giant strides in aircraft development came in a layered, incremental process. The design of an aircraft as advanced as the S-40 ought to be an outgrowth of proven concepts, he thought. Such a concept was the already successful S-38.

Sikorsky believed in the "art of the possible." He was also being realistic. The refinements urged by Lindbergh were costly in terms of structural weight. The luxury of cantilevered wings and empennage and integrally mounted engines added massive thickness and weight, upping the aircraft's basic operating weight and lowering available payload. Such penalties could only be offset by additional power, which, in 1930, was a scarce commodity. The S-40's four Hornet engines would deliver a total of no more than 2,300 horsepower.

Andre Priester shared Sikorsky's beliefs. Performance in Priester's book was always second to safety and reliability. He saw the S-40 as a building block toward more ambitious aircraft.

Lindbergh eventually let himself be persuaded. The two Europeans were, he thought, "a remarkable combination—the dynamic and demanding Priester with his Dutch accent and the imperturbable Igor and his Russian accent."[1]

Trippe, as impatient as Lindbergh, sided with the conservatives, but for pragmatic reasons. Pan American needed the S-40—and its huge payload capacity—without delay. There was no time on Trippe's agenda for protracted experiments with aircraft design. For now, Sikorsky would proceed with the "flying forest."

Lindbergh had other concerns, mostly about maintenance of the Sikorsky boats. Salt water was the curse of seaplanes. He complained to Sikorsky that the S-38 had been fitted with brass nuts on an aluminum framework, a match which, almost overnight, caused electrolysis, with white powder forming where the two metals met. Sikorsky agreed to make the changes.[2]

There was the matter of cockpit placement, always an issue with flying boats. In the original plans, the cockpit had been located high up in the center section of the wing, where it resembled the bridge of a ship. Lindbergh thought that the pilots' compartment belonged forward, about one-third of the distance from the bow to the leading edge of the wing. This would improve crash survivability and enhance the pilots' visibility. An inherent problem with the S-38 was the deluge of water that sprayed from the propellers onto the windshield during takeoff and landing.

The S-40, like the smaller S-38, was to be configured as an amphibian. This was an anachronistic notion, which still persisted in 1930, that just as it was deemed safer to fly over bodies of water with float-equipped airplanes, so it was equally prudent to equip seaplanes with wheels to fly over land. Since the S-40 was intended to fly over great stretches of Latin American land masses, so she would be burdened with a massive, retractable landing gear. Because no landing gear hardware existed for an aircraft of such dimensions, Sikorsky searched a railroad yard to find shock absorber springs of sufficient size. The springs he eventually installed on the S-40 had been designed for a medium-sized railway car.[3]

Sikorsky and his Russian engineers had a talent for "cut and try" methods to find correct solutions. To find the proper hull design, they tested different shapes by constructing miniatures and towing them behind a boom attached to a motorboat. These model hulls, about six feet long, were dragged about the Housatonic River at various speeds for around two thousand runs, a total of two hundred hours of testing.

By the spring of 1931 the S-40 neared completion. When the aircraft rolled out of her hangar, Sikorsky shared his pride with his employees. "Once again," he wrote, "we could feel gratified in watching one more ambitious dream materialized. It was grand to stand before a nearly completed airplane, and to attempt to recall the impressions created by the early ideas and sketches of the ship before it was built, or even designed."[4]

She possessed a size and presence unlike any aircraft on earth. Her wings, towering some twenty-three feet above the ground, spanned 114 feet and had a chord of sixteen feet. They had required 1,740 square yards of fabric in their covering. From bow to tail she measured nearly seventy-seven feet. Empty, she weighed 24,748 pounds, and when fully loaded she weighed 34,000 pounds. Her big, thick wings carried a load of just over eighteen pounds per square foot of wing area.

The cabin of the S-40 was designed to carry forty passengers, four abreast, in unprecedented comfort over a distance of 500 miles. With only twenty-four passengers, her range was extended to about 950 miles. Her four 575-horsepower Hornet engines would give her an advertised cruise speed of 115 miles per hour.

Flown by Sikorsky's chief test pilot and countryman, Boris Sergievsky, the S-40 underwent all her test series. After minor modifications, she went back to the hangar to be painted in Pan American colors. She had exceeded all expectations. As a pure flying boat, without the railroad springs and heavy wheels, her payload could be increased by 1,800 pounds. Even as an amphibian, she could climb to 6,500 feet on three engines and fly level at 2,000 feet on only two.[5]

On 25 September, Captain Basil Rowe and a Pan Am team arrived to perform the acceptance tests. Rowe liked everything about the airplane except for the heaviness in the aileron control. "We discussed several corrective measures," he recalled, "and finally decided upon a greater gear ratio. This was far from the ideal solution, but it was the best we could do at that stage of completion. The trouble with our compromise was constant winding of the wheel, but it was better than doubtful control in rough conditions."

On 10 October 1931, Basil Rowe and his crew ferried the S-40 to Anacostia for her formal christening. The day, appropriately, was Columbus Day. Twelve thousand people watched the ceremony. While Navy and Marine Corps bands played, two radio networks reported the proceedings. Juan Trippe made a short speech. Mrs. Herbert Hoover swung a bottle of what was declared to be Caribbean seawater against the S-40's bow. The new ship became, officially, the *American Clipper*.[6]

She lived a glamorous life. For the inaugural trip, her captain was America's premier hero, Charles Lindbergh. As with all Lindbergh's travels, the flight was attended by worshipful crowds, clamoring press, and the usual gaudy send-off from the Pan American base in Miami. With veteran Basil Rowe as first officer, the *American Clipper* took off with thirty-two passengers on board, bound for Kingston, Jamaica, then onward to Barranquilla, Colombia, and Cristóbal in the Canal Zone. Among the passengers was Igor Sikorsky.

During the overnight stops, Sikorsky sat at the dinner table with the crew. The discussions dwelt, inevitably, on the new clipper and the "next step." A creative chemistry had by now developed between Lindbergh and Sikorsky. "Lindbergh and I would take the menu," recalled Sikorsky, "turn it upside down and make sketches for a long-range flying boat. We both believed that scheduled transatlantic flying was possible, and at that time a flying boat seemed to be the right solution. At those dinners we laid down the basic principles around which to design a transoceanic flying boat. The problem was to combine speed with long range and a payload which would make transoceanic airline routes practical and economical."[7]

The inaugural flight continued to Barranquilla without trouble, arriving precisely on schedule. But on the following day the expedition nearly came to grief. While the aircraft lay tied to her dock, Lindbergh stood atop the wing supervising the refueling operation. A fuel tank overflowed, spilling gasoline over the wing and into the water. Lindbergh suddenly realized that a number of the spectators on the pier were smoking.

"Stop smoking!" he called from the wing. To his horror, he saw the obedient smokers extinguish their cigarettes—by tossing them into the gasoline-covered water.

It might have been disaster. Several tense seconds ticked past. The cigarettes fizzled, then snuffed out. Happily for the *American Clipper*, and Lindbergh, there was no inferno.

Lindbergh waited in Barranquilla while Rowe and First Officer Charles Lorber took the S-40 on down to Cristóbal and back again. Then he resumed command for the return journey to Miami.

The transit in Kingston resulted in a delay, which Lindbergh calculated would put them into Miami just before nightfall. The S-40 had no provisions for night flying and, in any case, there would be no lights on Biscayne Bay for a night landing. But Lindbergh took off, thinking that if all went well, they would arrive with still enough light left to make a normal landing.

He was wrong. Darkness came, and the *American Clipper* was still airborne. In the blackness, Lindbergh could not even determine the wind direction. When he finally settled the big ship onto the darkened water, it smacked the surface, porpoised, then lurched hard to the left, tossing a few unfastened passengers out of their seats.

Chagrined, Lindbergh apologized for the rough landing. Sikorsky, ever the nobleman, took personal blame for the landing. It wasn't at all Lindbergh's fault, he insisted. It must have been a problem with the design of the hull.

Lindbergh smiled. For the rest of their lives the two men would remain staunch friends.[8]

Over the years, Basil Rowe spent many hours in the cockpits of the S-40s. On one occasion during a flight to Colombia, he again had as a passenger the ship's builder, Igor Sikorsky. When Rowe went back to the cabin to pay his respects, he found the little Russian on his knees, feeling about the cabin floor, a worried expression on his face. The other passengers looked on with alarm. Rowe asked what the matter might be.

"I keep hearing a peep, peep, squeak, squeak."

Rowe listened, then assured him that a mechanic would attend to the matter when the Clipper landed in Kingston. Sikorsky, in the meantime, was upset. It was unthinkable that the *American Clipper*—*his* dreamship—should be afflicted with peeping and squeaking.

On the next leg of the journey, Rowe returned to the cabin. "Well, Mr. Sikorsky, do you still hear that peep, peep, squeak, squeak?"

"No, it's gone—what was it?"

"It was a thousand baby chickens in the cargo department. We unloaded them in Kingston."

Understanding, then relief, flooded Sikorsky's face. He turned to the window and laughed.[9]

On another occasion Rowe became involved in a publicity stunt. He was to race the *American Clipper* from Havana to Miami against an ancient cart drawn by oxen. The oxen were to plod along a four-mile route through the center of Havana to the outskirts of the city. The winner would be whichever vehicle arrived at its destination first.

Rowe didn't like the odds. "It proved much too wild because of three factors. The first and foremost was the method used by the Cubans in handling oxen: goading them along with a nail in the end of a pole. The second factor was a northeaster that I had to buck. The third was the Cuban himself and his inherent love of gambling."

Along the way Rowe was kept informed by radio of the oxen's progress. He heard that the crowds were betting heavily against the clipper and had begun pushing the cart until the beasts were moving at about ten miles an hour. When he was only halfway to Miami, he heard that the oxen were within a mile and a half of their goal.

Rowe decided to dispense with ethics. "I pulled the throttles closed and set the big flying clipper down on a smooth stretch of protected water in the lee of the Keys. I radioed 'Just landed,' planed along on the step for half a mile or so, then pulled up and continued the flight. It was a dirty trick, but so is sticking nails in oxen."

In 1931 Pan American posted its first annual profit—$105,452 on a revenue of $7,913,587. With the increase in passenger and mail revenues afforded by the capacious S-40s, the airline, at the height of the depression, would continue to show profits.

The *American Clipper* and her two sister ships, the *Caribbean Clipper* and the *Southern Clipper*, flew the routes to Central and South America, ranging as far south as Buenos Aires, Argentina, and Santiago, Chile, stopping regularly at ports like Rio de Janciro, Brazil; Bogota, Colombia; and Lima, Peru. In 1936 their capacity was increased to forty passengers with the installation of the more powerful 660-horsepower Hornet TB1 engines.

The sturdy S-40s provided a decade of faithful service to Pan American. After Pearl Harbor day they were requisitioned by the U.S. Navy and served as training ships until their retirement in 1943. The three aircraft logged an estimated ten million miles of flight, never experiencing a crash—a remarkable record for flying boats.

The S-40 was never a transocean flying boat. She was a lumbering truck of a transport aircraft, short-legged but sturdy, designed for the Latin American route system. She was a mammoth for her day, exceeded in size only by the less successful mammoth, the German Do X.

In her original configuration, the S-40's load-to-tare ratio (maximum payload versus empty weight of the aircraft) was 28:72, a far cry from the efficient numbers (nearly 50:50) of the next generation of over-ocean boats. But even this modest performance would have been impossible had Sikorsky incorporated the weighty streamlining features that Lindbergh had originally urged.

With the S-40, Sikorsky had practiced the "art of the possible." Now it was time for the next step. From the building block of the S-40 he would construct the world's most advanced flying boat.

The Next Step

The S-42 flying boat, in penciled outline, first appeared on the back of a hotel restaurant menu in Cienfuegos, Cuba. During the inaugural flight of the *American Clipper*, Lindbergh and Sikorsky had sketched the features of a new flying boat. By the time the inaugural trip returned to Miami, their menu-sketching had become a proposal for a transoceanic flying boat.

Lindbergh, it was agreed, would promote the idea to Pan American, whom he served as a technical consultant. Sikorsky would sell the plan to United Aircraft, the parent corporation of Sikorsky Aircraft Co.[1]

The S-42 proposal matched the ambitions of Juan Trippe, whose eye was now firmly fixed on the oceans. In Trippe's vision, Pan American was to become America's maritime service of the air. The historic Atlantic and Pacific trade routes, if Trippe had his way, would be plied by Pan American's flying merchant ships.

The competition had already begun. In the South Atlantic the adventurous French airline, Aéropostale, was sending mail from Africa to South America aboard their Latécoère flying boats. In the North Atlantic, the Germans had placed the *Graf Zeppelin* in regular service. In 139 flights across the Atlantic, the airship had carried an impressive total of 17,591 passengers without mishap. The age of transatlantic air travel was nearly at hand.[2]

On 1 October 1932 Pan American placed an order for three S-42 flying boats with options for seven more. The order specified features unprecedented in an airliner, including the technological advances sought by Lindbergh in the S-40 and the evolutionary "next step" development espoused by Andre Priester and Igor Sikorsky.

* * *

The final configuration underwent several alterations. In its original concept, the S-42 was a twin-engined, long-range flying boat. Early in the planning stage, the twin-engine concept gave way to a three-engine design. This idea, installing the engines on struts above the wing and fuselage, eventually yielded to a four-engine arrangement with the engines mounted directly into the leading edge of the wing which, in turn, was fixed atop a streamlined cabane in the upper fuselage.

The development of the S-42 became a collective effort. Priester and Lindbergh were the Pan American overseers of the project. Sikorsky's co-subsidiaries at United Aircraft—Pratt and Whitney, and Hamilton Standard—were to supply the engines and propellers. Although the new Pratt and Whitney Twin Wasp engine was the initial choice to power the S-42, it was later decided to stay with the upgraded, 700-horsepower versions of the reliable Pratt and Whitney Hornet engine instead of the unproven new Twin Wasp. The performance required in Pan American's specifications could only be achieved with a new device recently developed by Hamilton's brilliant engineer, Frank Caldwell—the controllable-pitch propeller.

The most advanced feature of the S-42 was her wing. To achieve the range and economy demanded in the performance requirements, Sikorsky realized he would need a wing of high-aspect ratio.* This meant a long, narrow wing, which would yield minimum induced drag and produce the highest coefficient of lift. But such a wing also presented serious problems of strength and weight. A "clean," cantilevered wing, one without external bracing, would be too heavy, with excessive thickness at the wing root, to satisfy Sikorsky's requirements. He chose instead a two-spar wing, braced to the fuselage by two extruded duralumin struts on either side. Despite the apparent clutter of the struts, this structure afforded a more efficient wing than would have been possible with a heavier, thicker, but more streamlined cantilever design.

Even more extraordinary was the load that would be borne by the S-42's wing. In the initial version, the new flying boat had a wing loading of nearly thirty pounds per square foot of wing area, a statistic that placed the S-42's wing in the same category as the hottest racing planes and fighters of 1934. Such a high wing loading not only delivered long-range fuel efficiency, but would provide better turbulence and storm

*Long wing span versus a narrow chord.

penetration. To the builders of the S-42, however, the wing-loading statistics spoke a single profound statement: *Less structure would be used to carry more load.*[3]

There were risks and penalties associated with high wing loadings. Excessively long takeoff runs and high landing speeds were problems that would have to be offset by new design features. A highly efficient airfoil, designated GSM-3, was developed by the brothers Michael and Serge Gluhareff in the Sikorsky wind tunnel. A trailing edge flap, 68 feet in span with 185 square feet of surface, was designed to reduce the landing speed of the S-42 to 65 miles per hour, the maximum certifiable landing speed specified by the Civil Aeronautics Authority. The new Hamilton Standard controllable-pitch propellers could deliver the full torque of the Hornet engines at takeoff and then coarsen their pitch to provide cruising economy.[4]

Much had been learned from the S-40. Although the empty weight of the S-42 was approximately the same as that of the S-40, her hull was 30 percent lighter, narrower by ten inches, and elongated by eight feet. Extensive testing in the wind tunnel and on the Housatonic River produced a cleaner, more efficient shape both in the air and on the water.[5]

The construction of the S-42 prototype was completed soon after Christmas, 1933, but ice in the Housatonic prevented a first launching until 29 March 1934. With test pilot Boris Sergievsky at the controls and a delighted Igor Sikorsky in the right seat, she quickly passed her water trials. The next day, in the air, she fulfilled her builders' hopes.

Throughout the spring and summer of 1934, the S-42 collected world records like flowers from a garden. On 26 April she lifted over eight tons of payload to an altitude of sixteen thousand feet, far exceeding the existing record. On 17 May she flew to a record altitude of 20,407 feet with a payload of 5,000 kilograms (11,023 pounds).

On 1 August 1934, the S-42 underwent her formal acceptance test for Pan American. On board were test pilot Boris Sergievsky, Captain Edwin Musick, Pan American's chief pilot, and Charles Lindbergh. Lindbergh had asked to be excused. "There is no advantage in my being on [the] plane," he telegraphed Trippe, "and I believe credit for breaking records should go to operating personnel." Trippe was adamant and persuaded Lindbergh to participate.[6]

A 311-mile closed course was laid out from the Sikorsky plant to the George Washington Bridge in New Jersey, over Staten Island and

Long Island to Point Judith in Rhode Island, and back to the departure point in Stratford, Connecticut. Taking off at near her maximum gross weight of 37,000 pounds, the S-42 flew four round trips over the course. For purposes of observation from the ground, she flew at relatively low altitude, using an average 69 percent of available power, cruising at an average speed of 157.5 miles per hour. When she arrived for the last time over Stratford after seven hours, fifty-three minutes, fifty-eight seconds, the S-42 had added eight more world records to her account. In a single flight, the S-42 had vaulted the United States into first place in the world in the number of aviation records held.[7] Significantly, the 1,242 miles she covered established her credentials as a true over-ocean airliner. The longest segment in the chain of transatlantic stepping-stones—Newfoundland to the Azores—was 1,240 miles.

The Atlantic would have to wait. Although the S-42 would have sufficed as a fast transatlantic mail plane, she lacked the capacity to carry the required fuel and a payload of more than six or eight passengers. She had been designed for the South American routes where she could carry up to thirty-two passengers.

The larger, longer-legged M-130, still on Glenn Martin's drawing boards, was intended to be the transatlantic airliner. The logical routes to Europe were either from Newfoundland to Iceland, thence to the British Isles, or from Newfoundland to the Azores, or the more southerly track from Bermuda to the Azores. Each of these routes required the consent and cooperation of His Majesty's government. Despite continued negotiation and political bargaining, Pan American remained unable to extract the necessary concessions from the British. The reason, despite the rhetoric from both shores of the Atlantic, lay in one simple truth: The British, in 1934, had nothing like the S-42 or the coming M-130. Until Imperial Airways, the British flag carrier, possessed an airplane that could commence scheduled flights from Britain to the United States, Pan American would find itself blocked from the British crown colonies.[8]

The S-42 entered Pan American service in the fall of 1934. Flying the eight-thousand-mile route from Miami to Buenos Aires, she reduced the travel time from eight days to five. She introduced a new standard of air travel to the South American market and firmly established Pan American as the premier flag-carrying American airline.

Meanwhile, Juan Trippe had taken a gigantic gamble. Betting on the Atlantic, he had ordered not only the Sikorsky S-42 flying boats, but he had also signed a contract with the Glenn L. Martin company for three of the even larger, more advanced M-130s.

More than ever, he needed an ocean.

Pacific

In his New York office on the fifty-eighth floor of the Chrysler Building, Trippe kept a large globe. It had become his custom to measure great-circle distances on the globe with a string, then translate the measurements into flight time for his flying boats. For Pan American publicity releases, Trippe liked to be photographed studying his globe.

The trouble with the picture was that a sizeable portion of the globe remained off-limits to Pan American. The world's most trafficked ocean, the Atlantic, remained blocked. Landing rights at each stop on both the northern and southern routes were closed while negotiations with the British government dragged on.

If not Europe, then where? Pan American was scheduled to take delivery of a fleet of oceangoing flying boats. Over what ocean would they fly?

The greatest, bluest, emptiest expanse on Trippe's globe bore the label *Pacific Ocean*. Named by Magellan, the Pacific belied its name, looming like a heaving void between America and the markets of the Far East. But the European airlines were already there. The French were flying to Indochina. The Dutch were in Java. Imperial Airways, in partnership with the Australian airline, Qantas, was on its way. An opportunity was about to be lost.

At a glance, the shortest route from America to Asia appeared to lie across the top of the world, over the Arctic, via Alaska and Siberia. That route had already been surveyed, at Trippe's behest, by Lindbergh in 1931. Though suitable during the summer season, the vital landing and docking facilities in the Arctic remained ice-blocked for half the year.[1]

That left the South Pacific. To the astonishment of his own directors, Trippe announced that Pan American would cross the world's widest ocean at its widest part.

Vast stretches of empty ocean lay between the tiny island stepping stones that formed the 8,700-mile route to Asia. The segment from California to Hawaii would be the longest commercial air route ever attempted. Beyond Hawaii, safe havens would have to be found on the atolls of Midway and Wake, mere dots on Trippe's globe. Farther west, only Guam and the Philippines were presumed to be satisfactory since the U.S. Navy had already established operating bases there.

The problems were immense. Even with the development of an airplane that could cover the great distances between islands, no aircraft or passenger-handling facilities yet existed. No one knew whether there was enough sheltered water to accommodate a flying boat. In the case of Wake Island, there was no habitation, no shelter, not even fresh water.

But it could be done. Six months earlier, six U.S. Navy P2Ys had flown from San Francisco to Hawaii in under twenty-five hours. Pan American already had the S-42, the most advanced long-range aircraft in the world, with improved models on the way. Trippe had recently concluded a deal with Glenn L. Martin for the construction of three M-130s, a third larger in size than the S-42. He needed an ocean now. The Pacific, even at its widest point, would do.

In June 1934, C. H. "Dutch" Schildhauer, a former navy pilot and flying boat devotee, became Trippe's agent to accumulate the knowledge needed to begin the Pacific operation. In Washington Schildhauer learned that the Pacific islands they wanted to use, particularly Midway and Wake, were administered by no specific authority. Who, he wanted to know, granted or denied aerial access? Who could authorize construction of aircraft and passenger facilities?

Midway, 1,300 miles west of Hawaii, had been developed as a cable station. Like most Pacific atolls, it was ringed with coral and had a lagoon of sufficient size to permit a flying boat to take off and land.

Wake was another matter. No one seemed to know anything about Wake Island. The tiny cluster of atolls was originally found by the Spanish in 1568, then rediscovered by a British captain, William Wake, in 1796. Since then it had been infrequently visited by various passersby, and since 1899 was claimed by the United States as a trophy of the Spanish-American War. Only twelve feet in elevation, the island was the summit of an undersea mountain. On all sides, the water deepened abruptly, and there appeared to be no break in the coral ring around the atoll. There was a lagoon, though its depth and suitability for flying boats had yet to be determined.

The question of authority was pursued in typical Pan American fashion. Hawaii, as well as Guam and the Philippines, posed little problem, but Midway and Wake were a gray area. Trippe launched a campaign to have them placed under U.S. Navy jurisdiction. In the fall of 1934 he petitioned Secretary of the Navy Claude Swanson for permission to operate through the island groups and to construct marine facilities on Midway, Wake, and Guam. To protect his investment in the facilities, he proposed a five-year lease at a rental of $100 per year.[2]

As it happened, Trippe's plans dovetailed with the navy's concerns in the Pacific. The growing belligerence of Japan following WW I had begun to raise an alarm in both the State Department and in the navy. Having appropriated the Micronesian chain of islands in the western Pacific, Japan then dropped a curtain of secrecy around them, developing harbors and airfields in defiance of the postwar treaties. Intelligence gatherers in the navy feared that the islands were being developed not only as a protective fence guarding the gates of Japan, but also as a staging base for a possible eastward assault on American interests in the central Pacific. At the same time, the Japanese government loudly protested each overt American military venture into Pacific waters.

So the timing of the Pan American proposal was fortuitous. The State Department found it desirable, in view of the Japanese attitude and considering the constraints placed on the United States by the treaty ceilings, to establish an American presence in the middle and western Pacific, directly beneath the noses of the Japanese. That presence would be somewhat legitimized in the form of a commercial airline.

On 13 December 1934, President Roosevelt signed the order placing Wake, Johnston Island, Sand Island in the Midway group, and Kingman Reef under navy jurisdiction. The same month, Secretary Swanson granted to Pan American the use of naval facilities at San Diego, Pearl Harbor, and three months later approved Pan Am's use of Midway, Wake, and Guam. Thus was cemented a relationship between the U.S.

Navy and Pan American Airways that continued to grow throughout the next decade. Technology would be exchanged, crews cross-trained, fields, harbors, and navigational facilities shared, personnel transferred from naval service to airline service and vice versa. In the empty skies of the western Pacific, Pan American would act as the surrogate eyes of the navy.[3]

On 27 March 1935, the SS *North Haven*, a freighter chartered by Pan American, steamed from San Francisco laden with tons of fuel, generating plants, construction materials, radio units, boats, prefabricated housing, foodstuffs, tractors, dynamite, storage tanks, windmills, and 118 men. The workers chosen for the project were adventurers with construction skills. Many were college students with engineering backgrounds. In overall charge of the expedition was William Grooch, a former navy pilot who had begun his airline career with NYRBA, been summarily dismissed by the hot-tempered Ralph O'Neill, then hired by Andre Priester as a Pan American pilot.[4]

Pausing in Honolulu to take on additional supplies and more workers, the *North Haven* steered westward for Midway. Because of the encircling reef and the shoal water on all sides of the island, the *North Haven* was forced to drop anchor four miles out at sea. There, while the ship heaved and tossed, the crew of adventurers labored to unload their heavy cargo onto barges. They had to cross the jagged coral reef, land the supplies, then muscle them across the fine sand of Midway.

While a construction crew remained at Midway to erect the airline village, the *North Haven* hoisted anchor and continued to the next island on the route, Wake.

Their worst fears about Wake Island were confirmed. There was no shallow water in which to drop anchor. The slope of the nautical mountain dropped steeply on all sides to the floor of the ocean. Contrary to plan, because of the low elevation of the southern island and the likelihood of flooding, they would have to erect their village on the northern island of Wake's hairpin. But due to the prevailing northerly wind the *North Haven* would remain off the southern side, with her anchor fixed to the reef, in order to unload the cargo. Worse, the lagoon was found to be precariously narrow and shallow for flying boat operations. Worst of all, they discovered that Wake's lagoon was filled with hundreds of protruding coral heads, each of which could gut the fragile duralumin hull of an airplane.

The adventurers, many now seasick and sunburnt, grimly went to work.

Aerial navigation was another problem. How was a flying boat to find a tiny speck of sage and sand in the middle of the Pacific? The aerial navigator's tools and techniques were little different from those used for centuries aboard sailing ships. Airborne navigation had never been practiced over a route this long. An error of only a few miles in the Pacific could cause an aircraft to miss its island target—an event guaranteed to end in calamity.

Trippe turned this matter over to his young radio wizard, Hugo Leuteritz. Since 1928, when Trippe had lured him to Pan Am, Leuteritz had enjoyed Trippe's unquestioning patronage while he labored to develop airborne direction-finding equipment.

Leuteritz's interest in aerial navigation amounted to more than a mere technical challenge. He had not forgotten his ditching experience aboard Pan Am's Havana to Key West Fokker land plane when the pilot had missed the Florida coast. Since that day, Hugo Leuteritz had felt an abiding passion for navigational precision.

The direction-finding system that Leuteritz now favored had been developed in England by a radio experimenter named Adcock. But Adcock's device, which consisted of an antenna stretched around four telephone poles oriented to the cardinal points of the compass, was a low-frequency radio and therefore of little use for long-range navigation.

Leuteritz experimented with the Adcock. He tried increasing the frequency, thereby shortening the wave length and increasing the range. He added a dipole to each of the four antenna poles, which further increased the device's range.

Leuteritz conducted his research in secret. He received Trippe's unfaltering support, since Trippe was convinced that the success of the operation hinged on the clippers finding their island bases, every time, without fail.

By early 1935 Leuteritz was able to send a secret message to his boss: *The long-range direction-finder was working*! They should begin building the devices immediately. If the DF were installed at each terminus of an overwater route, an aircraft would be able to fix its position by radio bearing over the entire distance.

There were skeptics in high places. To many of the aviation "experts" of the time, a Pacific air route was premature and foolhardy. No commercial flying boat had yet made it as far as Hawaii. The craft of aerial navigation was still inadequate. Trippe was advised by the chairman of the National Committee on Aeronautics to cancel his plans. The industry, declared the chairman, could not afford a disaster such as the one Trippe was preparing. Pan Am should pull back and wait until advancements in aircraft design and navigation made the Pacific a navigable route.

Worried, Trippe sought out Leuteritz. He told him about the doubters in Washington. Was the DF, in fact, reliable? What if the equipment failed? Were they biting off too much?

Leuteritz explained the extensive research he had performed on the system. The equipment, he told Trippe, had undergone thorough testing, first in the Caribbean and South America, and then on the West Coast. It worked. If Trippe wanted, he could come along and see for himself.

Trippe shook his head. He needed no further convincing. He gave the order to go ahead.[5]

The supply ship *North Haven* was already under way in the Pacific when Glenn Martin advised that delivery of the M-130 would be delayed. Trippe had already established a new Pan American Pacific base at Alameda, on the eastern shore of San Francisco Bay. Accords had been reached with the U.S. Navy and the State Department to use and develop existing facilities in Hawaii, Guam, and the Philippines. To anchor the western terminus of his Pacific route, Trippe had bought an interest in China National Aviation Corporation (CNAC) in March of 1933, thus establishing Pan American's presence on the Asian mainland.[6]

There was no time to wait for the Martin flying boat. To the Sikorsky S-42 would fall the task of pioneering the Pacific airways. The second of the S-42s delivered to Pan Am went back to the Sikorsky plant. There she was stripped of her cabin furnishings, fitted with extra fuel tanks and a maze of plumbing inside the fuselage, and two rest bunks in the after cabin. More powerful 800-horsepower Pratt and Whitney S1EG engines were installed, affording a 5,000-pound increase in gross weight, up to a new maximum of 43,000 pounds. Her wing span was lengthened to 118 feet 4 inches. The modified aircraft, now equipped as an S-42B, had a still-air range of nearly 3,000 miles, sufficient for the longest Pacific segment, San Francisco to Honolulu, some 2,400 nautical miles.[7]

Rechristened the *Pan American Clipper*, the modified S-42 went to Miami in February 1935 for endurance and navigation trials. Under command of Pan Am's chief pilot, Captain Edwin C. Musick, the *Pan American Clipper* rehearsed her Pacific journey. Long-range cruising techniques were developed using carefully calibrated fuel counters, installing carburetors with a new, automatic mixture control, experimenting to determine the most efficient power versus revolutions per minute for the new Hamilton Standard controllable-pitch propellers. Tests were performed with each engine shut down, one at a time, and the resulting fuel consumption noted. Emergency procedures were rehearsed. Multiple engine failures were practiced. The crew learned to hand-pump fuel from the fuselage tanks to the wings in the event of an electrical pump failure.

On the afternoon of 23 March 1935, Musick and his crew took off in the reconfigured S-42 and pointed the nose of the flying boat out over the Atlantic. Darkness came, and they continued southeastward, in the direction of the Virgin Islands. Throughout the night they flew, navigating by the stars, pumping fuel from the fuselage to balance the load in the wings, practicing the myriad tasks of long-range flight. The smell of fuel pervaded the cabin. Worried, the crew opened the windows.

This was the longest flight ever attempted by a flying boat. The craft of aerial navigation was a new skill, still being developed, but founded in centuries-old principles. Navigator Fred Noonan, who had worked aboard sailing ships before coming to Pan American, was perhaps the first professional aerial navigator in history. Now Noonan labored with his bubble sextant, shooting and reshooting his celestial fixes, checking and rechecking his calculations, while the S-42 cruised through the night sky at two-and-a-half miles a minute.

Six hours into the flight Musick sent for Noonan. A blinking light had appeared on the horizon. A lighthouse? How could there be a lighthouse in the middle of the empty ocean? Noonan stared at the blinking light, as perplexed as Musick.

Gradually, the light became steady. Noonan began to laugh. The light, which was not a lighthouse, happened to be the planet Jupiter rising from a low shelf of cloud over the rim of the earth. Then everyone laughed, including the taciturn Musick. But the relieved laughter betrayed their anxiety. The men realized that in this new flying boat they were entering an unexplored world where nothing was what it seemed. Planets became lighthouses. The ocean had become a trackless void.[8]

The dawn came. Musick had already turned and headed the flying boat westward. The S-42 continued past the Bahamas chain, over the Florida peninsula and back out to sea into the Gulf of Mexico. Again they turned and, after seventeen hours, sixteen minutes in the air, touched down in Biscayne Bay, back in Miami.

It had been proved. The *Pan American Clipper* had the necessary range, and her crew possessed the skills. They could fly to Hawaii.

"GIANT SILVER CLIPPER SHIP ARRIVES FOR TRANSPACIFIC SERVICE," reported the *San Francisco News*. Musick and his crew—First Officer R. O. D. Sullivan, Navigator Fred Noonan, Second Officer Harry Canaday, Engineering Officer Vic Wright, and Radio Officer Wilson Jarboe, Jr., made several preliminary flights out to sea, homing back to Alameda on Hugo Leuteritz's DF. They learned to identify by sight each of the bays and harbors on the California coast. They practiced blind landings in San Francisco Bay.

On the sunny afternoon of 16 April 1935, Musick taxied the *Pan American Clipper* out into San Francisco Bay. A few minutes before four o'clock, he pushed the four overhead throttles full forward. The big flying boat surged across the bay, lifted in a trail of spray and foam and climbed slowly westward. She disappeared in the low overcast over the coast, then broke clear at about six thousand feet.

Noonan's navigation kept the flying boat precisely on course. In smooth air the S-42's engines thrummed all night without missing a beat.

Soon after sunrise, the gray hump of Molokai came into view. Musick ordered his crew to shave and don fresh uniforms. Eighteen hours and thirty-seven minutes after leaving Alameda, he landed the *Pan American Clipper* in Pearl Harbor, one minute behind schedule. They had broken by six hours the record set a year earlier by the six navy P2Ys.

The return journey was another story. For almost the entire flight the clipper bucked unpredicted headwinds that slowed its ground speed to less than a hundred knots. As fuel and time were expended, the clipper neared the end of its endurance, which had been calculated at twenty-one-and-a-half hours. At Alameda Trippe and the crew's anxious wives waited in silence. On a wall chart they watched the *Pan American Clipper*'s painfully slow progress.

Musick tried different altitudes, searching for better winds. Vic Wright leaned the engines, slowing the RPMs, squeezing the most mileage from each drop of fuel. Fred Noonan struggled to pinpoint their exact position in the cloud-filled skies. His fixes showed their ground speed to be less than a hundred knots.

With less than half an hour of fuel remaining, they spotted the California coast. When Musick settled the *Pan American Clipper* down on San Francisco Bay, they had been airborne for twenty-three hours and forty-one minutes.

Nothing was said to the press about the scarcity of their remaining fuel, or the fact that for much of the night the *Pan American Clipper* was lost. The press release explained the delayed arrival as intentional. The crew had been conducting tests on three different ocean tracks during the long flight. Juan Trippe told the press that "the results fully justify early inauguration of through service to the Far East."[9]

During the summer months of 1935 Musick again flew to Honolulu, and then on to Midway where the new flying boat facility had been readied. There were no difficulties on this return voyage.

In mid-October, while Musick went to Baltimore to begin acceptance tests of the Martin M-130, Rod Sullivan took the *Pan American Clipper* again to Honolulu, onward to Midway, and then farther westward to the untried lagoon of Wake Island.

Rod Sullivan, in the opinion of his fellow airmen, was "a diamond in the rough." He was a burly, pug-nosed Irishman with a quick temper and a heavy-handed touch with both airplanes and people.[10]

When Sullivan arrived over Wake Island in the *Pan American Clipper*, the lagoon was still only partially ready for flying boat operations. From the air he could see the deadly coral heads still protruding like mushrooms through the greenish clear water.

For months a young ex-varsity swimmer from Columbia University, Bud Mullahey, had been assigned the risky task of dynamiting coral heads in the Wake lagoon. Daily Mullahey had dived beneath the surface, planted his charges and removed the obstacles, one by one. He had now exploded over a hundred coral heads. Hundreds still remained. But a channel of sorts had been cleared, marked by buoys, barely deep enough and long enough to accommodate a flying boat.

Sullivan brought the S-42 in, fighting the cross wind that ruffled the lagoon. His first approach was too fast and too long. He took the flying boat around for another try. Tension began to mount both in the cockpit and on the shore. There was no alternate landing site. Wake was surrounded by a thousand miles of ocean.

On the next attempt, Sullivan landed the flying boat, a bit too fast, and was able to stop only scant feet before running aground on the opposite shore of the lagoon.

Sullivan's explosion of temper, according to reports, continued from the dock up the sandy path and into the mess hall. His anger seemed sufficient to melt the icing from the cake especially baked for the occasion by the bedraggled builders of the desert island base.

The icing on the cake read "Welcome to Wake Island."[11]

Wings of Empire

G reat Britain in 1934 had nothing that could match the Sikorsky S-42. An official myopia had beset the British air transport industry. Colonial administrators and merchants still journeyed to the outposts of the empire aboard bi-winged anachronisms like the Short S.17 Kent and the Calcutta flying boats. As late as 1934, Arthur Gouge, Britain's eminent aircraft designer, was designing a new flying boat for Imperial Airways—a four-engined biplane. Like the empire it served, Imperial Airways was living in a bygone age.

The issue of American supremacy in the development of airline equipment had begun to rankle British sensitivities. Between 20–24 October 1934 the MacRobertson air race was conducted from Mildenhall, England, to Melbourne, Australia, a distance of 11,300 miles. The winner, not surprisingly, was a British De Havilland DH.88 Comet, three of which were specifically designed for the race. A shock, however, was the runner-up, a KLM Douglas DC-2. The third-place finisher was also an American-built airliner, a Boeing 247, which beat out another British entry.[1]

About concurrently came a pronouncement that changed everything. Henceforth, by decree of the postmaster general, all first-class Royal Mail was to be carried to empire countries on the air routes to South Africa, India, Burma, Malaya, and Australia, at no surcharge, *by air*. This decision galvanized the moribund British aircraft industry. It meant that the development of long-range transport aircraft, just as in America, was to be subsidized by the infusion of airmail revenues. Imperial Airways ordered the development of a new fleet of long-range flying boats.

To the slow-moving aircraft industry of between-the-wars Britain, the order for twenty-eight eighteen-ton flying boats landed like a lightning stroke. No aircraft order of that magnitude for airline equipment had ever been placed in Great Britain, nor had an aircraft of such size or complexity ever been constructed. The specifications were laid down by Major R. H. Mayo, Imperial Airways' technical adviser. Imperial wanted a flying boat with a capacity of twenty-four passengers and a normal range of 700 miles—long enough to serve the route to South Africa. Not yet specified—but clearly anticipated—was that a variant of Imperial's new aircraft would soon be flying over the North Atlantic.

There was never any doubt as to whom the flying boat order would go. The Short Brothers firm of Rochester was a venerable company that had produced numerous flying boats both for the military and for Imperial Airways.[2]

But there were severe time constraints imposed by the contract. The Shorts complained that there was insufficient time to develop an aircraft as advanced as the huge flying boat specified by Imperial. It would take years to make the giant leap from the plodding Calcutta-class boat to the ship Mayo wanted. There was no time for such luxury. Oswald Short, unwilling to forego the most lucrative deal in Shorts' history, signed the contract. Thus began one of the most intense development projects in British aviation history.

Arthur Gouge (whose accomplishments would eventually win him knighthood) was the guiding hand in the design of the new flying boat. Beginning with the cubic capacity specified by Imperial, Gouge produced a design for an aerodynamically clean, cantilever-winged monoplane with a span of 114 feet and a fuselage length of eighty-eight feet. Her empty weight would be 24,000 pounds, and her maximum gross weight 40,500 pounds. She would be powered by four Bristol Pegasus engines of 920-horsepower each, turning De Havilland controllable-pitch propellers.

The new lineage of Shorts' flying boats took a regal name—Empire class. Beginning with the S.23, the Empire class advanced the British flying boat standard an entire generation in one leap. Altogether, some forty-one S.23s were constructed. Each was given a name beginning with the letter C, and the series was collectively called the C-class flying boats.

Gouge's design incorporated features hitherto unseen on transport aircraft. Because of the S.23's size, a new hull design radically different from the Shorts' earlier flat planing bottoms, had to be constructed.

Gouge experimented with various hull tapers and beams until arriving at a narrow and effective shape that would allow the fully loaded ship to free herself from the water on takeoff.

Another innovation was a trailing edge flap design, patented by Gouge, that increased wing area by 30 percent with virtually no increase in drag. In actual use the Gouge flap succeeded in decreasing landing speed by twelve miles per hour.

The seventeen-foot-deep hull allowed space for two decks. On the upper deck was the cockpit, called the "bridge," adopting the same nautical vein as Pan American. It was a businesslike, spacious compartment equipped with the latest instrumentation of 1936, including an autopilot, Sperry artificial horizon and directional gyro, Hughes turn indicators and compasses, Kollsman altimeters, and a Marconi homing indicator. Abaft the cockpit on the upper deck was a long compartment containing space for freight and mail and, on the starboard side, the ship's clerk's office. In the forward section of the bottom deck was a spacious marine compartment containing the ship's mooring equipment. The rest of the lower deck was devoted to passenger accommodations. The forward passenger saloon was connected to the midship cabin by a central corridor that contained toilets on one side and the galley on the other. Abaft the midship cabin was a luxurious promenade cabin that could be configured both for seats and for sleeping berths. On the port side was a rail so that passengers could observe the outside scenery through the cabin windows. Yet another cabin, directly over the after step of the hull, contained seats for six passengers or more sleeping berths.[3]

Canopus, first of the regal Empire boats, first flew on 4 July 1936. Produced at a rate of about one a month, the C-class boats began carrying passengers and mail throughout the Imperial Airways network. For the remainder of the decade, wherever the Union Jack waved, the Empire-class boats flew. S.23s began serving the long route from Southampton to Alexandria, then southward across the African continent to Durban. An S.23 commenced the first flying boat service from England to Australia. Yet another opened service to Karachi.

The Empire boats' speeds, as advertised by the Air Ministry, were impressive. They had a maximum cruise speed of 165 miles per hour, with a maximum speed of 200 miles per hour at 5,500 feet. At a maximum gross weight of 40,500 pounds, the S.23 required a relatively brief takeoff run of twenty-one seconds.

But for all their elegance and aesthetically pleasing lines, the Empire boats lacked the hard-nosed operating efficiency of their American contemporaries, particularly the Sikorsky S-42 and the Martin M-130. The S.23's still-air range, with the medium-range tanks installed, was only 760 miles. In terms of load-to-tare ratio, the S.23 was an iron eagle. She was a weighty machine whose range and capacity never matched her builders' expectations. Although her maximum takeoff weight was 40,000 pounds, this included a disposable load of no more than 10,250 pounds, a load-to-tare ratio of only 25:75. In contrast, the Sikorsky S-42's load-to-tare ratio was 42:58, meaning that nearly half the aircraft's total weight amounted to fuel and payload. The S.23's "uncluttered" profile, including the cantilevered wing (regarded as an aerodynamic ideal in the 1930s) came at a dear price in structural weight. The great thickness required at the wing root to support the unbraced wing resulted in a dramatic increase both in weight and profile drag.[4]

There was more, however, to the economic equation. The Empire boats, appropriately named, were built to serve an empire. To Arthur Gouge and Oswald Short and the directors of Imperial Airways, the North Atlantic route was not the crown jewel of the airways as it was to Igor Sikorsky and Juan Trippe. Imperial Airways' routes were across the Mediterranean, over the Sudan and the jungles of Africa. They were the ancient routes to India. Passengers expected—and received—accommodations of unequaled luxury aboard the double-decked, lushly appointed S.23s and S.30s and, ultimately, the mighty S.26s. Imperial's competitors were not the flying boats of Pan American, but the DC-2s flown by KLM from Europe to the Far East, and the new Dewoitine D.333s entering the Europe-to-Southeast Asia service of Air France.[5]

Nonetheless, pressure would continue to build for a British-built, transoceanic aircraft to make its appearance on the Atlantic. Not only was the United States in the lead with their S-42, Britain's European rivals were now sending their own flying boats over the Atlantic.

The French Flair

The shortest and most benign route to the Americas lay beneath the equator. Only 1,890 miles separated Dakar and Senegal from Natal, on the eastern salient of South America. The prevailing weather on the South Atlantic was balmy. In contrast, the air distance from Shannon, on the coast of Ireland, to Botwood, Newfoundland, was 1,980 miles. The North Atlantic, with its ice-filled harbors and howling winter winds, was ill-suited to flying boats.

Both the German airline, Deutsche Luft Hansa, and the pioneering French company, Compagnie Générale Aéropostale, began to extend their routes to the Americas. As early as 11 May 1930, the famous French aviator, Jean Mermoz, and his crew took off from Dakar in a Latécoère 28 single-engined twin-float seaplane, the *Comte de la Vaulx*, landing in Natal nineteen-and-a-half hours later. With this flight, Aéropostale accomplished the first delivery of transatlantic mail and established a new distance record for hydroplanes.

The return voyage was less successful. With his copilot/navigator Jean Dabry and radio operator Léopold Gimie, Mermoz had been airborne for six hours when an oil leak forced him to make an open-sea landing. Still five hundred miles from Africa, Mermoz managed to set the *Comte de la Vaulx* down beside the Aéropostale weather ship, *Phocée*. Mermoz, his crew, and the mail were saved. The *Comte de la Vaulx*, damaged by the rough seas, was lost in the Atlantic.

The adventure convinced Aéropostale and the French Air Ministry that single-engined aircraft were inappropriate for South Atlantic operations. A requirement was issued for a transoceanic mail plane that could carry a 1,000-kilogram (2,304 pounds) payload between Dakar and Natal. Orders were placed for one model each of two advanced flying boats, the Latécoère 300 and the Blériot Model 1590. Thus was launched a decade of ambitious French flying boat development.[1]

The Laté 300 was a handsome craft, her long and slender hull fitted with Dornier-style sea wings and the large parasol wing-mounted on W struts above the fuselage. In appearance she bore a close resemblance to her two-engined Latécoère predecessors, the Laté 32 of 1927, and the Laté 38 that appeared in 1931.

The Laté 300 was powered by four Hispano-Suiza twelve-cylinder, water-cooled engines of 650 horsepower each, mounted in tandem configuration atop the wing's center section. Each engine turned a fixed-pitch, three bladed metal propeller. The trailing edge of the center section was recessed to permit clearance for the aft propellers.

In overall dimensions, the Laté 300 was comparable to the Martin M-130, though she preceded the American craft by nearly four years. Her large, low-aspect-ratio wing yielded a loading, at a maximum gross weight of 50,706 pounds, of 15.9 pounds per square foot of wing area, a kitelike statistic that contributed to her unimpressive cruise speed of only ninety-nine miles per hour. But in terms of efficiency, the French boat was constructed with disciplined use of weight. Her empty weight of 25,000 pounds afforded a fuel capacity of nearly 23,000 pounds *and* a mail load (as specified in her design requirements) of 2,204 pounds.[2] These were impressive statistics for 1931 and placed the Laté 300 in a class shared by few transport aircraft of the day.

Though the prototype first flew in 1931, the aircraft sank after a takeoff accident, disrupting the project's timetable. Not until October 1932 was the reconstructed and modified flying boat again flown. On 31 December 1933, bearing her new name *Croix du Sud*, she took off from Etang de Berre, near Marseille, and established a world's record by flying to St. Louis, Senegal, on Africa's west coast, a distance of 2,285 miles, in just under twenty-four hours. Two days later she made her first ocean voyage, crossing the South Atlantic to Natal, then continuing southward to Rio.

The success of the *Croix du Sud* prompted orders for three production aircraft, designated the Laté 301, for Air France, and another three, the Laté 302, for the French Navy. These aircraft differed only slightly from the original, their tail surfaces being enlarged and a greater dihedral added to the wings.

Air France's Laté 301s took the names, *Ville de Buenos Aires*, *Ville de Rio de Janeiro*, and *Ville de Santiago de Chile*. By January 1936 all three had been delivered. A month later, the *Ville de Buenos Aires* was lost on the Dakar-Natal route. The other two Laté 301s continued in service until the occupation, as did the French Navy's Laté 302s.

Aéropostale, in the meantime, had suffered financial straits. After an ongoing public scandal involving the company's directors, the airline sank into bankruptcy. On 30 August 1933 a unified French airline, Air France, was formed from the assets and operations of five independent French airlines, including Compagnie Aéropostale.[3]

Air France's most famous pilot was Jean Mermoz, who had become a French equivalent of America's Lindbergh. He was a charismatic figure, a war hero and pioneering airmail pilot whose life had been a continuous tale of adventure. He had survived capture by Moors after a forced landing in the Moroccan desert. In South America, he had once been forced to land his mail plane atop a twelve-thousand-foot-high mountain mesa. Realizing that he would have to be his own rescuer, Mermoz and his mechanic finally rolled their damaged airplane, themselves in it, off the sheer precipice of the mountain, gathering airspeed as the airplane dropped, and flew to safety.

It was Mermoz who had made the initial pioneering transatlantic flight in the *Comte de la Vaulx*—and the ocean ditching on the return flight. It was Mermoz, again, in January 1933 who flew the Couzinet 71 land plane, *Arc-en-Ciel*, nonstop to South America (an event that foreshadowed the coming demise of the transoceanic flying boat).

On 7 December 1936 Mermoz and his crew of four took off from Natal, bound for West Africa, in the *Croix du Sud*. It was the twenty-third Atlantic crossing of the famous Latécoère flying boat. During the night, a message was transmitted from the *Croix du Sud*: "*Coupons moteur arrière droit. . .*" ("Shutting down the right rear engine. . ."). And then silence. Despite an intensive search, no trace of Mermoz or the *Croix du Sud* was ever found.

The loss of Mermoz was a heavy blow. "We were haunted for hours by this vision of a plane in distress," wrote Antoine de Saint-Exupéry. "But the hands of the clock were going round and little by little it began to grow late. Slowly the truth was borne in upon us that our comrades would never return, that they were sleeping in that South

Atlantic whose skies they had so often ploughed. Mermoz had done his job and slipped away to rest. . ."[4]

Also designed to meet the French Air Ministry's requirement for a South Atlantic mail transport was the Blériot 5190 *Santos Dumont*. Because of financial troubles at the Blériot-Aéronautique company, this aircraft did not make her maiden flight until August 1933. By the middle of 1934 her test series had been completed, and on 27 November 1934 the *Santos Dumont* made her first Dakar-to-Natal flight.

The one-of-a-kind Blériot flying boat, though nearly equal in size to the Laté 300 and powered by the same engines, lacked the range and load capacity of the Latécoère boat. She was a metal-hulled aircraft, with the wing mounted on a turret-like cabane that housed the pilots' cockpit and the engineer's station. She had outrigger floats, which were attached to the hull by horizontal struts and to the wing by diagonal braces. Two of her four Hispano-Suiza, twelve-cylinder, 650-horsepower engines were mounted in tandem on the aircraft's centerline, and the other two were installed on either side in the wing's leading edge. Each engine drove a three-bladed, adjustable-pitch propeller and was accessible to the flight engineer while in flight.

The *Santos Dumont* was a large aircraft for her time. Her wings spanned 141 feet, and her fuselage was over eighty-five feet long. At her maximum gross weight of 48,502 pounds she could carry nearly 19,000 pounds of fuel with a payload of 1,322 pounds. With a wing loading of 20.3 pounds per square foot and the advantage of controllable-pitch propellers, she cruised at a respectable 118 miles per hour over a distance of 2,000 miles.

Though it was contemplated that on the Mediterranean routes she could carry up to forty passengers, she remained in service on the Atlantic. During her career, the *Santos Dumont* completed thirty successful Atlantic crossings.[5]

A medium-range flying boat, designed for service in the Mediterranean, the prototype Lioré et Olivier H 242 appeared in 1933 and was certificated in early 1934. Air France put this four-engined flying boat to work, staging from Marseille to Athens, Algiers, Ajaccio, Tunis, Tripoli, and Beirut.

The LeO H 242 was a high-winged monoplane with four 350-

horsepower Gnome Rhone Titan radial engines mounted in tandem pairs and braced by an ungainly arrangement of N struts atop the wing's center section. In the original configuration, the air-cooled Gnome engines, both front and rear, were uncowled. Twelve models of the H 242-1 then followed, and these had circular nacelles, an increased maximum gross weight, and a slightly greater speed.

The H 242's wings were wooden with ply covering, attached to a single-step, V-bottomed, duralumin hull. In her bow were the usual mooring compartment, a traditional two-pilot cockpit, and radio and navigation compartments. Her main cabin accommodated ten to fifteen passengers and was equipped with a lavatory and separate baggage hold.

With her blunt features and plethora of struts and braces, the H 242 was an aerodynamic ox. At best, she plowed through the sky at a stately cruise speed of 111 miles per hour. The H 242-1's maximum weight of 19,180 pounds provided a respectable disposable load of 7,357 pounds, and her 3,714-pound fuel capacity allowed a still-air range of 633 miles.

Except for the loss of two aircraft in operational accidents, all the H 242s stayed in service on the Mediterranean until the German occupation brought an end to their commercial careers.[6]

The Blériot and Latécoère boats, for all their range and advanced technology, were courier craft. They were the world's first transoceanic aircraft, but their function was limited to the transport of mail. As early as 1930, however, Latécoère had begun work on a large, passenger-carrying, transatlantic flying boat, designated the Laté 520. This giant craft was to be powered by four of the yet-unbuilt Hispano-Suiza 1,000-horsepower engines. With these power plants, the flying boat would have a maximum gross weight of 67,000 pounds—a statistic placing it in the behemoth class for 1930. When Hispano-Suiza peremptorily shelved their plans for the powerful new engine, Latécoère was then compelled to redesign the aircraft, using six of the available Hispano-Suiza 800/860-horsepower engines. This modified version was given the designation Laté 521.

At Etang de Biscarosse, near Bordeaux, the Laté 521 made her first flight on 17 January 1935. She had been designed to carry thirty passengers on transatlantic routes. On the shorter Mediterranean segments, she could be configured for as many as seventy. On her bow was the name: *Lieutenant de Vaisseau Paris*. Her aft fuselage bore the inscription *37 Tonnes* (81,571 pounds).

Glenn Hammond Curtiss, "father of the flying boat." (Smithsonian)

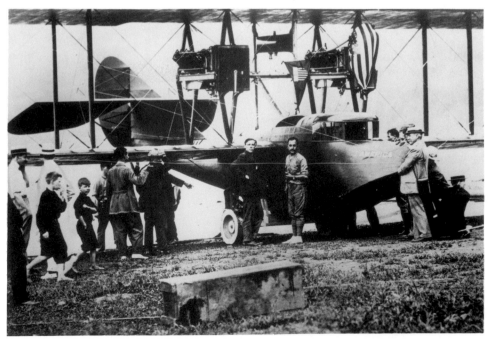

The Curtiss *America* on the day of her maiden flight. (Smithsonian)

The U.S. Navy's NC-4, first airplane to cross the Atlantic. (Smithsonian)

Cy Caldwell and the Fairchild FC-2, *La Niña*. Caldwell flew Pan American's first scheduled mail flight from Key West to Havana. (Pan American)

(*Right*) Ensign Juan Terry Trippe, who would later head Pan American. He was designated Naval Aviator Number 1806. (Pan American)

Weeks Faster to
SOUTH AMERICA
BRAZIL - URUGUAY - ARGENTINA

BY THE ROUTE *of the* GIANT FLYING YACHTS

NYRBA
NEW YORK RIO & BUENOS AIRES LINE Inc.

(*Above*) The graceful Consolidated Commodore was the flagship of the New York, Rio & Buenos Aires Line. (General Dynamics)

(*Left*) Though Ralph O'Neill's dream of an international airline came true, his creation, NYRBA, was gobbled up by Pan American. (Smithsonian)

The little two-engined workhorse, the S-38, firmly established the Sikorsky company in the aviation business. (Pan American)

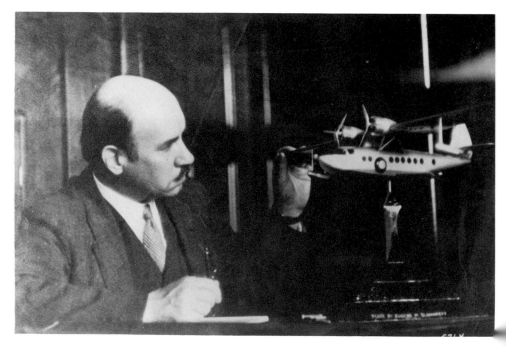

Igor Sikorsky with a model of the S-43 amphibian. (Smithsonian)

(*Above*) Dornier's sturdy little Wal, like Sikorsky's S-38, found employment around the world. (Dornier GMBH)

(*Right*) Professor Dr. Claude Dornier, German builder of a generation of advanced flying boats. (Dornier GMBH)

A Dornier Wal launches by catapult from the depot ship *Westfalen*. (Lufthansa)

Dornier's four-engined Super Wal entered the service of Lufthansa in 1928 on the Germany-to-Scandinavia routes. (Lufthansa)

The three-engined Rohrbach Romar, a medium-range boat operated by Lufthansa on Baltic services. Adolf Rohrbach, like Claude Dornier, pioneered the use of metal structures for flying boats. (Lufthansa)

The Dornier Do X, the world's largest airplane when it was constructed in 1929, was intended to carry a hundred passengers in ocean-liner comfort over the Atlantic. (Lufthansa)

The Do X configured with its original power plants, twelve 500-horsepower Siemens air-cooled engines. These were soon replaced with the more powerful Curtiss Conqueror water-cooled engines. (Dornier GMBH)

Despite its great size and complexity, the Do X's cockpit was ascetically equipped even by 1929 standards. (Dornier GMBH)

The Do X under construction at Altenrhein, on the Swiss shore of the Bodensee. (Dornier GMBH)

(*Above*) The Sikorsky S-40 was the forerunner of a generation of American-built, four-engined, long-range flying boats. (United Technologies Corporation)

(*Left*) Andre Priester, Pan American's chief engineer, oversaw every aspect of the airline's operations. (Pan American)

Charles Lindbergh and Juan Trippe in 1929. Trippe recruited Lindbergh as technical advisor to Pan American. (Pan American)

Because of its plethora of wires and braces, the S-40 was dubbed by Lindbergh the "flying forest." (United Technologies Corporation)

Pan American chief pilot Edwin Musick shunned the publicity that attended his record-breaking flights. Despite his reticence, he became the most famous airline pilot in the United States. (Clyde Sunderland)

When it appeared in 1934, the Sikorsky S-42 set new standards for over-ocean airliners. (Pan American)

Sikorsky S-42 in foreground with her older sister ships, a pair of S-40s, all on beaching gear. (Pan American)

The Shorts S.23 was designed to fulfill the ambitious requirements of the Empire Mail Scheme, but it lacked the range to be a transatlantic airliner. (British Airways)

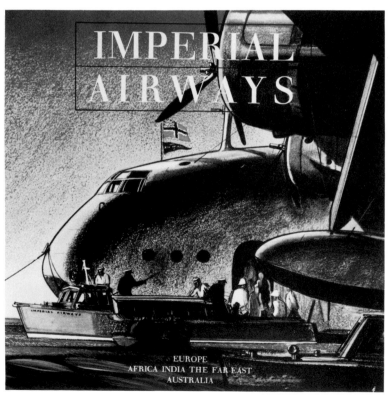

Imperial Airways' fleet of elegant Empire-class boats carried the Union Jack to the outposts of the empire. (Smithsonian)

IMPERIAL AIRWAYS

ENGLAND
EGYPT
'IRAQ
INDIA
HONG KONG
MALAYA
AUSTRALIA

SUMMER TIMETABLE
IN FORCE FROM 16 AUG. 1938 UNTIL FURTHER NOTICE
This timetable cancels all previous editions and is
subject to alterations without notice

(*Above*) The first of the Empire-class boats, *Canopus,*
in 1936. (British Airways)

(*Left*) Imperial Airways timetable. (Smithsonian)

Latécoère 300 *Croix du Sud.* (Musée de l'Air)

Latécoère 521 *Lieutenant de Vaisseau Paris.* (Musée de l'Air)

Jean Mermoz, pioneer airmail pilot and French national hero. In December 1936 he and his crew vanished in the South Atlantic with the *Croix du Sud.* (Musée de l'Air)

Antoine de Saint-Exupéry, writer and pioneer airmail pilot. (Museé de l'Air)

Lioré et Olivier 242. (Musée de l'Air)

Didier Daurat, legendary operations boss of the pioneering French airline, Aéropostale. Daurat was the model for Rivière in Antoine de Saint-Exupéry's novel, *Night Flight*. (Musée de l'Air)

Blériot 5190 *Santos Dumont*. (Musée de l'Air)

The Latécoère 631 was the largest passenger-carrying flying boat ever to enter commercial service. (Musée de l'Air)

Glenn Martin's mother, "Minta," was his lifelong companion and only confidante. (Smithsonian)

Transpacific inaugural of the *China Clipper* 22 November 1935 in Alameda, California. (Pan American)

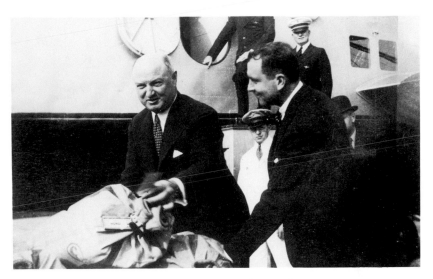

Postmaster James Farley and Juan Trippe during the *China Clipper* transpacific inaugural, 22 November 1935. Because mail subsidies provided the incentive for the Pacific route development, cynics called the Martin boat the "Taxpayer Clipper." (Pan American)

During the takeoff for the transpacific inaugural flight, Ed Musick changed the script. At the last instant, he chose to fly *beneath* the spans of the still-unfinished Bay Bridge. (Pan American)

The *China Clipper* over the unfinished Golden Gate Bridge, 1935. (Pan American)

The *Manila Tribune* heralds the inaugural voyage of the *China Clipper*. (Pan American)

The *China Clipper* being serviced. The cowling flaps were an innovation to cope with the heating problems of the R-1830 engines. (Pan American)

The *China Clipper*'s second passenger compartment, aft of the main lounge. (Pan American)

Cockpit of *China Clipper*. Ed Musick sits on the left. Only in publicity photos did pilots wear their uniform caps in the cockpit. (Pan American)

Glenn L. Martin, builder of the *China Clipper,* remained a devotee of the flying boat until long after the era had ended. (Smithsonian)

The M-156 *Russian Clipper*. After Pan American declined to order derivatives of the M-130, Glenn Martin sold this only *China Clipper* variant to the Soviet Union where it entered the service of Aeroflot in the Far East. (Martin Marietta)

The *Mercury-Maia* composite was one of several schemes to provide Imperial Airways a transatlantic capability. (British Airways)

Mercury separating from *Maia*. (British Airways)

The G-class S.26 *Golden Hind*. The G-class boats were ordered for Imperial Airways' North Atlantic service. (British Airways)

The Dornier Do 26 *Seeadler* (Sea Eagle) was a fast, long-range, four-engined courier plane. It transported mail over the North and South Atlantic, landing and launching from depot ships in mid-ocean. (Smithsonian)

Refueled and serviced, the Do 26 *Seeadler* is catapulted from the depot ship *Friesenland*. (Dornier GMBH)

Weighing over 100,000 pounds at takeoff, the six-engined BV 222 Wiking would have been one of the most impressive commercial aircraft in the world. Though designed in 1936 as a North Atlantic airliner for Lufthansa, the big boat did not fly until 1940. All fourteen models went to war as supply and reconnaissance aircraft. (Lufthansa)

The last of the Sikorsky flying boats, the VS-44A *Excambian* of American Export Airlines, 1942. (F. L. Wallace)

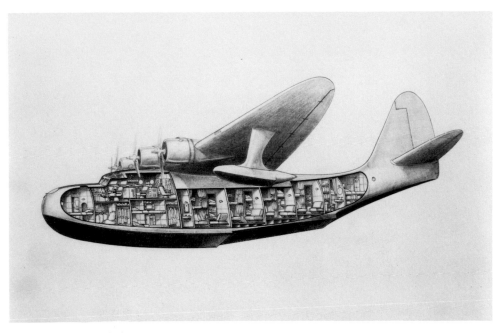

Only three models of the VS-44A were constructed. All were delivered to American Export Airlines. (United Technologies Corporation)

Cutaway of 314 in its original single-finned configuration. (Pan American)

A dual-finned 314 "on the step." This model, like the single-finned version, had directional stability problems. All were eventually configured with three vertical stabilizers. (Pan American)

A Pan American 314 arrives in West Africa. (E. F. Blackburn)

The bubble octant was the flying boat navigator's primary tool for over-ocean celestial navigation. (E. F. Blackburn)

With the entry of the United States in WW II, the *China Clipper* was placed in the service of the U.S. Navy. Here she appears in camouflage war paint. (Pan American)

The 314 *Capetown Clipper* at anchor at New York's La Guardia airport. Her glory days have come to an end as the faster, more efficient DC-4 replaces her on the route to Europe. (Pan American)

While developing the jet-age De Havilland Comet I in the late 1940s, Britain was simultaneously producing an airliner from the past—the behemoth Saunders Roe Princess flying boat. (British Airways)

While the Latécoère 631 spent the war years mouldering on the assembly line, the age of the flying boats passed her by. (Musée de l'Air)

To Glenn Martin, the Mars was to be the forerunner of a new lineage of commercial flying boats. Instead, it became the highly successful JRM series of the U.S. Navy. (Martin Marietta)

China Clipper "on the step." (Pan American)

Orient Express. On her way to Asia, the *China Clipper* stops at Pearl Harbor. (Pan American)

The Laté 521's hull was a deep two-decker. In the lower deck, behind the mooring compartment, were a twenty-seat cabin, six two-berth cabins, and another twenty-six-seat compartment. A companionway led to the upper deck and the galley, lavatory, and baggage compartments. Another eighteen-seat cabin and a space for three flight engineers occupied the upper deck.

The prow of the flying boat resembled the snout of a dolphin. In a style peculiar to French flying boats, the "bridge" of the aircraft was recessed backwards from the bow, and atop this structure, recessed farther aft, was the pilots' compartment.

The broad, slightly swept back upper wing was mounted atop the fuselage and braced by struts to the lower, stubby sea wing. This Dornier-style surface, which contained most of the ship's fuel, was attached to the hull near the waterline and fitted with shallow floats.

The Hispano-Suiza engines were suspended from the wings in four nacelles, with the inner engines mounted in the customary tandem, pusher-puller configuration. Each engine drove a three-bladed Ratier propeller with electrically controlled pitch.[7]

By the time the Laté 521 made her first voyage to the New World in December 1935, the Martin-built *China Clipper* had already captured the imagination of the world with her inaugural Pacific flight. The larger and, in many respects, more capable Laté 521 arrived in the United States, via Dakar, Natal, and Martinique, only to rendezvous with calamity. On 4 January 1936 she was sunk by a hurricane while at her mooring in Pensacola, Florida. Not until mid-1937, when she had been rebuilt in France, did her career resume.

Commanded by the veteran airmail pilot, Henri Guillaumet, the *Lieutenant de Vaisseau Paris* set a seaplane distance record in October 1937, flying a 3,586-mile nonstop journey from Morocco to Brazil. Before the end of the year she had garnered three more speed records with various loads, and an altitude record (6,561 feet) carrying a load of 39,771 pounds.[8] All these records were set by Guillaumet, who, after the death of Mermoz, was France's most prominent aviator.

Beginning in 1938 the Laté 521 made three round-trip flights to America over the North Atlantic route, flying from Biscarosse, via Lisbon and the Azores, to Port Washington in New York. In April 1939, the *Lieutenant de Vaisseau Paris* was joined by a sister ship, the *Ville de Saint-Pierre*. This new ship, designated the Laté 522, was powered by 920-horsepower Hispano-Suiza engines, and soon thereafter the prototype

Laté 521 was refitted with the larger engines. Though owned by the government and on loan to Air France's Transatlantique Division, neither of these flying boats entered regular service. With the onset of war in 1939, both were pressed into duty with the French Navy.

Though the Laté 521 and 522 had the same dimensions, the latter ship had a maximum weight of 92,594 pounds, nearly 9,000 pounds more than the prototype, and an empty weight of 52,911 pounds. This represented a respectable load-to-tare ratio of 43:57. With a maximum fuel load of 31,967 pounds, she could carry a payload of 7,716 pounds over a distance of 2,485 miles. Her broad, round-tipped wings supported a load of 26.1 pounds per square foot.[9]

These statistics made the Laté 521 and 522 formidable flying boats, well ahead of their time. They might have entered the record books as significant players in maritime aviation. But like most French transport aircraft of the period, they were tied to the Hispano-Suiza engine, a power plant of dubious reliability. And then at the apex of their careers, war intervened. Bad timing and, worse, bad luck, denied the elegant Laté 520 series a prominent role in the history of air transport.

With a firm footing on both shores of the South Atlantic, Air France began to cast an ambitious eye toward the North Atlantic. In 1936 the French Air Ministry issued a specification for a large flying boat that would transport forty passengers over a route of 3,730 miles (6,000 kilometers) against a thirty-seven-mile-per-hour headwind. Although three manufacturers—Lioré et Olivier, Potez, and Latécoère—constructed prototype examples of such a flying boat, only the Latécoère actually went into production and entered commercial service.

The prototype was ordered in 1938, but it had not yet flown when war interrupted her construction. Not until 4 November 1942, after the fall of France, did the prototype fly, and at that time two more aircraft were placed on order by the Vichy government.

The Laté 631 was, arguably, the most beautiful flying boat of all time. Her long, slender lines and finely tapered wings gave her an elegance unlike any transport aircraft of the era. In her original configuration, the Laté 631 was powered by six 1,650-horsepower Gnome Rhone engines and had a maximum takeoff weight of 145,505 pounds.

She had a high, tapered, cantilevered wing with a span of 188 feet and full-span ailerons. She was of all-metal, stressed-skin construction. The horizontal stabilizer had a marked dihedral with twin vertical stabilizers and rudders mounted at each tip. The cockpit was mounted far aft of the bow, just forward of the wing's leading edge, and contributed to the Laté 631's rakish good looks.

The production version did not appear until after the end of the war. Four aircraft were produced, each powered by six American-built 1,600-horsepower Wright Cyclone GR-2600-A5B, twin-row radial engines. These engines had two-stage superchargers and drove three-bladed, fully feathering Ratier three-bladed propellers.

In July 1947 three Laté 631s entered the service of Air France, Africa, and began flying the route from Biscarosse to Port-Etienne, Africa, to Fort-de-France, Martinique. Their cabins were configured to carry forty-six passengers in the lower deck of the spacious hulls, which were compartmented with lavatories, a galley, a restaurant and bar, and a central corridor. On the upper deck, just forward of the wing, was the flight deck with widely separated pilots' seats and, farther aft, the navigation compartment and the flight engineer's station.

With their Wright power plants, the Laté boats had a maximum gross weight of 157,300 pounds and an empty weight of 71,280, yielding a remarkable load-to-tare of 55:45. The long, low-aspect-ratio wings supported a loading, at maximum weight, of forty-one pounds per square foot of wing area, equal to that of a Douglas DC-4. The advertised cruising speed of the Laté 631 was 185 miles per hour with a range of 3,750 miles against a headwind of thirty-five miles per hour.[10]

These were impressive statistics and should have placed the Latécoère 631 among the front-ranking transport aircraft of the world. But it was too late; the age of the flying boat passed.

In the story of the great flying boats, the six-engined Latécoère 631 would earn one lasting distinction: She was the largest passenger-carrying flying boat ever to enter commercial service.

Martin

The giant, passenger-carrying flying boat had its share of devotees in 1935. None of these was more zealous in his devotion than the builder of America's largest aircraft, the Martin M-130.

Glenn L. Martin was a midwesterner by birth and by disposition. Fiercely independent, prudish and conservative, stubborn as a prairie mule, he embodied the best and the worst qualities of his generation of American entrepreneurs.

Born in Macksburg, Iowa, 17 January 1886, he was the only son of Clarence and Araminta Martin. Early in his life his family moved to Liberal, Kansas, then to Salina where Martin worked as a garage mechanic between semesters at Kansas Wesleyan University. His mother, "Minta" Martin, made her son's welfare her personal mission, becoming his lifelong advisor and constant companion.

In 1905 the family moved to Santa Ana, California, where, at age nineteen, Martin worked briefly in a hardware store before opening up his own shop and sales agency. It was here that he was first drawn to the newborn craft of flight. In 1907 he began to build gliders and, in 1908, designed and built his own pusher biplane. Along the way he taught himself to fly, becoming the third man in history to fly a heavier-than-air machine of his own design.[1]

Thereafter, Martin's name figured prominently in the records of American aviation. Known as "The Flying Dude" for his dapper dress and fastidious manner, Martin barnstormed about the country setting speed and altitude records with aircraft of his own manufacture. In May of 1912 he made headlines with a round-trip flight between Newport Beach, California, and Catalina Island in a Martin-built floatplane. In another floatplane he called the *Great Lakes Tourer*, he made a business of taking passengers for thrill flights over Lake Michigan.[2] He incorporated the Glenn L. Martin Company in 1911 and the next year moved the factory to Los Angeles.

The first of a generation of Martin military aircraft, the Martin TT, appeared in 1913. New versions of this training aircraft were then produced not only for the army but for the governments of the Netherlands and their East Indies colonies. In 1917 Martin briefly merged his corporation with the Wright Company, resulting in the Wright-Martin Corporation of New York. Soon, though, Martin withdrew from this partnership and moved the Glenn L. Martin Company from Los Angeles to Cleveland.

Martin's cantankerousness was already legend. Photographs of the period show his sober expression, eyes set in a razor-thin face, peering intently through rimless glasses. Neither a smoker nor a drinker, he was known as a humorless, prissy, hardheaded businessman who quarreled frequently with his associates and employees. One such was his chief engineer, Donald Douglas, who left Martin to build his own family of famous aircraft.[3]

With the approach of WW I, Martin became a builder of heavy bombers, designing the first multi-engine airplanes to mount the new Liberty engine. In the early twenties he continued to develop new bombers, including the MB-2 employed by General Billy Mitchell to sink the "unsinkable" German battleship *Ostfriesland*.

The U.S. Navy became a Martin customer in 1929 with the purchase of the PM-1, the first of a Martin-built lineage of navy flying boats. Powered by two Wright Cyclone engines, this sturdy biplane had a wing span of seventy-two feet, ten inches, and an overall length of forty-nine feet. First delivered in 1930, a total of thirty PM-1s were operated by the navy during the early thirties. In 1931 an improved aircraft, the PM-2 appeared, powered by improved engines and fitted with twin rudders.

Although neither of these designs showed particular innovativeness, the success of the PM series emboldened Glenn Martin to test new waters. He had become convinced that the future belonged to the flying boat. "Great new markets will open up all over the world," he predicted. "Especially in the Orient."[4]

The first great market he had in mind was the transocean service now being envisioned by Pan American's Juan Trippe. When he received Trippe's request for a bid for the construction of a giant flying boat, Martin had already convinced himself that he could fill the order.

Glenn Martin's vision, however, tended to outreach day-to-day reality. One such reality was that his company was nearly on the rocks. As Martin entered the negotiating battle with Pan American, he faced opposition from his own business manager, C. A. Van Dusen, and chief engineer Lassiter Milburn. It was their conclusion that Martin could fill Trippe's specifications for three flying boats for a total of no less than two million dollars. Juan Trippe, the quintessential poker player, had in mind a number half that amount.

But Glenn Martin was a man driven by a dream. He wanted to make money, but even more did he want to join in a venture that would make history. He was determined that he would build Pan American's flying boat, even at a loss. Against the advice of an angry Van Dusen and Lassiter Milburn, he signed a contract with Trippe for a price of $417,201 per airplane.[5] Three aircraft would be built in the initial order, with options for more. Martin, unwisely as it turned out, was gambling that he would recoup his losses on re-orders of the flying boat.

Despite Martin's financial problems, construction of the new flying boat began in November of 1932, even before the contract was signed with Pan American. Given the company designation M-130, the three aircraft began to take shape at the plant at Middle River, Maryland, near Baltimore, under the direction of Milburn and W. K. "Ken" Ebel, who served in the unique dual roles of engineer and chief test pilot. The keel of the first aircraft, NC 14714, was laid in May 1933 and would be given the Pan American name *Hawaii Clipper*. NC 14715, the *Philippine Clipper*, and NC 14716—"Sweet Sixteen"—the most famous of flying boats, the *China Clipper*, followed.

Glenn Martin was ill on 9 October 1935, the day of the official acceptance ceremony. Lassiter Milburn took his place, delivering a brief speech about "this great flying boat, the largest airliner ever developed in America . . . the first airliner in the world developed to carry swiftly and safely men and mail and merchandise across the oceans."[6]

Trippe, with Lindbergh at his side, then gave the great ship a name. "This flying boat will be named the *China Clipper*, after her famous predecessor that carried the American flag and crossed the Pacific a hundred years ago."

Though Pan American's publicity department had credited Lindbergh as the developmental mastermind behind the M-130, the Lone Eagle had been preoccupied with other matters. He had recently undergone the ordeal of his son's kidnapping and murder and the subsequent trial of the accused kidnapper, Bruno Hauptmann. Hounded by the press, Lindbergh and his wife had become virtual recluses and would soon leave the country to take up residence in England.

Pan American's guiding genius was, in fact, Andre Priester. From his office in the Chrysler Building, the little Dutchman issued a steady barrage of instructions and specifications to the Martin engineers. He conceived ideas for improved engine cowlings, for redundant electrical and hydraulic systems (features that would become standard on future designs), and for a strengthened hull design. He wanted to cure the old electrolysis problem encountered on the Sikorsky aircraft—the corrosion resulting from dissimilar metals (brass nuts fastened to aluminum) exposed to salt walter—by coating the metal surfaces and incorporating impregnated fabric between parts. His requirements specified a sound-proofed, luxuriously appointed cabin that equalled the stateroom of an ocean liner.

By any standard, the M-130 was in a class by herself. She was, in 1935, the largest flying boat ever constructed in America.

The M-130's empty weight was 25,363 pounds. Fully loaded to her maximum weight of 52,252 pounds, the *China Clipper* could carry *more* than her own structural weight in useable load. This translated to a load-to-tare ratio of 52:48, a remarkable engineering achievement for 1935. Her advertised passenger load was forty-one, though that load would be severely restricted for the long San Francisco–Honolulu route.

She had a fuselage length of over ninety feet. Her wings, braced at the center section by two struts on either side and cantilevered from the outboard engines, spanned 130 feet. With an area of 2,315 square feet, the broad wings supported a loading of 22.46 pounds per square foot.

The new Pratt and Whitney Wasp R-1830 engines, the first twin-row, air-cooled engines to enter commercial service, were the most advanced power plants of their day. Geared and supercharged, each delivered 830 horsepower (later upgraded to 950 horsepower). The *China*

Clipper came equipped with the new Hamilton Standard constant-speed propellers.

Aesthetically, the Martin clipper pleased the eye. The wings perched atop a streamlined cabane on the upper fuselage. Her lines were clean. Except for the tail group, she was constructed without wires and protuberances and without the usual cumbersome outrigger floats. Instead, she had Dornier-style "sea wings." These sponsons served as fuel tanks and afforded both stability in the water and, in the air, additional aerodynamic lift.

To depression-weary Americans, the new Martin clipper possessed magical qualities. She conjured up visions of the exotic East, of faraway places and mysterious lands. She was a fantasy craft, a magic carpet built and flown by Americans, destined for adventure.

Following the ceremony, the *China Clipper* was turned over to Ed Musick. Time was short because Trippe, certain that Pan American would receive the new transpacific mail route award, FAM 14, had already announced the commencement of service within the next month. Musick had only six weeks to ready his new flying boat and crew for the Pacific inaugural.

He took the clipper to Miami, where a series of publicity and test flights were performed. Then, with his crew and a pair of NBC broadcasters, Musick flew the *China Clipper* across the Gulf of Mexico, over the narrowest portion of Mexico at the Isthmus of Tehuantepec, stopping at Acapulco, then onward to San Francisco. There, while excitement mounted, Ed Musick prepared to cross the ocean.

16

China Clipper

E d Musick was a reluctant hero. He abhorred the flash-
bulbs and handshakes and the constant clamor for re-
marks about what, to him, was simply a job.

But as the day neared for him to take the *China Clipper* across the
Pacific, Ed Musick's life changed. Each day became a steady torment of
interviews and photographs and public speeches. The press wanted to
know about his private life (prosaic), his tastes in spirits (none), his
outside interests (minimal). *Time* would report in its cover story only
that "he lives quietly with his blonde wife, Cleo, has no children, likes
baseball, Buicks, apples, ham and cheese sandwiches, vacations in Manhattan."

There was little about Musick that would fill space in the tabloids.
In photographs he appeared as a man medium in height and slight of
build, slightly stoop-shouldered, with thinning black hair. He had a
permanent five-o'clock shadow that defied any razor.

Musick's shy, laconic comments to the press had become the particular
frustration of Pan American's public relations department. When he
flew the S-42B on the proving flight to Hawaii, the press director had
pleaded for newsworthy reports. Would Musick please send something—anything—that was publishable?

Musick balked. "I'm a pilot, not a newspaperman. I wouldn't know
what to send."

"Send something about the sunset over the Pacific."

Okay, Musick agreed. From over the ocean he radioed: "SUNSET,
0639 GMT."

That was Musick.[1]

* * *

Born in 1894 in St. Louis, Musick had grown up in Los Angeles where, like Glenn Martin, he became obsessed with the craft of flight. His first airplane, which he built himself, crashed without flying. Musick worked as a mechanic, first on racing cars and then at Martin's new Los Angeles aircraft factory. After he learned to fly, he became a professional air-show pilot. He performed along the Pacific Coast as "Monseer Mussick, the famous French flier," or, at other times, as "Daredevil Musick." Along the way Musick was acquiring a passion for precision. He studied the causes of the accidents that befell his colleagues and began to devise his own methodical, meticulous procedures.

With the onset of WW I, Musick worked as a civilian flight instructor for the army, then received his commission as a second lieutenant in the Marine Corps Reserve. Designated Naval Aviator Number 1673, he spent the rest of the war instructing navy student flyers in Miami.

In the postwar years Musick, like most professional aviators of the day, took whatever flying jobs he could find. What he found was usually dangerous and frequently illegal. He flew flying boats to the Bahamas and to Cuba for the over-water airline Aeromarine until the company folded. It was the era of Prohibition. For lack of better employment Musick made a living flying booze from offshore supply boats to clandestine fields on the East Coast.

In 1926 his name came to the attention of the operations manager of Philadelphia Rapid Transit Airline. The manager, whose reputation for meticulousness equaled Musick's, was a Dutch immigrant named Andre Priester. When Priester moved on to a new airline called Pan American, he took Musick with him.

On the afternoon of 22 November 1935, twenty-five thousand people had crowded onto the Alameda seaplane base on San Francisco Bay. On the speaker's platform, Postmaster General James Farley read a message from the president: ". . .Even at this distance, I thrill to the wonder of it all. . ." The wonder to which FDR referred lay at her mooring, her bow directly behind the platform.

Farley launched into his own speech. ". . . A person or letter will arrive in China within six days after leaving New York. This is, indeed, an epoch-making achievement and one which rivals the vivid imagination of Jules Verne. . ."

Juan Trippe, beaming from his place of honor on the reviewing stand, knew precisely to whom the credit for the achievement should go. In only eight years, from a company with no assets or airplanes or routes of its own, Trippe had built Pan American into America's premier international airline.

"Therefore," Farley said, "I anticipate that our friendly relations and our commerce with the countries of the Orient will be strengthened and stimulated by the transpacific airmail service."

Airmail had made it possible. Trippe had taken a colossal gamble, proceeding with his Pacific plans before he had a mail contract in hand. Not until 21 October 1935, only a month before the inaugural flight, did the Post Office Department award FAM 14—Foreign Air Mail contract number fourteen—to the sole bidder, Pan American Airways, at the highest allowable rate of two dollars per mile.

Today's inaugural flight—and all to follow for the next year—would be mail flights. The *China Clipper* would carry 110,000 letters in her bulging mail sacks. Only after sufficient experience had been gained on the Pacific would Pan Am commence passenger service to the Orient.

Farley concluded his address. A radio announcer took over, heaping hyperbole on the occasion, praising the Post Office, the aviation industry, Pan American, and the seven airmen who would fly the *China Clipper*. "On the wings of these sturdy clipper ships," he said to his radio audience, "are pinned the hopes of America's commerce for a rightful standing in the teeming markets of the Orient."

Trippe listened with a sanguine expression. The script had been created by his publicity director, William Van Dusen, an imaginative young man hand-picked by Trippe himself. For this occasion, Van Dusen had outdone himself.

The crew marched aboard. The radio announcer, reading from Van Dusen's script, eulogized the crew members, Trippe, the Post Office, the airplane, and the country in general. "What a thrilling sight she is! So confident, so sturdy. Her gleaming hull and wings glistening in the sunshine, her great engines ready to speed her on her way!"[2]

The five ocean bases in the Pacific—Honolulu, Midway, Wake, Guam, and the Philippines—precisely on cue, each signaled by radio its readiness to commence the transpacific service.

The lines were cast off. While the band struck up "The Star Spangled Banner," Musick powered the *China Clipper* out into the bay. Radio audiences heard the national anthem punctuated by the throaty rumble of Pratt and Whitney engines.

After a couple of circles on the bay while the engines warmed, the *China Clipper* surged forward. Rockets blazed from shore. From overhead, a swarm of light airplanes buzzed down to escort the clipper on her departure.

During the past eleven days Musick and his crew had rehearsed heavy-weight takeoffs. Each time the *China Clipper* had lifted her great load into the air precisely on schedule. Today, with a final tick on the water, she again broke free and was airborne.

Ahead loomed the San Francisco-Oakland Bay Bridge, which was still under construction. It was Musick's intention, taking off to the west, to soar up and *over* the bridge. From the cockpit he could see the unfinished pylons and the dangling cables and the girders still festooned with scaffolding.

The *China Clipper* was flying, but barely. With her great burden of fuel, she had gained no more than fifty feet. Despite Musick's best efforts, the clipper would climb no more. She skimmed across San Francisco Bay, roaring hellbent toward the Bay Bridge.

At the last instant, with the steel mass of the Bay Bridge filling the clipper's windscreen, Musick changed the script. He nosed the *China Clipper* down toward the water. The flying boat zoomed *beneath* the bridge, between the massive girders and under the hanging cables. Directly on her tail came the escorting airplanes, their pilots all thinking this was part of the show. To the astonishment of the few on the shore who knew better, they all made it.[3]

While the crowd cheered from the shores of the bay, the *China Clipper* slowly gained altitude and vanished beyond the rim of the Pacific Ocean.

For the westbound flyers, nightfall came slowly. When darkness finally enveloped the *China Clipper*, she was flying between layers of cloud. Musick chose the southernmost of the surveyed oceanic tracks, skirting the towering cumulus buildups that lay along the route to Hawaii.

Fred Noonan labored over his chart table, plotting radio direction finder bearings and celestial fixes that he managed to shoot through breaks in the overcast. In the red-lighted cabin Noonan looked like an alien creature in his fur-lined flying suit and leather helmet. He needed the costume to take celestial shots with his sextant from the opened after hatch atop the clipper's fuselage. Like most aerial navigators, Noonan did not trust the accuracy of celestial fixes taken through the glass of an aircraft hatch. It was believed that the aircraft glass might refract the light of his celestial target.

Each crew member alternated two hours on duty with a period in the crew's rest bunk. Musick and the first officer, Rod Sullivan, rotated command in the cockpit. The junior flight officer, George King, took over the navigating duties while Noonan catnapped.

The radio operator, Wilson Jarboe, passed Noonan's position reports at half-hour intervals to Alameda where, in the lobby of the seaplane base, Van Dusen had mounted a gigantic wall map. The prolific Van Dusen produced a fresh press release for every position report from the *China Clipper*.

Dawn overtook the clipper as slowly as the night had fallen eight hours earlier. Still 200 miles from their destination, Sullivan spotted farther to the south the dark mass of Mauna Kea jutting from a layer of cloud. When they were thirty miles from Honolulu they recognized Diamond Head.

At 1010 A.M., 20 hours and 33 minutes after taking off from San Francisco Bay, Ed Musick landed the *China Clipper* in Honolulu's Pearl Harbor. The longest leg of the 8,210-mile transpacific route had been flown.

Following a flower-strewn reception and gala welcome, the *China Clipper* was loaded with staples for the island bases—twenty-one crates of fresh vegetables, twelve crates of turkeys for the first Thanksgiving on the atolls, cartons of cranberries, sweet potatoes, mince meat, and crates of material including paint, typewriter ribbons, baseballs, a complete barber's outfit, and tennis racquets.

The 1,380 miles from Honolulu to Midway were the easiest leg on the route to Asia. When the weather was clear, as it almost always was, navigators needed only to follow the strand of islands spaced along a northwestward arc toward the atolls of Midway.

In the ripple-free air even the Sperry autopilot, normally given to wild fits of cantankerousness, kept the *China Clipper* on a steady course. Leaving Oahu, the clipper flew over the island of Nihoa, then Necker, French Frigate Shoals, Gardner Pinnacles, and Laysan Island. The strand of islands pointed like signposts to Midway.

Midway had changed. The buildings were now brightly painted, the grounds landscaped, flags flying at their masts. The white-uniformed Pan Am staff stood at their posts on the landing float. The clipper swooped low over the base, touching down in the lagoon at 2:01, one minute off schedule.

At dawn the *China Clipper* was again westbound. There were no signposts marking the 1,260-mile route to Wake. After Kure Island, only twenty minutes past Midway, there were a thousand miles of trackless ocean. No landmarks, no chain of atolls pointed to the destination. There was only Wake Island—two-and-a-half square miles of sandspit—barely awash in the Pacific.

It was the most demanding feat of aerial navigation in the world. There were no alternate landing sites and not enough fuel for a return to Midway. The only aids to navigation were the sun, sometimes a glimpse of Venus, the driftsight, the navigator's own dead reckoning, and the Adcock Direction Finder, a capricious device not fully trusted by navigator Noonan.[4]

From his bag of navigational tricks, Fred Noonan produced a technique called "aim off." "Aim off" was a tricky but effective way to ensure that a vessel or aircraft did not overshoot a tiny target like Wake.

The navigator would deliberately fly a course to one side of his destination. Then, when he had intersected a precomputed line of position he would obtain by sun sight, he would turn and fly down the sun line to his target. "Aim off" was not infallible, but it solved half the navigational problem—that of knowing on *which* side, north or south, the *China Clipper* might be from Wake.[5]

Two minutes before the crew of the clipper spotted Wake, the Pan Am base on the island radioed that they had sighted the inbound aircraft. Five minutes ahead of schedule, the *China Clipper* glided to a touchdown on the marine runway in the Wake lagoon, now lengthened and deepened since Rod Sullivan's visit in August.

At sunrise the next morning, the *China Clipper* lifted from Wake's lagoon, bound for Guam, 1,560 miles to the west. With the clipper's cabin windows open, warm tropical air filled the cabin. Musick regularly changed altitudes, seeking the tailwinds that would shave time from the long flight. Flying at 8,000 feet, the clipper covered the last 160 miles to Guam in less than an hour.

There they discovered that their precision flight planning had been in vain. Though they had arrived in Guam's Apra Harbor exactly on schedule, the crew learned that the arrival celebration in Manila was scheduled for *two days* hence. Someone in the public relations department had become confused about the international date line. It was now too late and too embarrassing to reschedule the event.

Musick and his crew, grumbling, spent an unwanted day off in Guam, trying to be inconspicuous, ignoring the clamor of questions over the radio.

On Friday, November 29, the *China Clipper* embarked on the last leg of her journey to the Orient. The Guam–Manila segment was the only portion of the voyage never flown during the feasibility testing. By now the crew had confidence in themselves and in the sleek new Martin flying boat. The *China Clipper* had proven herself. She was a faithful and sturdy vessel. She made the journey to Manila without incident.

None of the hoopla of the inaugural flight quite matched the celebration in Manila. A hundred thousand excited greeters watched the *China Clipper* appear on the horizon. After a circle of the city, the giant craft landed in Manila Bay. A swarm of fighter planes flew overhead in salute. Hundreds of small launches escorted the clipper to her landing barge. Through flower-bedecked arches the crew walked ashore. Newsreel cameras whirred while Ed Musick presented a letter from President Roosevelt to Governor Quezon.

There was a motor parade, a banquet, an official reception. The man of the hour was Ed Musick. The press hounded him for comments. He was asked to describe the historic flight across the Pacific. True to form, Musick described in two words one of the most momentous feats in aviation history: "Without incident," he explained.

But the spotlight remained on Musick. Despite his wishes, he could no longer escape fame. The first transpacific flight of the *China Clipper* earned for him the prestigious Harmon Trophy, previously won by only two other Americans: Wiley Post and Charles Lindbergh. The cover of *Time* magazine featured his face. He was besieged by requests for interviews. Ed Musick, whether he liked it or not, had become an authentic American hero.

Orient Express

Not only was Musick a celebrity, so were the *China Clipper* and her two sister ships. Whenever one of the Martin M-130s lay at her mooring in Alameda, crowds gathered. The very name—*China Clipper*—conjured up a spell of adventure. California to Asia in six days! The sense of wonder was the same Americans would feel half a century later for the orbiting space shuttle.

A *China Clipper* craze swept the country. A song appeared, written by Norma Morton and Ethel Powell. Then came a dance step to the same music. Restaurants and night clubs adopted the name. Magazines featured articles about the famous flying boat. First-person accounts were published in newspapers by passengers who had flown in her.

Hollywood lost no time cashing in. In 1936 Warner Brothers produced *China Clipper*, starring Humphrey Bogart and Pat O'Brien. In the film, scripted by former naval aviator Frank Wead, Bogart played an aviator loosely fashioned after Ed Musick. O'Brien portrayed a tough, single-minded airline boss whose real-life counterpart was clearly Juan Trippe.

Though the film lacked artistic excellence, it played to sell-out audiences. Besides the dramatic footage of the *China Clipper*, clipped mostly from newsreels, the movie was perhaps most notable as the first major aviation movie produced without loss of life.

The movie contained an ironic scene in which cinematic art imitated life. Bogart had just managed to fly the *China Clipper* through a typhoon, narrowly making a critical deadline that saved the airline. When he emerged from the cockpit, he referred to his visionary but insensitive boss: "I was just thinking how swell it would have been if he'd said thanks."

The irony was probably lost on Trippe, who rarely said thanks to anyone. It did not pass unnoticed by the pilots who flew for him.[1]

Almost a year had passed since the inaugural mail flight. All three of the Martin M-130s had entered service. Joining the *China Clipper* were her sister ships, the *Philippine Clipper* and the *Hawaii Clipper*. It was time to commence passenger service.

In his global strategy, Trippe planned to link his Pacific air route to Pan American's Chinese subsidiary, China National Airlines Corporation. The ideal connecting point was the busy market port of Hong Kong. Pan American, however, still had rights only to Manila and then to the Portuguese colony of Macao, about 40 miles west of Hong Kong. The British government, recalcitrant as ever in their dealings with Pan American, had denied landing rights in the crown colony of Hong Kong, Trippe's wished-for destination. The matter was stalled on the familiar issue of reciprocity, since the British Air Ministry demanded landing rights in the Philippines.

Trippe's tactic was one he would use repeatedly in his dealings with foreign governments. He let the powerful merchants and *taipans* of Hong Kong worry that their traditional markets were being bypassed in favor of Macao. He let it be known, too, that they had their own government to blame for this travesty. To fuel their worries, Trippe ordered construction of radio and docking facilities at Macao, and showed every intention of making the sleepy Portuguese colony the new aerial hub of the Far East.

It was a typical Trippe charade, but it worked. Immense pressure came from the trading houses, banks, and colonial administration of Hong Kong to the British Air Ministry. By September 1936, His Majesty's government had reconsidered its position on the matter. Pan American was granted landing rights at Hong Kong's Kai Tak airport and the marine facilities of Victoria Harbor. The first passenger flight was scheduled for 21 October 1936.[2]

Though the M-130 was designed to carry thirty-two passengers, it could do so only on short-range segments. The California-to-Hawaii leg of 2,410 miles required such a burden of fuel that the load for the first crossing was restricted to eight passengers. Trippe selected seven notables, matching his own political priorities, to accompany him on the first Pacific passenger flight: Senator William McAdoo of California;

William Roth and Wallace Alexander, the two who headed the Matson Steamship Line; Cornelius Vanderbilt "Sonny" Whitney, Trippe's old friend and chairman of the Pan American board of directors; Roy Howard, who directed the Scripps-Howard newspapers and who wrote favorably about Trippe's ventures; Paul Patterson, president of the *Baltimore Sun*; and Amon Carter, publisher of the *Fort Worth Star Telegram*.

The remaining passengers, including Betty Trippe and two other wives, would travel ahead on the SS *Lurline* and join the flying contingent in Honolulu.

The morning before their arrival in Hawaii, the passengers on the *Lurline* rose before dawn. From the rail they scanned the horizon. In a dramatic rendezvous, the *Philippine Clipper*, commanded by Captain John Tilton, appeared in the eastern sky. The flying boat swept over the steamship. Betty Trippe, watching from the rail of the *Lurline*, was moved to tears.

The Pacific air route was in business. The supply ship, the *North Haven*, had returned to the islands, and the bare shelters on Midway and Wake were now expanded into elaborate overnight inns. On Midway great refrigerators were installed that contained six months' supply of food. Long deplaning docks were constructed with electric lights and a pergola. The hotels were sprawling, forty-five-room structures, incongruously Georgian in architecture, with white pillars and a plat of grass on each side of a brick walkway. The two wings of the inns spread like giant claws in either direction. While a wild surf crashed against the encircling reef outside, the guests in the hotel were served exotic cuisine by white-uniformed Chamorro stewards. There were Simmons beds in the rooms, bathrooms with hot showers, spacious verandahs, elegant lounges with wicker furniture.

Gooneyville was the name given to the bright, bleached little village on Midway. It was named for the baldheaded, turkey-sized Laysan albatrosses who migrated there from the Aleutians. The gooney bird provided endless entertainment for the travelers at Midway. Dusky-colored young gooneys would run wildly along the beach, flapping their wings in an effort to fly, then suddenly nose over and crash in a flurry of feathers and sand. Passengers enjoyed Midway.

Wake was different. Not everyone enjoyed the barren, relentlessly tropical atoll. Until the coming of the flying boats, Wake had been uninhabitable. Wake had no fresh water, no edible vegetation, no shelter, no shade, no harbor, no protection from the howling typhoons that periodically scoured the sparse brush from the sand dunes.

Nor did it have gooney birds. Instead, Wake had hermit crabs, armored creatures that clanked like mechanical toys across the sand. And Wake had rats. Wake's rats had short front legs and elongated rear legs and seemed specially constructed for scuttling over the island's wind-blown surface. Sporting guests were offered air rifles and the opportunity to go "hunting" during their layover.[3]

From Wake Island the clippers flew on to Apra Harbor in Guam. Guam in the 1930s was a scruffy, tropical U.S. Navy–administered territory in the middle of the Japanese-mandated Marianas group. The harbor, ringed by low cliffs, served as an anchorage for navy warships and passing freighters. Clipper passengers were taken to a facility rented from the U.S. Navy. There they sat on shaded verandahs, sipped their drinks, and waited until four o'clock the next morning when their clipper would take off for Manila.

The next link in the over-ocean chain, Manila, had been the original terminus of the transpacific service. After extending the route to the Chinese mainland, and then abandoning Macao in favor of Hong Kong, Pan American sent a Sikorsky S-42B to the Far East to fly the Manila–Hong Kong segment. The Sikorsky workhorse was given the official name *Hong Kong Clipper*. To her irreverent pilots, she was "Myrtle."

To the public, *China Clipper* became a generic name and was generally applied to all three of the Martin M-130s and, later, even to the Boeing B-314s. During the 1930s the *China Clipper* became an airborne Orient Express, embarking diplomats and spies, generals and journalists, the famous and the infamous.

Passage aboard the *China Clipper* was not cheap, at least in 1930s dollars: $278 from San Francisco to Honolulu. All the way to Hong Kong, one way, cost $950.

For her time, the *China Clipper* was a flying palace. Forward of the main passenger space was the galley, eventually fitted with steam cookers. Abaft the galley was the crew cabin, which contained the navigator's station as well as the crew rest berths. Farther aft was the largest compartment, the passenger lounge, which seated as many as fifteen. Then came two smaller cabins, each with ten seats or six berths. Behind these compartments were dressing rooms and wash rooms, with hot running water. The last space aft was the rear cargo hold.

The cabin seating configuration varied. Though the seats in the main lounge were sometimes arranged five abreast, they were large, comfortable, and afforded more space and moving room than latter-day big jets. The cabin soundproofing permitted conversation in a normal voice, a remarkable feature in an airplane of 1935.

Usually one steward flew on the Pacific flights, but sometimes two. He (there were no stewardesses at that time) served dinner on white tablecloths with real china, silver, and heavy water goblets. No liquor was served. No smoking was permitted. Only on the all-night San Francisco-to-Honolulu leg were the sleeping berths used.

As a cargo ship, the *China Clipper* carried day-old chicks to a Pacific island for a poultry colonization experiment. To another island she carried queen bees. She transported spare tires for trucks on the Burma Road, gowns for Hollywood stars vacationing in Hawaii, Thanksgiving turkeys for construction workers on Wake.[4]

Ernest Hemingway, riding the wave of his recent success with his novel *For Whom the Bell Tolls*, traveled to China to view firsthand the Sino-Japanese conflict, and then returned to America on the *China Clipper*. General Douglas MacArthur, by then a field marshal of the Philippine Army, arrived in Manila aboard a clipper. Major General Claire Chennault, commander of the volunteer Flying Tigers, crossed the Pacific three times aboard the Martin clippers. Most of his fighter pilots, en route to the air war in China, also traveled by clipper. Ambassador Maxim Litvinoff of the Soviet Union flew aboard the *China Clipper* on his way to the United States on the eve of the attack on Pearl Harbor.

By late 1941, desperate, eleventh-hour negotiations were taking place to avert war in the Pacific. Journalists, military leaders, and diplomats winged between America and the Orient aboard the Pan American clippers. The *China Clipper* had become an instrument of geopolitics.

In China, the Sino-Japanese war was dragging into its fifth year, stalemated in the vastness of the Asian countryside. In 1941 Japanese troops marched unopposed into French Indochina. Tensions had heightened further when President Roosevelt retaliated by freezing all Japanese assets in America and proclaiming an embargo on Japanese trade in oil and steel.

In November of 1941 a Japanese diplomat, Saburo Kurusu, flew from Tokyo to Hong Kong aboard a Japan Airways flight, then boarded the *Hong Kong Clipper*. Kurusu was on his way to Washington in a last-minute attempt to negotiate an accord between Japan and the United States.

Kurusu boarded the *China Clipper* in Manila. Between Wake and Midway one of the M-130's engines failed. The diplomat was forced to spend two idle days in Midway waiting for the clipper to be repaired. Then, in Honolulu, he stepped aboard the waiting *California Clipper*, a Boeing B-314, for the last leg of his Pacific mission. Even with the delay, he had managed to reach America in nine days instead of the customary month by ship.

Kurusu arrived in Washington 15 November 1941. On 26 November, an armada of Japanese vessels sailed in secret from the chilled waters of the North Pacific. They were warships of the *Kido Butai*, Admiral Yamamoto's carrier strike force, bound for Pearl Harbor.

Losses

E d Musick was a man who seldom used profanity. But when he looked down for the first time at Pago Pago harbor, he loosed an untypical flurry of expletives. Beneath the nose of the S-42B, he could see green Samoan hills swelling to 1,500 feet at each end of the harbor. An ocean breeze piled up the waves in a white froth at the mouth of the bay. Pago Pago harbor was ill-suited for landing a twenty-ton flying boat.

To alight in the harbor, Musick would have to descend along the slope of the encircling hills, using full flaps, then flare at the last instant and slap the Sikorsky down on the water before he ran out of harbor. If he glided too far, he would coast into the ocean combers at the mouth of the bay.

In the specially outfitted S-42B, Musick and his crew were surveying the route from San Francisco to Auckland, New Zealand. They had followed an improvised course that stopped in Hawaii, then continued southwestward to a tiny Pacific atoll called Kingman's Reef, then on to American Samoa with its treacherous Pago Pago harbor. Because all three Martin M-130s were committed to the San Francisco-Far East route, and because the awaited Boeing B-314s were not yet delivered, the Sikorsky workhorse, the S-42B, was again pressed into service.

No one liked the operation. Kingman Reef, like Wake Island, was the summit of an undersea mountain, but it was less than a tenth the size of Wake. The island amounted to a single sand dune, barely visible above the waves, encircled by a coral reef. Inside the reef was a sizeable lagoon, suitable for the landing of a flying boat. The tiny desert island had no room for a hotel or hangars or a radio facility as on Midway and Wake. A chartered tanker, the *North Wind*, lay at anchor in the lagoon. Laden with aviation gasoline, the *North Wind* served as a mother ship, transmitting radio directional signals to the inbound aircraft.

As with the first Pacific proving flights, the cabin of the Sikorsky was stripped and extra fuel tanks and plumbing installed. A new feature had been added, a fuel-jettison system with dump valves under the wings so that in the event of an engine failure the heavily loaded flying boat could reduce its great weight. Named the *Samoan Clipper*, the ship was dubbed by the crew the "flying gas tank." The ever-present smell of gasoline pervaded the cabin.

The danger of fire preyed on Musick's mind. On the first leg of the initial survey flight, midway between San Francisco and Hawaii, Number One engine had overheated. Musick ordered the engine shut down. He told flight engineer Vic Wright to open the wing dump valves and jettison fuel. A short while later, the crew became aware of gasoline vapor inside the cabin. To his horror, navigator Harry Canaday discovered that drops of fuel were appearing on his charts. Somehow gasoline had blown inside the cabin, making the S-42B a potential incendiary bomb. Hurriedly Wright shut off the ship's electrical supply. All the windows were opened. For the rest of the night Musick and his crew flew on three engines, with no lights, radio, or electrical equipment, praying that a spark would not ignite the combustible atmosphere inside the *Samoan Clipper*.[1]

The route to New Zealand was the most demanding feat yet undertaken by Pan American. The risks were considerable: the hazard of fire in the fuel-laden Sikorsky, the microscopic target of Kingman's Reef, the tortuous approach to Pago Pago harbor. As Pan American's chief pilot, Ed Musick had been responsible for selecting the crew of the *Samoan Clipper*. It was typical of Musick that for the job of captain on the survey flights he assigned himself.

The New Zealand operation had political overtones. Though Pan American now served the mid-Pacific route to China, the real prize—the Atlantic—still eluded Juan Trippe. The gateway to Britain was still blocked by the restrictive Clause H of the Pan American–Imperial agreement, which denied Pan American the right to commence scheduled transatlantic flying until Imperial Airways was ready to fly a reciprocal service.

It was 1937 and Imperial was still not ready. Until Imperial Airways possessed a true transatlantic airliner, the British Air Ministry was not inclined to give the Americans a chance to demonstrate their technical superiority on an ocean so bound to British prestige as the North Atlantic.

So, in the meantime, Trippe sought other opportunities. One such was the 7,000-mile route from California to New Zealand and Australia. Even from Europe, traveling westward by air over the Atlantic and Pacific to Australia was quicker than the traditional route over the Mediterranean, the Suez Canal, and the Indian Ocean. Trippe believed this could be a lucrative route, initially for a postal service and eventually for scheduled passenger flights.

Again the British lion stood in the way. Imperial Airways was already flying through the Middle East, Malaya, and Burma. Imperial's Australian partner, Qantas, was extending its own routes through the Pacific and had ambitions to fly all the way to Canada. The sticking point was Hawaii, essential as a refueling stop for any Pacific crossing. The U.S. War Department had refused landing rights to any foreign carriers. The British, tit for tat, closed the gates to Australia and New Zealand. Once again Pan American's plans foundered on the reciprocity issue.

Trippe, the tireless finagler, dispatched Harold Gatty, the pioneer Australian navigator, to Auckland. There Gatty played upon New Zealand's historical sense of isolation not only from the empire but from the rest of the world. With the proposed air route, Gatty pointed out, New Zealand would be separated by only four flying days from modern civilization. Instead of being a junior and generally ignored partner of Australia, New Zealand could sit astride a major new commercial artery.

The government of New Zealand considered the matter, and then made a bold decision. New Zealand would break ranks with Britain and Australia. On 11 March 1937, Pan American received the concession to operate a commercial route from San Francisco to Auckland. Six days later, Ed Musick was preparing to fly the first trip.

The first approach to Pago Pago harbor was not to Musick's liking. He was too high, and the lightly loaded Sikorsky, at the end of the 1,600-mile flight from Kingman's Reef, tended to float too far before touching down. Ahead, Musick could see the spray from the combers at the mouth of the bay. He pulled up for another try.

On the next pass he flew at treetop height, diving down the slope of the hills. Flaring abruptly, almost at stall speed, he smacked the

Sikorsky down on the water. As the big flying boat slewed to a halt in the harbor, it was quickly surrounded by outrigger canoes filled with Polynesian natives who had never before seen a flying boat.

Taking off from Pago Pago was the same ordeal in reverse. But this time the S-42B was heavy, loaded with fuel for the 1,800-mile flight to New Zealand. Musick made two trial runs across the harbor before attempting a takeoff. With a good wind on the nose, he then lifted the S-42 off the water, clearing the breakers by only a few feet, and climbed out to the southwest.

The reception in Auckland was unlike anything Musick had experienced before, exceeding Manila's reception of the *China Clipper*. To Musick's astonishment, thirty thousand New Zealanders turned out to cheer him and his crew. Some wept openly when the American flyers took the reviewing stand. The New Zealanders were colonists, a people grown weary of isolation from the mother country and from the rest of civilization. Their lives, it seemed to them, had been changed overnight by the accomplishment of Musick and the *Samoan Clipper*. In a single epic flight, Ed Musick had propelled them into the twentieth century.

Musick took the reviewing stand. When the cheering finally abated enough for him to speak, Ed Musick remained in character. "We are glad to be here," he said and, having nothing more to say, broke into a grin. The crowd cheered all the more.

Musick came to Pago Pago again on his third South Pacific survey flight. He liked the narrow harbor no more than when he had seen it the first time.

The *Samoan Clipper* took off from Pago Pago at dawn, 11 January 1938. Two hours and twenty minutes later, Musick radioed that an oil leak had developed in number four engine. A short while later he reported that he intended to dump fuel to lighten the ship, then return for a landing in Pago Pago.

Ed Musick never made it back to Pago Pago. The *Samoan Clipper* exploded in mid-air and fell to the sea like a flaming comet.

That evening the U.S. Navy ship *Avocet*, searching the area, recovered from an oil slick the charred flotsam of the *Samoan Clipper*. There were pieces of the crews' uniforms, pages from the engineering log, fragments of wood.

The death of Ed Musick stunned the aviation world. Musick had been the world's most famous airline pilot. He had just been awarded the

Harmon Trophy. In New Zealand, where he was worshiped as a hero for linking that small country with the continent of North America, they had just named an aeronautical station in his honor.

What happened? It was revealed that Pan Am had already conducted dye tests of the Sikorsky's fuel-dumping system and determined that the fuel jettisoned from the valves beneath the wing circulated *forward*, over the *top* of the wing. Worse, experience showed that after dumping, fuel vapors somehow collected *inside* the wing structure. Although a bulletin from the Bureau of Air Commerce was issued prohibiting fuel dumping from the S-42, the ban applied only to passenger flights and not to Musick's survey flight.[2]

Why had Musick elected to dump fuel? Though he may have been unaware of the recent prohibition against dumping from the S-42, he had already experienced the vapor hazard during his first South Pacific survey flight. It seems likely that Musick's concern about the tiny Pago Pago harbor probably overrode his fear of fuel dumping. A landing with the overloaded Sikorsky, still glutted with fuel for the flight to Auckland, would almost certainly end in the combers at the mouth of the bay and probably destroy the aircraft.

When he commenced dumping, either jettisoned fuel was sucked into the engine exhaust and ignited or, more likely, collected as a vapor inside the wing. When the electric flap motor was actuated to extend the flaps for his approach to Pago Pago, the vapor detonated, turning the *Samoan Clipper* into an incendiary bomb.[3]

The disaster struck closest to the airmen of Pan American. They were a lighthearted, normally irreverent bunch. The death of a pilot was nothing new. But this was different. This was Musick. Musick was the most conservative, most meticulous, most professional pilot in the profession. Ed Musick, they had thought, was indestructible.

Captain Leo Terletsky had never been thought indestructible. Terletsky, in fact, had been the particular worry of his former chief pilot, Ed Musick.

Leo Terletsky was a White Russian, a man of considerable charm on the ground. In the air his easy charm left him. In command of a flying boat, Terletsky seemed beset by fears and uncertainties. He performed erratically, issuing and countermanding orders, infecting his crew with his own anxiety. Some copilots and engineers refused to fly with him.

Soon after the inauguration of the transpacific service, Leo Terletsky was transferred to San Francisco to fly the M-130s. His checkout over the Pacific was given by the chief pilot, Ed Musick. There had been no significant weather, no en route problems, and Terletsky's performance was judged acceptable. Later, it would be thought by his colleagues that Terletsky, who seemed to fear flying, would always perform competently so long as an experienced captain like Musick was with him. Alone, Terletsky became the victim of his own lack of self-confidence.[4]

On 23 July 1938 Terletsky took off from San Francisco Bay in the *Hawaii Clipper*. His copilot for the flight was "Tex" Walker, a competent aviator whom Terletsky often asked for as his first officer.

The *Hawaii Clipper*'s Pacific crossing was normal, transiting Honolulu, then Midway, Wake, and Guam on schedule. On 29 July, Terletsky and his crew of eight, with six passengers, prepared to take off from Guam's Apra harbor.

Before dawn Terletsky and Walker checked the en-route weather. There were occasional rain showers, scattered thunderstorms, cumulus tops at eight to ten thousand feet. This was typical summer Pacific weather. The airmen foresaw no difficulties.

Shortly before 6:00 A.M., the patrol launch fired a star shell signaling that Apra harbor was clear. The *Hawaii Clipper* roared across the bay, smacking the evenly spaced waves, then lifted into the dawn sky.

Throughout the morning the clipper droned toward Manila, diverting slightly to the south of a tropical depression. Radio Officer McCarty tapped out regular position and weather reports: "Rainy flying conditions, head winds, cruising at 10,000 feet."

At noon, when they were 565 miles from Manila, McCarty signaled that the *Hawaii Clipper* was flying in rough air through the tops of cumulus buildups, still bucking head winds, still in rain. Panay, on the Philippine coast, acknowledged the report, then asked to transmit the midday weather sequence. "Stand by for one minute before sending," replied McCarty, "as I am having trouble with rain static."

It was the last message received from the *Hawaii Clipper*. Fourteen navy vessels and long-range army bombers from the Philippines swept the ocean between Guam and Manila. On the second day, an army transport, the *Meigs*, found a large oil slick near the *Hawaii Clipper*'s last reported position. Nothing more was ever found. On August 5, after a week-long sweep, the search for the *Hawaii Clipper* was abandoned.

There was speculation that the Japanese had interdicted the Pan American flying boat. It was conjectured that Japanese hijackers had stowed away on board the *Hawaii Clipper* in Guam, then forced the airplane to divert to a Japanese base where the crew and passengers were killed.

The year before, Amelia Earhart had vanished in the South Pacific during her round-the-world flight. With her was the pioneer navigator Fred Noonan, who had flown with Musick aboard the *China Clipper* and on the early Pacific flights.[5] Earhart and Noonan had taken off from Lae, New Guinea, on 2 July 1937, bound for Howland Island, a tiny island on which the U.S. government had recently constructed a landing strip.

They never made it. Earhart's last worried radio communication reported that her fuel supply was nearly exhausted and estimated their position to be a hundred miles from Howland.

Despite the largest air-sea search in history, no trace was ever found of Earhart and Noonan. There was—and continues to be—conjecture that she was on an intelligence-gathering mission for the United States government. Her route brought her in close proximity to Japanese fortifications in the Micronesian islands. Clues were uncovered supporting a theory that Earhart and Noonan died while in Japanese captivity. No conclusive evidence was ever offered, and the fate of Amelia Earhart became an appealing mystery.[6]

Japanese sabotage was suspected on earlier occasions. Before the first transpacific flight in 1935, two Japanese nationals had been caught trying to sabotage the airborne direction finder. Later a Honolulu-bound clipper was forced to return when the crew was unable to transfer fuel from the bilge tanks. Though this problem was traced to a fuel line plugged with a cork left in place after an overhaul, Japanese saboteurs were again blamed.

The press embraced these rumors. Villainy, particularly by the Japanese, made a better story than an unsolved mystery.[7] But to the airmen who regularly flew the oceans, the probable culprit in the *Hawaii Clipper*'s disappearance was the Pacific and its vast, brooding storms. Clipper pilots had reported anvil-topped cumulonimbus clouds that towered above 60,000 feet, far higher than any storm was previously believed possible. To blunder into such a storm in a man-made craft like the *Hawaii Clipper* would be an intolerable risk. In the case of the *Hawaii Clipper*, it was fatal.[8]

19

The Right Vehicle

Meanwhile, in Britain the need for a transoceanic flying boat could no longer be ignored. The Empire-class boat, despite its load-carrying limitations, would be made to fly the North Atlantic.

By mid-1937 the long-standing recalcitrance of His Majesty's government to enter a reciprocal rights agreement with Pan American began to dissolve. Imperial Airways and Pan American scheduled a series of survey flights to prove the feasibility of sending mail by air between the two continents.

Caledonia and *Cambria*, the second and third production aircraft of the S.23 series, were modified for these flights. Their standard fuel capacity of 4,680 pounds was increased to 17,864 pounds by adding fuel tanks in the wing bays and along the wing spars in the hull. Their wing spars and planing bottoms were reinforced and all passenger accommodations, including even the cabin flooring, were stripped from the cabins.[1]

On 5 July 1937, the *Caledonia* lifted from the Shannon River at Foynes, Ireland, bound for the bay of Botwood on the Newfoundland coast. Three hours later, the *Clipper III*, a Pan Am Sikorsky S-42B, took off from Botwood, bound for Foynes. The clipper, commanded by Pan American Captain Harold Gray, flew a great circle course, arriving in Ireland after a flight of twelve hours, thirty-four minutes. The *Caledonia*, flown by Captain A. S. Wilcockson, flew a slightly longer rhumb-line course and, bucking the prevailing westerly wind, took fifteen hours, three minutes to reach Botwood.[2]

Though the simultaneous flights were hailed as a milestone in the progress of commercial aviation, their real importance lay in the ending of a political stalemate. Since 1935, had the British government seen fit to grant the concession, Pan American's S-42Bs could have conducted a scheduled mail service between America and Britain and even transported a small passenger load. Though the British made much in their own press about the S.23's slightly superior speed and "breakthrough" design features, the truth lay in the numbers. Even with the complete removal of all cabin accommodations, the S.23, fully fueled, could not transport a ton of payload. The S-42B, with only one of its four passenger compartments reconfigured to carry extra fuel, also fully fueled, had a payload capacity of nearly 7,000 pounds. For its first Atlantic survey flight, the *Clipper III*, in fact, carried a kit of maintenance spares for the English base. The kit, which weighed 1,995 pounds, could as easily have been eight commercial passengers.[3]

After the ceremonies and celebration of the Atlantic survey operations had faded from the press, a grim melancholia settled over the directorship of Imperial Airways and the British Air Ministry. They were compelled to face an unhappy truth: Britain *still* did not possess a true transatlantic airliner. The Empire boats, for all their futuristic appearance and reasonable speed, were severely limited. Worse, Pan American not only had the transpacific Martin M-130 but was advertising the arrival of its next generation of flying boat, the Boeing B-314, which would transport both cargo and a substantial passenger load nonstop over the Atlantic.

An inescapable fact about long-range flying boats was that such airplanes could *fly* at a far greater weight than that at which they could take off. Crucial amounts of energy—and weight—were sacrificed simply to lift the flying boat from the water.

The inherent problem of the Empire-class flying boat was one of weight control. The structurally heavy S.23 simply could not accommodate the great weight of fuel required to take off and then cross an ocean.

Thus was conceived one of the most bizarre efforts to lengthen the range of the flying boat. The Shorts' technical director, Major Robert Mayo, devised a scheme that involved mating two four-engined aircraft, using their combined power and lift for takeoff and climb, then separating the smaller machine to continue the ocean journey alone. The larger aircraft of the composite took the name *Maia* and was designated S.21. The upper aircraft, mounted on a frame above *Maia*, was a sleek, twin-float plane christened *Mercury*, which became the S.20.

Mercury was a high-winged monoplane powered by four Napier Rapier V engines of 340 horsepower each. Her 1,200-gallon fuel tanks in the wings provided a still-air range of 3,800 miles. Her maximum weight taking off alone was 12,500 pounds, but this increased to 20,800 pounds when launched from *Maia*.

Though the design work on the two aircraft began before the arrival of the S.23 series, *Maia* was a derivative of the Empire boats, differing from the S.23s by the extra width in her fuselage, a greater area in her vertical stabilizer and rudder, and 250 square feet more wing surface. To provide clearance for *Mercury*'s floats, the outboard engines were mounted farther out.

Extensive flight tests were conducted throughout 1937, at first with individual aircraft, and then with the two machines coupled. On 6 February 1938, over the Short plant at Rochester, *Mercury* made her first in-flight separation from *Maia*. In July, after separating from her mother ship near Foynes, Ireland, *Mercury* continued nonstop to Montreal in twenty hours, twenty minutes, completing the first nonstop commercial flight over the North Atlantic. In October she established a world distance record for seaplanes, leaving *Maia* near Dundee, Scotland, and flying 6,045 miles to the Orange River in South Africa in a time of forty-two hours, five minutes.[4]

The scheme received much public praise, though its only true function amounted to the fast transport of mail. At best, the *Mercury-Maia* composite served an interim role, that of flying the flag over the Atlantic, while the British Air Ministry awaited the arrival of a true long-range airliner.

On 10 August 1938, the Germans, who had been generally excluded from the British-American transatlantic negotiating, startled the world. A Deutsche Luft Hansa Focke-Wulf Condor took off from Berlin on a 3,800-mile nonstop flight to America. In just under twenty-one hours, the Condor arrived in New York. Three days later the airliner made the return journey to Berlin, without problem.

The Condor was a rakish, four-engined, 39,000-pound *land plane*. It could transport twenty-six passengers over a distance of 1,000 miles, or nine passengers for 2,500 miles. It cruised at 220 miles per hour at 12,000 feet—numbers that were unattainable by any contemporary flying boat.

To prescient observers of 1938, the flight of the Condor was a glimpse into the future. The "right" vehicle for the North Atlantic was not the flying boat. Not only had DLH turned to land planes, Air France Transatlantique was experimenting with high-altitude land planes and was already flying regular schedules over the South Atlantic with their four-engined Farman land planes.

To Charles Lindbergh, still a technical advisor to Pan American, the flying boat had always been an expedient. As early as 1933 he predicted "that land planes would eventually replace flying boats wherever airports could be built within practical range of one another." He believed that the seaplane–land plane debate, from the safety aspect, was a matter of psychology. "If passengers would fly in a land plane through storms and over fog-covered mountains, surely they would also be willing to fly in a land plane over water. But the first years of transoceanic airline operations would have to be with flying boats."[5]

Lindbergh was nudging Pan American toward the age of the land plane. In his diary he wrote that "they have eventually come round to the ideas I have been advocating for so many years, in regard to using land planes for the North Atlantic route."[6]

The age of the great flying boats had barely begun. Now it was almost over.

The British, committed to the Empire mail scheme and the development of the Empire-class boats, were not ready to be converted. In 1938 they produced an upgraded C-class boat, the S.30, powered by 1,010-horsepower Pegasus 22 engines. Eight of these aircraft were ordered by Imperial Airways, and though they were intended for the Bermuda–New York route, four were configured for in-flight refueling with tanks of 2,750 gallons and assigned a maximum takeoff weight of 53,000 pounds.

After lengthy trials, a weekly transatlantic mail service commenced on 5 August 1939. Handley Page Harrow tankers, staging from Ireland for westbound flights and out of Newfoundland for the eastbounds, refueled the S.30s en route. Sixteen of these flights were carried out before the outbreak of WW II. Thereafter the commercial in-flight refueling scheme, like the *Mercury-Maia* composite, was abandoned.

The final C-class boats, the S.33 series, combined the Pegasus XC engines and short-range tanks of the S.23 with the strengthened hull of the S.30. They were ordered in 1938 by Imperial Airways for the short-haul segments of the Poole–Karachi service. Like all other flying boat projects of the late 1930s, the final production models were abandoned in favor of military construction.[7]

In 1939 appeared the S.26, an enlarged derivative of the C-class boats, designed to fly mail nonstop across the Atlantic. First of these was the *Golden Hind*, delivered in September 1939, followed by her two sister ships. These ships, called the G-class flying boats, were powered by four Bristol Hercules engines of 1,380 horsepower each. With a gross weight of 75,000 pounds and an intended range in excess of 3,000 miles, they were designed to compete with the newly introduced Boeing B-314s of Pan American.

Golden Hind. The romantic name conjured up images of imperial glory, of full-rigged merchant ships and pith helmets and Bengal Lancers. From the cabins of the Empire-class flying boats passengers could gaze down on the Nile, on the vastness of India, on nomadic desert caravans. The Empire boats carried the flag to the outposts of the world. They maintained, briefly, the illusion that Britannia still ruled not only the waves but perhaps even the skies.

Boats of the Reich

E lsewhere in Europe, swastikas had begun to adorn the tails of Deutsche Luft Hansa aircraft. With the rise of the Third Reich, the general suspicion of all things German deepened in Britain, France, and the United States. Germany's flag-carrier, DLH, found itself largely ignored in the negotiating of North Atlantic air facilities.

Britain controlled the landing rights in Shannon, Bermuda, and Newfoundland. France's Aéropostale, prior to its demise, had negotiated exclusive access to the Azores base at Horta. The Americans, in the person of Juan Trippe, controlled the rights to the eastern shore of the United States. The Germans had no card of their own to play.

But ambitious Germany had already launched what was the first transatlantic commercial air service with the airships *Graf Zeppelin* and, later, the *Hindenburg*. With catapult ships in the South Atlantic, Wal flying boats were flying a regular mail service.

Now the Third Reich placed its bets on a new series of Dornier flying boats. The first of these, the Do 18, was a direct descendant of the Wal. Her seventy-seven-foot nine-inch tapered wing was parasol-mounted on a faired centerline pylon. The two tandem-mounted Junkers Jumo 540/600-horsepower diesel engines were slickly cowled into the center section of the wing. Six of these handsome aircraft went to DLH, and the remainder of the production series were marked for Luftwaffe duty.[1]

In the summer of 1936 DLH obtained agreement from the British and the Americans to operate an experimental mail service in the North Atlantic. The agreement contained numerous restrictions, including lim-

124

its on the amount and type of mail and allowing the use of Newfoundland bases *only* in the event of inclement weather.[2]

Two DLH Do 18s, christened *Zephir* and *Aeolus*, were stationed aboard the depot ship *Schwabenland*. In September the pair took off from the Azores on separate headline-grabbing flights. *Zephir* flew nonstop to New York in twenty-two hours twelve minutes, arriving with a reserve of ten hours' fuel. On the same day *Aeolus* flew directly to Bermuda in eighteen and a quarter hours and then continued on to join her sister ship in New York.

In March 1938 a Do 18, modified for a heavier maximum weight and given an extended wing span, was catapulted from the *Westfalen* in the English Channel. The Dornier flew southwestward over the Atlantic, nonstop to Brazil, an astonishing journey of 5,214 miles in a flight time of forty-three hours. This feat captured the world's straight-line distance record, which had been set at 4,447 miles by a Japanese Kawanishi H8K2 Emily flying boat.[3]

The depot ships dragged behind them a large canvas apron that was used to flatten the water for the landing mail plane. In rough seas, oil was poured on the water to calm the waves. The mail plane would be hoisted aboard by crane, refueled, then catapulted on her way again. The German catapults used propellants of compressed air, accelerating the flying boats down a 110-foot track from zero to ninety-five miles per hour in two seconds. To stretch their range, the mail planes would often fly for the next several hours only a few feet above the sea, riding the cushion of air beneath their wings called ground effect.

Despite the politics of the North Atlantic, the German mail planes received en-route support from both the French and the Americans. The weather ship *Carimare*, halfway between the Azores and Bermuda, supplied weather reports and direction-finding assistance. The approach to New York was on the radio guard of Pan American.[4]

While the Do 18 was still undergoing her proving flights, an even larger boat, the Do 24, was being designed for the Dutch government for service in the Dutch East Indies. Though similar in lines to the Do 18, the Do 24 was slightly larger. Her wings spanned eighty-eight feet, eleven feet greater than the Do 18, and she was powered by three tractor-mounted 1,000-horsepower BMW Bramo Fafnir 323R-2 radial engines. Her tail group featured twin outboard vertical stabilizers. Soon after the aircraft began her commercial career, however, war had begun and the Do 24 was produced exclusively for Luftwaffe use.

In 1937 DLH ordered three models of a new Dornier flying boat, the Do 26. This elegant machine represented the culmination of Claudius Dornier's flying boat designs. She had a slender, all-metal fuselage with a two-step hull. Instead of the usual Dornier sea wings, outrigger floats retracted into the wing and were completely enclosed while airborne. The cantilevered wing, instead of being mounted atop a pylon as in earlier Dornier boats, was joined to the upper fuselage and swept upwards in a graceful gull design. The four Junkers Jumo 205C 600-horsepower liquid-cooled six-cylinder diesel engines, tandem-mounted in sleek above-wing cowlings, drove three-bladed controllable-pitch metal propellers. The front propellers turned on a direct drive, and the rear propellers were driven on extension shafts. A unique engineering feature of the Do 26 allowed the rear propellers to tilt upwards six degrees to avoid spray during takeoff. When the aircraft was airborne, the propellers could then be lowered to their normal position.

The Do 26 was a superb flying boat both in aesthetics and performance. Her fuel-efficient diesel engines and race-plane wing (bearing at takeoff weight a load of 34.12 pounds per square foot of wing area) provided a range of 5,592 miles. She could comfortably fly any over-ocean segment on the planet. She boasted a short-range cruising speed of 192 miles per hour and, for extended flights, could maintain an economy cruise of 164 miles per hour. Her empty weight of 23,589 pounds versus an all-up weight of 44,092 pounds produced an impressive load-to-tare of 49:51. Her gross weight and dimensions—a ninety-eight-foot wing span and eighty-foot fuselage length—were comparable to those of the Sikorsky S-42, the Martin M-130, and the Short Empire-class boats. But the Do 26, at least in her inception, was not intended to carry passengers. Her 14,881-pound maximum fuel load left little capacity for them. She was a high-speed mail plane designed to be catapulted from depot ships on the high seas.

In late 1938 DLH deployed the Do 26 to the South Atlantic. There the Dornier flying boats made eighteen mail-service crossings before war ended their civilian careers.

Towards the end of 1936 Deutsche Luft Hansa solicited designs from German aircraft manufacturers for a giant transatlantic, passenger-carrying flying boat. Winner of the competition was the Hamburger Flugzeugbau (Blohm und Voss), who produced plans for a clean-lined, six-engined flying boat with a range of 4,630 miles.

At a takeoff gross weight of 100,530 pounds, the BV 222 Wiking was one of the most formidable commercial craft in the world. Powered by six BMW Bramo 323 Fafnir 1,000-horsepower engines, the Wiking boasted a maximum speed of 193 miles per hour and could cruise at 157 miles per hour. Its empty weight of 62,810 pounds produced a load-to-tare of 37:63.

Despite the Wiking's great size and capacity, DLH specified cabin accommodations for only *sixteen* passengers. This paradox reflected, presumably, the growing German determination to gather prestige in all matters aeronautical. It had been ordained by the Third Reich that DLH's passengers would fly the North Atlantic in unequaled aerial opulence.

Nearly four years passed before the BV 222 made its maiden flight, 7 September 1940, from the Elbe River at Finkenwerder. In the meantime the world had changed. DLH did not commence its North Atlantic service, nor did the mighty Wiking ever transport her eminent would-be passengers to the New World. Instead, the Luftwaffe put the new boat, as well as her thirteen sister ships, into war service as supply and reconnaissance aircraft.

A 1940 DLH order for a behemoth Dornier-built flying boat also went unfilled. Though hull construction had already been completed, the project was canceled in 1942. This would have been the Do 214, an eight-engined, double-deck transoceanic flying boat. Designed with a wing span of 197 feet and a gross weight of 319,670, this Dornier airplane, had she not become a casualty of war, would have been one of the last and, perhaps, the most successful of the oceangoing flying boats.[5]

21

American Export Airlines

I n the reciprocity negotiations between Imperial Airways and Pan American, Juan Trippe had negotiated from the premise of exclusivity. It was presumed by both parties that Pan American, in its *de facto* role as "chosen instrument," had an American monopoly on the North Atlantic air routes.

By the second half of the 1930s, this premise was being challenged. The development of bigger and more advanced long-range aircraft made it clear that commercial airline service to Europe would soon become a reality. With the reality would come, to a favored few, enormous profit, particularly if the profit were sweetened by U.S. mail subsidies.

One of the challengers was a steamship company, American Export Lines. In the spring of 1937 the shipping line incorporated a subsidiary company, American Export Airlines (AEA), and made immediate application to commence a series of survey flights to European ports. Their rationale was simple: Since American Export already plied the historic trade routes with their steamships, was not their airline subsidiary, supported by the same corporate and logistical network, imminently qualified to serve the public interest on the Atlantic?

Juan Trippe, for one, didn't think so. With the tenacity of a bulldog Trippe had held on to Pan American's Atlantic monopoly even though he had not yet broken the constraint of the odious Clause H, which forbade Pan Am to commence service between America and Britain until Britain was ready to do the same. But times were changing, and Trippe and his high-handed, unilateral dealings with foreign governments had cost him support in Washington. The Roosevelt administration, no

128

friend to the Republican-oriented Trippe, made clear its opposition to a monopoly by any single carrier, particularly Pan American, on the forthcoming Atlantic routes.

In the spring of 1939 a new Consolidated Model 28 Catalina twin-engined flying boat was delivered to American Export Airlines. That summer AEA conducted a series of survey flights with the Catalina over six different routes over the Atlantic. With the experience gained from these operations, AEA filed its application for a route to the United Kingdom and a route to France. In December, smelling success in the air, the airline placed an order with the Vought-Sikorsky division of United Aircraft for the preliminary engineering, and option for construction, of three four-engined, long-range S-44-type flying boats configured for nonstop transatlantic service.

By the time hearings on these applications commenced in October 1939, war had broken out in Europe. Because the recently passed Neutrality Act prohibited commercial flights into belligerent countries, the Civil Aeronautics Board (CAB) then permitted AEA to amend its application to include temporary permission to operate to Rome, via Lisbon.

On 15 July 1940, the CAB granted a Certificate of Convenience and Necessity to AEA to serve Lisbon, via Bermuda and the Azores. The Rome destination was deleted because of Italy's entry into the European conflict.[1]

The news landed like a thunderclap at the Pan American offices in the Chrysler Building. AEA had the Atlantic route! Pan American's lock on the Atlantic had been breached, at least on paper.

There were more battles to be fought, however. One inescapable truth about international airline routes still remained: Such an operation, to be profitable, depended on the infusion of mail subsidy, which required the approval of Congress. On Capitol Hill Pan American mounted an all-out campaign to block the upstart airline that had intruded into their exclusive territory. Thus Trippe's lobbyists, wielding far more influence in Congress than in the White House, managed to deny the crucial mail subsidy to AEA. The new airline could have its Atlantic route, but without the boon of mail revenues.

Trippe's victory would be only temporary. In a few months the rules by which Pan American had so successfully played the game were about to change.

* * *

With the Atlantic route award in hand, AEA immediately exercised its option for the three Sikorsky flying boats.

AEA's three S-44s were to be the last of the lineage of Sikorsky flying boats. The prototype aircraft, the XPBS-1 Flying Dreadnought, was the product of U.S. Navy contract No. 42868, dated 25 June 1936, for a four-engined, cantilevered high-wing monoplane flying boat. The XPBS-1 made her maiden flight from the Housatonic River, near Stratford Lighthouse, on 13 August 1937. Her test pilot was Edmund Allen, who would later perform the demanding test series of the new Boeing B-314.

The "Dreadnought," featuring nose, dorsal, and tail-gun turrets, an auxiliary power unit producing 110-volt AC electricity, had a gross weight of 47,455 pounds and, with a war load of 4,000 pounds, boasted a range of 3,170 miles. She mounted four Pratt and Whitney XR-1830-68 engines of 1,500 horsepower.

But she was to be one of a kind. In the course of her construction, the navy approved a second experimental aircraft, this one built by Consolidated. In the subsequent competition for a production order, the contract went to Consolidated. The winning aircraft was the PB2Y, a patrol plane similar in lines to the famous B-24 Liberator bomber.[2]

Design work on AEA's transatlantic flying boat, designated the VS-44A, began in February 1940. By this time Sikorsky's parent corporation, United Aircraft, had moved its Chance Vought division to Stratford, combining it with Sikorsky as the Vought-Sikorsky Aircraft Division and prefixing the aircraft designation with VS. The combination lasted from 1 April 1939 until 31 December 1942, the Vought company producing fighters and scout aircraft while Sikorsky constructed the last of his flying boats. Already under development in another wing of the plant was a mysterious new contraption called a helicopter.

AEA's three Sikorsky flying boats, collectively called the Flying Aces, were the *Excalibur*, *Excambian*, and *Exeter*. On 17 January 1942, in a ceremony at the Sikorsky plant, Mrs. Henry Wallace, wife of the vice president of the United States, bounced a bottle of champagne against *Excalibur*'s duralumin-skinned bow. The bottle refused to break. Mrs. Wallace delivered another blow. Again the bottle didn't break. When it seemed that the ship's nose would crack before the bottle, a thoughtful Sikorsky employee interceded. He taped a length of angle iron to the bow. Mrs. Wallace swung once more, the champagne gushed, and *Excalibur*, now officially blessed, began her career.[3]

The next day Captain Charles F. Blair, AEA's chief pilot, began testing the VS-44A. After two proving flights from freezing Long Island Sound, Blair and his crew took the new flying boat to the warmer waters of the St. Johns River at Jacksonville Naval Air Station in Florida. For two months *Excalibur* underwent her shakedown.

In the meantime, the world was changing. The new Sikorsky flying boats had to comply not only with performance specifications for AEA, but also for the U.S. Navy. With the United States officially at war, all three VS-44As had been requisitioned by the navy.

Thus was solved AEA's problem of subsidy, which, because of peacetime politics, had been denied them. On 12 January 1942 AEA signed a contract with the Naval Air Transport Service (NATS) to operate a wartime transatlantic route and on 12 February received its temporary certificate to fly between New York and Foynes, Ireland.

The first nonstop proving flight from New York to Foynes was made by *Excalibur* on 26 May 1942. Regular service began on 20 June with weekly round trips until the other two VS-44As arrived, and then three weekly trips began. *Excambian* was delivered to AEA in May 1942, and her sister ship, *Exeter*, arrived the next month. All the Flying Aces wore the subdued navy camouflage of sky blue on top and light gray underneath. Large American flags were painted on their bows.

The first westbound trip, flown on 22 June 1942, encountered powerful headwinds. Charles Blair, commanding *Excalibur*, descended to minimum altitude over the water, taking advantage of "ground effect" and a resultant lessened fuel burn, and continued nonstop to New York. *Excalibur*'s flight time from Foynes to New York totaled twenty-five hours forty minutes. "Remarkable voyage," reported an astonished passenger, Admiral Cunningham, Royal Navy.[4]

AEA's Flying Aces proved to be the longest-legged airliners of the era. In their time they alone possessed the capability of flying nonstop commercial flights with a capacity payload in both directions over the Atlantic. Early Atlantic operations in winter favored a more southerly route, but as wartime weather forecasting became more accurate, nonstop eastbound flights of 3,100 miles were regularly flown in twenty hours or less. Wintertime westbound flights were often routed as far south as the west coast of Africa and then west to Trinidad.

Records fell regularly. The Flying Aces established new times for the fastest flight from the United States to Europe (New York to Foynes, 3,329 miles) in fourteen hours, seventeen minutes, and the fastest westbound flight, over the same route, in sixteen hours, fifty-seven minutes. The VS-44As made the first nonstop flights along the wartime supply routes between Bermuda and North Africa, Africa and Trinidad, and between Africa and Puerto Rico.[5]

The brilliant record of the VS-44As was marred on October 1942 by the loss of AEA's flagship, *Excalibur*. During a hurried takeoff from Botwood's Bay of Exploits on the coast of Newfoundland, the VS-44A's flaps were inadvertently lowered to the fully extended position, normally only used for landing. As the big flying boat gathered speed, the improperly set flaps caused a nose-heavy, downward pitching moment. The aircraft porpoised across the surface of the bay, trying to bury her nose into the water. The captain, a pilot known for manhandling airplanes, hauled mightily on the yoke, yanking *Excalibur* into the air. She flew briefly, then plunged nose first back into the bay. In the ensuing crash, half the passengers and one crew member, Flight Engineer Mike Doyle, lost their lives.[6]

The VS-44A correctly owes a part of her success to her Pratt and Whitney power plants. The R-1830 Twin Wasp engine became known as one of the most reliable reciprocating aircraft engines of all time. This power plant produced 1,200 horsepower at takeoff, driving a three-bladed Hamilton Standard hydromatic quick-feathering propeller.

With the VS-44A, Sikorsky finally abandoned his preference for the structural economy of strut-braced wings, as with the S-42 and its predecessors. The VS-44A had sharply tapered, fully cantilevered wings, spanning 142 feet. As with the S-42, the VS-44A's wings were loaded like a fighter's. Their 1,670 square feet of wing area bore a highly efficient loading of 34.43 pounds per square foot. The fully cowled Pratt and Whitney engines faired smoothly into the leading edge. Sikorsky's design retained the outrigger floats instead of adopting Boeing and Martin's aesthetically pleasing but less stable sea-wing configuration. The trailing edge, flaps, and ailerons were covered with a fire-proofed fabric. Her 3,900 gallons of fuel were carried in the wing center section, which was compartmented into three separate tanks.[7]

The VS-44A's fuselage had an overall length of nearly eighty feet. The tail surfaces, similar in shape to the wings, were also fully cantilevered. The fin and horizontal stabilizer had duralumin covering, while the rudder and elevators were fabric covered. The hull was of aluminum alloy, semi-monocoque construction with six watertight bulkheads.[8]

The VS-44A's original maximum takeoff weight was 57,500 pounds (later raised to 59,534). With an empty weight of 30,200 pounds, this afforded a useful load of some 27,300 pounds, impressive numbers for any airliner of the 1940s. Her transatlantic performance was evidenced by her load-to-tare ratio of 47:53.

Was the VS-44A a successful flying boat? To the airmen who flew her—and compared her to other seagoing aircraft—she was the ultimate flying boat, the best and the last.

But her timing was bad. In the form of the XPBS-1, she first appeared on Sikorsky's drawing board in 1936. Six years amounted to a lifetime in the evolution of the flying boat. By the time of her launching as a commercial airliner in 1942, she was already obsolete because of her size. The VS-44A, fueled for an Atlantic crossing, could carry only sixteen passengers. With a filled cabin on a short haul, she had a maximum load of forty-seven. The Boeing 314, even with its limitations of load versus range, could carry twenty-four paying passengers across the Atlantic and, on shorter legs requiring less fuel, could transport seventy-four.

In 1945 the Civil Aeronautics Board approved the purchase of AEA by American Airlines, renaming the overseas carrier American Overseas Airlines. In September the airline acquired six Douglas C-54s, and on 23–24 October flew the first commercial scheduled transatlantic flight by land plane, from New York to Bournemouth, England. On the previous day, flying from the opposite direction, *Excambian* had journeyed westbound from Foynes to New York. It was the last transatlantic flight of a VS-44A.[9]

The VS-44A came too late, and when she arrived she lived her life in the shadow of the larger, more glamorous Boeing 314.

22

Boeing

With the Sikorsky S-42 and the new Martin M-130, Pan American had intercontinental flying boats that its competitors could only dream about. But carrying sacks of mail long distances between land masses had never been Juan Trippe's ultimate goal. Neither the Sikorsky nor Martin flying boats possessed the capacity to carry a profitable passenger load across an ocean. Profit, if any, came only from the artifice of mail subsidies. On its longest segment, California-to-Hawaii, the M-130 could transport a maximum of fifteen paying passengers. Such loads, without the cushion of taxpayers' dollars, did not translate to black ink in airline ledgers.

Even before the *China Clipper* entered commercial service, Trippe was shopping for a new airplane. He ordered his purchasing department to send specifications to aircraft manufacturers for a new flying boat with a range of 4,800 miles, that could carry 8,000 pounds of cargo and mail, with accommodations for no fewer than fifty passengers. As an inducement, a prize of $50,000 would go to the winning design. The expenses of the losers would not be reimbursed. "I believe in tying the bag of oats out front," said Trippe.[1]

Glenn L. Martin's entry, an enhanced version of the M-130, was summarily rejected. The Martin design was judged to be unambitious, short of the desired passenger capacity, and lacking the futuristic innovations Pan American sought in their next flying boat. In any case, it was too expensive for Juan Trippe's parsimonious taste.

Glenn Martin, with some justification, was outraged. He had taken a loss on his deal with Trippe to build the M-130. The shortfall, he had expected, would be recouped with subsequent orders of the M-130 or its derivatives. Trippe, by declining to exercise options on Martin flying boats, was dealing Martin a nearly fatal economic blow. Dismissing any notions of loyalty, Trippe had opened the field to all newcomers.

The design submitted by Igor Sikorsky was clearly the most advanced of all the entries and won the vote of Lindbergh, head of Pan American's technical committee. But a flying boat as advanced as Sikorsky's would require at least four years of development time. Such a luxury could not be afforded if Pan American were to proceed with its plans. Sikorsky's proposal joined Martin's in the trash bin.

One of the newcomers, the Boeing Company of Seattle, Washington, had not responded to the design request. Boeing's engineering department was preoccupied with the development of the Model 294, the Army Air Corps "Project X" that was to become the XB-15, and the Model 299 that would be the prototype B-17. But then an engineer named Wellwood Beall, who had been diverted to sales work, came home from an assignment in China where he had gone to deliver ten export versions of the Boeing P-26 "Peashooter." When Beall heard of Pan American's expired deadline, he made the flying boat request his personal project.

On his own, Beall produced a preliminary design study for a Boeing flying boat. His proposal incorporated the already-built XB-15 wing. Pan American's requirements stipulated the new Wright R-2600 Double Cyclone fourteen-cylinder, twin-row engine, producing 1,500-horsepower at takeoff. Indeed, the only other proven engine in use on large airliners was the R-1830, installed on the Martin M-130, which would be inadequate for a flying boat of the size required by Pan American.[2] Pan American had also specified the newly developed Hamilton Standard full-feathering constant-speed, three-bladed propeller. Beall mated these features to a double-deck hull, tail assembly, and Dornier *Flossenstummel* (sea wings).

As his plans developed, Beall became an impassioned advocate of the new flying boat. His zeal finally won over Boeing's president, Clair Egtvedt, who directed Beall to petition Pan American for an extension of the design competition deadline. On 9 May 1936, Beall, Egtvedt, and aerodynamicist Ralph Cram officially delivered the proposal for Boeing Model 314 to Pan American's technical committee. Thereafter ensued the predictable head-butting with Pan American's tight-fisted deal makers. On 31 July 1936, Juan Trippe announced that Boeing had received a contract for six 314s with an option for six more. Each aircraft carried a price tag of $618,908 with another $756,450 for spare engines and parts.

Wellwood Beall, from whose vision the new flying boat was conceived, was named project engineer for the 314, heading a team of eleven engineers. The Beall team's task began by mating a cantilevered, monoplane wing, derived from the XB-15, to an aircraft of slightly over 80,000 pounds maximum weight. This raised the original loading of the wing from twenty-five pounds per square foot of wing area on the XB-15 to twenty-eight pounds per square foot on the 314, a performance enhancement that would be accommodated by the powerful new Wright R-2600 engines.[3]

The Wright engines, specified by Pan American in its original design request, were still untested on commercial aircraft, though they had been used in military airplanes. The new engines, if Wright's specifications proved correct, would have the lowest specific fuel consumption (measured in pounds of fuel consumed per horsepower/hour) of any engine in service. They would also be the first commercial engines to require 100-octane gasoline.

The Hamilton Standard full-feathering propeller negated one of the worst nightmares of over-ocean airmen. Even though controllable-pitch propellers had been in use for several years, there was still no way to prevent them from "windmilling" in the event of engine failure except by using a propeller "brake." A windmilling propeller increased the total drag of an aircraft by a quantum factor and usually destroyed an already-damaged engine. The full-feathering propeller allowed the blades to turn edgewise to the airstream, stopping rotation and virtually eliminating the drag of the propeller.

The problem of sufficient propeller clearance from the water—a constant since the first flying boats—had been addressed in earlier aircraft by either mounting the engines atop the wing, as with the Dornier series, or by installing the engines in the wing and mounting the wing above the fuselage on a faired pylon, as with the Sikorsky S-42 and the Martin M-130. This choice demanded the use of struts to stabilize the wing, which, combined with the superstructure atop the fuselage, added drag and weight to the structure. The Boeing team chose to follow the lead of more recent designs like the Sikorsky XPBS-1 and the Consolidated XPB2Y-1 that used a deep, streamlined hull with sufficient height from the water to mate the wing directly to the upper fuselage. The engine nacelles could then be smoothly faired into the wing's leading edge.

A feature seen on the Dornier Do X but never used before on an American transport was an in-flight access to the engines. The 314's wing had sufficient thickness to allow the flight engineer to crawl through a passageway to the accessory section of each engine and perform in-flight maintenance.

In her initial configuration, the 314 had a maximum weight of 82,500 pounds (later 84,000). Her 152-foot wing tapered to smoothly rounded tips and was aluminum-covered from the rear spar forward and fabric aft. With an area of 2,867 square feet, the broad wings supported a load of 28.78 pounds per square foot (later, 29.30). The outer bays of the wing were watertight compartments—a feature that would prove fortuitous during the 314's first trials. The fuselage, measuring 106 feet long, was constructed as an integral unit with the wing's center section and inboard nacelles. Her hull, instead of being compartmented to prevent flooding as with most flying boats, was given a double bottom like a ship's hull.[4]

The fully cantilevered horizontal stabilizer was metal-skinned and attached as one unit to the top of the after hull. In the initial configuration, a single oval-shaped vertical stabilizer and rudder were attached to the top of the horizontal surface.

The great depth of the hull permitted a double-deck configuration with compartments for passengers and crew members on separate levels. In a short-range configuration, the 314 was intended to carry seventy-four passengers. For long trips she could accommodate thirty-four in sleeping berths as plush and roomy as Pullman compartments.

On the upper level was the flight deck, separated by a door from the crew quarters, baggage, and mail compartments. This level alone contained more space than the entire cabin of a DC-3. The flight deck was a roomy compartment—twenty-one feet long and nine feet wide—with a curtain that could be drawn between the pilot and copilot. The after flight-deck compartment was shared by the navigator, flight engineer, and radio operator. A spiral staircase, thirty years in advance of the Boeing 747's winding stairway, led from the radio operator's station down to the main passenger deck.

Though the 314 did not equal the Dornier Do X in overall size, she was the largest commercial flying boat ever constructed in the United

States. She was destined to become the most successful of all the great flying boats.

By early June 1938, the 314 was ready for launching. In Puget Sound off Duwamish Head, Boeing's chief test pilot, Edmund Allen, powered the big flying boat into the open water. Behind the aircraft trailed a procession of picket boats carrying photographers, technicians, and in one of them Wellwood Beall and Pan American's Andre Priester.

During a taxi test with a strong breeze off the port wing, the flying boat suddenly heeled to the right, submerging the right wingtip and nearly dousing the outboard engine. Though Allen managed to raise the wing with thrust from the right engines, the left wing then dipped. Allen was forced to cut all four engines. To maintain stability, he sent life-jacketed crewmen out the navigation hatch and onto the wing to level the aircraft.

It was hoped that this bizarre tendency could be attributed to the light fuel load and the fact that the sea wings were empty of fuel. But during the next day's tests, the same problem occurred. It became increasingly obvious that the fault lay in the position and planing angle of the sea wings.

The trials proceeded nonetheless. On the evening of 7 June, Allen opened the four throttles and the 314 skimmed briefly across Puget Sound, then lifted. To observers from below, the maiden flight appeared uneventful. For thirty-eight minutes Allen kept the big boat airborne, then gently returned her to the smooth waters of Lake Washington.

There were problems. "We had power to spare," Allen said, "but when I got off the water I couldn't turn." He had been forced to use differential thrust on the four Wright engines to maintain directional control. The single rudder on the big flying boat's tail had been ineffective.[5]

Beall's engineering team went back to work. A new empennage configuration was tested, this one with the single vertical fin replaced by twin vertical stabilizers mounted at each outboard tip of the horizontal surface. But more flight testing proved that the double fin still lacked adequate directional control. Finally the center vertical stabilizer was restored with the twin outboard fins still in place. This triple-fin arrangement worked—to the great relief of Wellwood Beall and his team—providing full directional authority to Boeing's big boat.

Meanwhile, the earlier problem, the disturbing matter of lateral instability on the water, required an alteration in the position and planing angle of the sea wings. The fix was duly accomplished, and further tests showed that the 314 had, in fact, shed the irksome tendency to plunge her wingtips into the ocean.

These were costly changes both in time and development funds. Not until January 1939, nearly a year behind schedule, was the first 314 delivered. By June 1939 all six 314s in the initial order had been delivered. In order of construction, they were the *Honolulu Clipper*, the *California Clipper*, the *Yankee Clipper*, the *Atlantic Clipper*, the *Dixie Clipper*, and the *American Clipper*.

On 3 March 1939, at the Tidal Basin in Washington, D.C., Eleanor Roosevelt smacked a bottle of what was said to be water from the seven seas against the bow of the *Yankee Clipper*. Three weeks later the newly christened flying boat left New York to fly its first transatlantic round trip.

The second series of six were already in production. These were 314A models and would differ from the first series with their larger fuel tanks (25,500 pounds), more powerful Wright Double Cyclones (1,600 horsepower), and increased maximum gross weight (84,000 pounds).

The 314A, with her empty weight of 49,149 pounds, possessed a load-to-tare ratio of 41:59, a seemingly unremarkable ratio until it is considered that the giant ship could carry a useful load of 34,851 pounds, an astounding capability that outclassed any airliner in the world. Included in this useful load was a fuel capacity of 4,200 gallons, which, at normal cruising speed (280 gallons per hour) and weight, translated to a still-air range of over 3,000 miles.[6]

Juan Trippe now had the ultimate weapon in his clash with the European governments. For three years His Majesty's government had remained steadfast in upholding the onerous Clause H, which bound Imperial Airways and Pan American to simultaneous introduction of transatlantic service. Despite Britain's *Mercury-Maia* project, their experiments with in-flight refueling, and the continued development of the Empire-class boats, Imperial Airways still lacked commercial transatlantic capability. And Pan American, bound by Clause H, could not unilaterally begin service.

Pan American's rights to France had likewise been tethered to the reciprocity issue. But at the end of 1938, almost as the first 314 was passing into Pan American's custody, the French government relented, giving Pan American temporary landing rights in Marseille. In return, Air France, which still had no transatlantic passenger-carrying capability, would have rights to the United States whenever they were ready. Thus, Pan American would fly the new 314 to mainland Europe, to a port only three hours from Paris. Though Trippe still had no landing rights in Britain, he had outflanked the British.

A sigh of resignation could be heard in the halls of the British Air Ministry. With more hope than faith, the Ministry announced that Imperial Airways, on an experimental basis, would begin service over the North Atlantic in June 1939. If Pan American was prepared to commence service sooner, they could proceed. Clause H was waived.[7]

A certificate of public convenience and necessity was duly issued by the Civil Aeronautics Authority (CAA) granting Pan American operating authority to Great Britain and France, with London and Marseille as terminal points. As intermediate stops, Pan American was entitled to use the Azores, Shediac, Botwood, and Foynes.

On 20 May 1939, the twelfth anniversary of Lindbergh's solo Paris flight, the *Yankee Clipper* waited at her moorings at Port Washington in Manhasset Bay, New York. It was noon on a sunny Saturday. After years of frustration, Pan American was about to operate a scheduled flight over the North Atlantic. Like the Pacific inaugural of the *China Clipper*, a script had been produced that invoked symbolism and hyperbole.

"The *Yankee Clipper* is ready, sir," reported Captain Arthur Laporte. Before a gathered throng at Pan American's new marine terminal, Trippe handed over the ship's documents. He ordered the captain to cast off. Laporte and his crew of fourteen marched two by two down the ramp to the waiting *Yankee Clipper*.

In brilliant sunshine, the *Yankee Clipper* lifted from the bay, then veered toward the New York World's Fair, passing 500 feet over the heads of the gawking spectators. Radiotelephone communications had recently come into use in terminal areas. The *Yankee Clipper*'s crew received congratulations over the air from the chairman of the CAA. Laporte replied, following his script, "We are proceeding for Europe."[8]

Carrying 1,800 pounds of mail, the *Yankee Clipper* reached Marseille, via the Azores and Lisbon, on 22 May 1939. Three days later Laporte and his crew flew the 314 on the return trip, transporting a ton of

United States–bound mail, thus completing the inaugural round trip transatlantic air mail service.

There were more firsts. In June the *Yankee Clipper*, commanded by Captain Harold Gray, who had succeeded Ed Musick as chief pilot, flew the northern route to Europe, this time carrying non-revenue passengers including Juan Trippe and a contingent of official government and business guests. On 28 June, amid fanfare and newsreels, the *Dixie Clipper*, flown by Captain R. O. D. Sullivan (who had taken the first S-42 to Wake Island and who was Ed Musick's first officer on the M-130 inaugural) took off for Marseille with the first paying transatlantic passengers. The event made page one of the *New York Times*.[9]

Two of the new 314s, the *Honolulu Clipper* and the *California Clipper*, were tagged for the Pacific service, depleted by the losses of the *Hawaii Clipper* and Ed Musick's *Samoa Clipper*. By the time the second group of six, the 314As, were completed, war had come. Three of the flying boats were sold to British Overseas Airways Corporation (recently nationalized airline composed of the former Imperial Airways and British Airways) and would be christened *Berwick*, *Bangor*, and *Bristol*. Pan American took possession of the remaining three 314s, the *Pacific Clipper*, the *Anzac Clipper*, and the *Capetown Clipper*.

Like the Martin M-130 four years earlier, the 314 bathed in a brief shower of publicity. Each of her inaugural flights was attended by gala fanfare and media coverage. But as her ocean crossings became as routine as a railroad timetable, the public's attention waned. There were more urgent matters in the headlines. The peaceful conquest of the oceans had been overshadowed by another war.

23

War Day

S unday morning, 7 December 1941. It was business as usual in the central Pacific. Captain H. Lanier Turner, commanding the Boeing 314 *Anzac Clipper*, was inbound to Honolulu with his crew of ten and seventeen passengers. In the cabin, breakfast was being served to the passengers, mostly vacationers. They were an hour out of Pearl Harbor when radio officer W. H. Bell received the electrifying news: Pearl Harbor, their destination, was under attack by Japanese aircraft.

Farther to the west, the *Philippine Clipper*, a Martin M-130 commanded by Captain John Hamilton, had just lifted from the lagoon of Wake Island, bound for Guam. Hamilton expected a routine flight in clear skies all the way to Guam. But then, twenty minutes into the flight, Hamilton received new orders by radio. He was to return immediately to Wake and prepare to evacuate all Pan American personnel. Pearl Harbor, he was told, had been bombed.

In Hong Kong, beyond the international date line, it was already Monday, 8 December. Captain Fred S. Ralph and his crew of six had been alerted before dawn by the Pan American station manager. A Japanese attack on Hong Kong was expected. Ralph should muster his crew at Kai Tak airport and prepare to take off as soon as possible in the *Hong Kong Clipper*, a Sikorsky S-42B. Ralph had completed his preflight preparations. But as he stood on the ramp at Kai Tak waiting for the Sikorsky to be loaded, he heard the unmistakable drone of incoming warplanes.

For Captain Robert Ford, the thirty-five-year-old captain of the *Pacific Clipper*, the news came while he was midway between New Caledonia

142

and New Zealand. The Japanese, he learned by radio, were on the move throughout the Far East. Ford immediately posted lookouts and ordered the Boeing 314's radios silenced. Grimly he continued toward Auckland, not knowing what to expect.

And in New York, where it was still Sunday, Juan Trippe went to his office in the Chrysler Building. He knew that the American base at Pearl Harbor had been ravaged. He knew, too, that everything had changed, that his fleet of commercial flying boats would be diverted toward another, yet undefined wartime mission. But what Trippe did not know was what had become of his four flying boats out there in the Pacific on this December morning. He only knew that they were in extreme danger.

For several weeks all Pan American flying boat captains had carried sealed orders on board their aircraft. In the event of a war emergency, they were to open the orders and proceed accordingly. Lanier Turner, commanding the *Anzac Clipper*, opened his orders and learned that he was to divert to Hilo, on the island of Hawaii, about 150 miles to the south of embattled Pearl Harbor on Oahu.

For the next two hours Turner flew on to Hilo, hoping that this new route would not bring him into the scrutiny of the Japanese task force. Not until they had safely landed in the bay at Hilo did Turner inform his passengers about the events at Pearl Harbor. He advised them that they could either stay in Hawaii or return to San Francisco with the *Anzac Clipper*. He intended to depart, he said, just as soon as the flying boat could be serviced and refueled. All elected to stay.

All day Turner and his crew worked to make the *Anzac Clipper* ready to fly. There was no Pan American ground staff in Hilo, nor were there pressure fuel pumps. Fueling was done by gravity, laboriously pouring each gallon into the over-wing receptacles. By nightfall the job had not been completed, and so Turner and his crew were obliged to stay over all the next day. That night, Monday, 8 December, they departed Hilo in blackness and radio silence. By the time the *Anzac Clipper* reached San Francisco eighteen hours later, Lanier Turner and his crew had neither shaved nor slept in a bed for seventy-two hours.[1]

John "Hammy" Hamilton, thirty-four, was a bull-necked, muscular man, sometimes given to postures of bravado. But he was known as a solid pilot, navy-trained, a veteran of nine years on Pan American flying boats. Now, as captain of the *Philippine Clipper*, sister ship of the *China Clipper*, Hamilton was about to face the severest test of his career.

Bound for Guam when he received news of Pearl Harbor, Hamilton was now en route back to Wake. He ordered flight engineer T. E. Barnett to dump 3,000 pounds of fuel from the heavily loaded M-130. Landing in Wake's sheltered lagoon, Hamilton taxied to the pier and then went to confer with the senior naval officer on the island, Commander W. S. Cunningham, and the ranking marine, Major James Devereux.

Wake now possessed a landing strip, built earlier that year to accommodate a squadron of Marine Corps F4F-3 Wildcat fighters. The Wildcats, however, had no navigational capability. Now it was an urgent necessity to sweep the seas around Wake for an approaching enemy force. Without homing devices, the Wildcats could not patrol far enough from Wake without risking becoming lost. Would Hamilton take the *Philippine Clipper* on patrol, escorted by the fighters?

Hamilton consented, but with conditions. He insisted that the Martin M-130 be fueled not only for the patrol but for the onward flight to Midway, plus a four-hour reserve. He would take his load of civilian refugees along with him. Even though high-octane fuel was now a critical commodity on Wake, the officers agreed.

An hour later Hamilton was standing on the loading dock with the Pan American station manager, John Cooke. The two men watched the final fueling of the flying boat. As they talked, they became aware of the rumble of engines. They looked up. Out of a low, rolling scud line they could see two formations of airplanes. Cooke thought they were American B-17s. Hamilton knew better.

The two formations split, the first going for the airstrip. The second formation bore down on the north fork of the island, toward Hamilton and Cooke and the freshly fueled *Philippine Clipper*. The men felt the thud of bombs hitting the island. A trail of bullets kicked up the sand, coming toward them. Hamilton and Cooke and their Chinese chauffeur, Tommy, dived into an unfinished foundation hole. Twenty feet away a bomb exploded, showering them with sand and debris. More bullets whined across the sand, kicking spray.

In the next few minutes the Wake Island airline colony, built with the sweat and spirit of the adventurers from the *North Haven*, was blown to bits. The hotel, Pan American's oasis on a desert island, was hit and set afire. John Cooke's house was flattened. The clipper loading dock disappeared in a geyser of debris. Hugo Leuteritz's Adcock antennas crashed to the sand. A fuel dump took a direct hit, gushing flames and smoke.

The attackers finished their work and withdrew. John Hamilton climbed out from his ditch and peered through the smoke and dust. The island was ablaze. Columns of oily smoke curled into the low clouds. Hamilton ran toward the *Philippine Clipper*, expecting the worst.

The flying boat was still at her mooring, rocking in the waves from a bomb that had exploded a hundred feet away. Hamilton could see holes where a Japanese gunner had stitched a line of bullets across the fuselage. With flight engineer T. E. Barnett, Hamilton climbed on board to assess the damage. The fuel tanks seemed intact. The engines had not been hit, nor were the control surfaces damaged. She was flyable.

Hamilton told Cooke to round up all the passengers and Pan American employees. At the same time he gave the order to strip every nonessential item from the clipper—every piece of cargo, baggage, passenger amenity.

Ninety minutes after the Japanese attack, the *Philippine Clipper* was ready. She carried thirty-four people on board—twenty six Pan American station personnel plus eight crew members. Two were seriously wounded from the air attack. The Adcock direction finder was down, and Hamilton had no idea what to expect when he arrived at Midway. For all he knew, the Japanese would already be there.

One thing was certain: The Japanese wanted Wake. They would return soon. For the Americans still on Wake, the only means of escape was the *Philippine Clipper*.

Hamilton taxied the heavy ship out into the lagoon. The Martin flying boat rode low in the water, filled beyond her design capacity with fuel and human cargo. Hamilton opened the throttles, and the *Philippine Clipper* began to gather speed. But as she plowed across the narrow lagoon, it became clear that she would use up her sea room before reaching flying speed. Hamilton closed the throttles and turned the clipper around for another try.

Once again the *Philippine Clipper* labored to reach flying speed. Hamilton pumped the yoke trying to make her unstick from the water. Again he was forced to abort the takeoff.

On the third attempt the clipper's hull skipped free from the surface. She skimmed along, trailing a cascade of spray, struggling to remain airborne. Clinging to her few feet of altitude, the *Philippine Clipper* roared over the sandy beach, barely clearing the dwarf magnolias and scrub brush, and pointed her bow to the open ocean.

It was a bittersweet moment. From their gun positions, the marines watched the *Philippine Clipper* become a speck on the horizon. On board were thirty-four of their countrymen, now on their way to safety. Left behind on Wake Island were the marines and the civilian construction workers who had come to build the air strip. They would remain to face the Japanese.[2]

In the meantime, Midway, too, had come under attack. Warships of the Japanese *Kido Butai*, the same task force that struck Pearl Harbor, were shelling the island. While the *Philippine Clipper* was droning across the central Pacific at near sea level to avoid enemy contact, Japanese gunfire destroyed the Adcock direction finder on Midway. Hamilton and his crew had no way to find their tiny island target except by celestial navigation.

Darkness came, and Hamilton climbed the *Philippine Clipper* up into the night sky. Now there were stars by which navigator J. A. Hurtsky could take celestial fixes. Over the radio Hamilton broadcast his intentions to reach Midway and transmitted the names of those he had airlifted from Wake.

Midway stood out like a beacon. Fires still blazed from the afternoon's attack. With all his lights on to avoid misidentification, Hamilton made a reconnoitering pass over the blacked-out base, picked a landing area on the debris-strewn lagoon, and set the *Philippine Clipper* down.

When refueling was completed, the flying boat was airborne again. Navigation was no longer a problem as they followed the familiar chain of island signposts on the 1,304-mile route to Hawaii. Though Hamilton was prepared to divert to Hilo, he was instructed by radio to come on into Pearl Harbor. Despite the devastation to the base and the moored vessels, the Pan American facility had escaped destruction.

The escapees from Wake, most of them still wearing the standard island uniform—shorts and sneakers— disembarked at Pearl Harbor. The full realization of what happened now struck them. The military complex was in ruins. Fires still raged. Smoke blotted the tropical sky. The navy's battleship row had become an oil-slicked gravesite.

Two days later, on 10 December 1941, John Hamilton flew the Martin M-130 back to San Francisco. The 2,402 mile trip was, he said, "like any other we have ever made with the exception that we maintained radio silence."[3]

For the *Philippine Clipper* and her famous sister, the *China Clipper*, it was the end of an era. The six-year adventure of the "Pacific Highway" was now a romantic memory. Both remaining Martin clippers would acquire military paint and finish their careers performing wartime logistical duty. The *Philippine Clipper* would wear a "wound" stripe as testimony to her machine-gunning on Wake. The glory days were over, and neither of the Martin clippers would survive the war.

Captain Fred Ralph, thirty-four, had a special affection for the *Hong Kong Clipper*. Her nickname was Myrtle. She was an S-42B, an aging Sikorsky flying boat brought to the Far East in November 1941 to fly the Manila–Hong Kong segment of the transpacific air route. She had now completed eleven shuttle flights.

Fred Ralph had just finished preflighting Myrtle. It was Monday morning, 8 December 1941, a few minutes before eight o'clock. An eerie stillness lay over the colony. Ralph had planned to fly the Sikorsky and her passengers that morning to the presumed safety of Manila, but he had just been told that Manila, like Pearl Harbor, was under Japanese attack. Now Ralph had new orders. He was to fly Myrtle out of Hong Kong to an inland lake near Kunming in the interior of China.

But it was too late. The rumble of aircraft engines split the morning stillness. Looking to the north, Ralph saw the silhouettes of airplanes descending over the Sha Tin Pass. They were coming directly at Kai Tak airport.

The first bombs struck Kai Tak. Bullets chewed up the tarmac where Fred Ralph and his working party stood watching. They ran for cover. Most of them jumped into the water behind concrete dock pilings.

Fred Ralph sprinted to the end of the dock, and as the bullets pinged against the concrete, he leapt into the water and ducked behind a piling. Too late he realized that he had chosen an open sewer for his shelter.

Ack-ack bursts smudged the sky, hitting nothing. Air raid sirens began to wail. Explosions rocked the colony. The Zeros roared low over Kai Tak, dropping their externally mounted bombs, cratering the runways, firing on the CNAC (China National Airline Corporation, Pan American's affiliate) transport aircraft parked on the tarmac, strafing the buildings and hangars.

From his shelter Fred Ralph watched the Zeros dive on the *Hong Kong Clipper*. He counted six passes, and each time the incendiary bullets stitched a path over the dock and across the water, missing the flying boat. Then, on the seventh pass, the bullets found their target. Myrtle erupted in flames. While Fred Ralph and his crew watched helplessly, the big Sikorsky flying boat burned to the waterline.

The warplanes withdrew, soaring northward back toward occupied Kwangtung province. Fred Ralph climbed from the foul water. Dripping wet, he stared at the burned-out hulk of the *Hong Kong Clipper*.

Meanwhile, William Langhorne Bond, Pan American's boss of CNAC, was already busy dispersing the undamaged CNAC aircraft. Three of his transports had survived the bombing, and he ordered these aircraft camouflaged and pushed off into the vegetable gardens that surrounded the airport.

That night Fred Ralph and his crew escaped Hong Kong aboard a CNAC DC-2. For a month they were not heard from. They wound their way across Asia and Europe, finally arriving in New York in January 1942. Hong Kong, they learned, had fallen to the Japanese on Christmas Day.[4]

In Auckland, Captain Robert Ford pondered his situation. His way home—the Pacific island route to San Francisco—had become a battleground. Between New Zealand and Hawaii there were no safe harbors.

Ford and his crew of nine had flown the Boeing 314, the *Pacific Clipper*, to Auckland without incident. For a week he waited for orders. The big flying boat was the most advanced long-range aircraft in the world. Ford knew that it would be desperately needed back in the United States. Pan American, like the rest of America, was at war.

Finally, Ford received instructions, such as they were. He was to fly the *Pacific Clipper* home the long way, via Asia and Africa and the South Atlantic. The specific route was up to him. So was everything else, including the details about obtaining fuel, maintenance, navigational aids, weather reports, and, incidentally, protection from the Japanese.

No one had yet made a round-the-world flight with a commercial aircraft. Although Bob Ford had no abiding wish to enter history, he now had little choice. If he wanted to go home with his crew and the *Pacific Clipper*, he had to take the 23,000-mile-long way around.

He received an extra assignment. Before commencing the westward journey to America, he was to fly part way north across the Pacific, to

Nouméa, pick up the Pan American personnel stranded there, and fly them to Australia.

Ford landed at dawn in Nouméa. An hour later, with twenty-two company people and their families on board, he took off again. Six and a half hours later he arrived at the Australian east coast town of Gladstone.

Throughout the next day the *Pacific Clipper* droned over the waterless stretches of Australia. Darwin, their destination, was a raucous, rowdy north-coast port town, now in the throes of a war emergency. A Japanese air attack was expected at any time. All night, while a tropical storm spat lightning and drunks fought in the streets, they fueled and serviced the flying boat. At dawn they were airborne again, bound for Surabaja in the Dutch East Indies.

Flying in radio silence over the island of Java, the *Pacific Clipper* was suddenly intercepted by fighters—Dutch—whose pilots had never seen a Boeing flying boat and were unable to identify the aircraft. For several tense minutes the fighter pilots debated by radio whether to shoot the intruder down. Finally one of the Dutchmen thought he could discern part of an American flag on the top of a wing. The fighters stayed on the Boeing's tail, their guns armed, until the entire entourage arrived in Surabaja—with the clipper landing in a minefield.

Not until later, when they chatted with the young fighter pilots in the officers' mess, did the flying boat crew realize how close it had been. The Dutch in the Far East had been badly mauled by Japanese air raids. The fighter pilots were anxious to retaliate. They wanted to shoot something down. It had almost been the *Pacific Clipper*.

The Boeing's Pratt and Whitney engines needed one-hundred-octane aviation gasoline. The only fuel available on Java was automobile gas. With no other choice, Ford topped off his tanks with the auto fuel. On the afternoon of 21 December 1941, he headed out over the Java Sea.

The next twenty-one hours were the longest flight that Ford or his crew had ever made. The engines popped and complained because of the low-grade fuel, but they continued to run. Flying low over the Bay of Bengal at dawn, Ford flew directly over a surfaced Japanese submarine. Before the surprised enemy sailors could man their deck gun, Ford managed to climb up into the low clouds. With no charts to make an accurate landfall, Ford managed to find Ceylon and landed the Boeing in the tropical harbor with the romantic sounding name of Trincomalee.

On Christmas Eve the strange odyssey was under way again, now bound for Karachi. An hour later they were back in Trincomalee with oil gushing from a failed number three engine. The engine had gotten them across the Indian Ocean—twenty-one hours of flight time on improper fuel—and then failed only thirty-four minutes into the next leg. Bob Ford was beginning to believe that luck was, after all, on his side.

Flight engineers Jocko Parrish and Swede Rothe, working without special tools or parts for the complex engine, labored for two days. For the rest of Christmas Eve and all of Christmas Day they worked, fabricating parts and tools from material borrowed from the Royal Air Force base.

On 26 December 1941, Ford made his second takeoff from Trincomalee. The overloaded Boeing climbed slowly in the hot, tropical morning air, barely clearing the groves of palms that lined the harbor. All day they flew over the vast brown landscape of India, landing that evening in Karachi. From there, on 28 December, Ford flew the Boeing along the coast of the Gulf of Oman, over the Persian Gulf to the island of Bahrain.

Again no high-octane aviation fuel was to be found. Fueling once more with automobile gasoline, and once more hearing his engines knock and ping, Ford pointed the flying boat westward over the Arabian desert, across the Red Sea, into the Sudan. That evening he landed in the confluence of the Blue Nile and the White Nile, below Khartoum.

From the Sudan they flew over the interior of Africa, past barren hills to the equatorial jungles of the Congo. At Léopoldville Ford put the Boeing down in the fast-flowing muddy waters of the Congo River. It was New Year's Day, 1942.

The next leg, and the next takeoff, were the most perilous of the journey. The day was humid, hot, without a breath of wind. The high-density altitude, due to the tropical temperature, deprived the Boeing of her maximum takeoff performance. She carried a load of 5,100 gallons of gasoline—33,660 pounds—for the long flight across the South Atlantic to Brazil.

Ford opened the throttles and headed downstream, taking advantage of the six-knot current in the river. Ahead lay a series of cataracts. A few feet before the rapids, Ford coaxed the Boeing off the water, by scant inches, then mushed along in the air cushion over the water. He discovered then that he had no aileron control. For several minutes he was forced to fly at full power down the gorges below the cataracts, using only the rudder to turn the Boeing. Cautiously he gathered speed and altitude. Grudgingly, the heavy ship began to climb in the jungle air. The ailerons returned to service, and Ford banked the ship westward, toward the South Atlantic. Not until later did he determine that the great load of fuel in the wing tanks had bent the wings enough to bind the ailerons, locking them in place.[5]

Twenty-three hours and thirty-five minutes later, after an ocean journey of 3,100 miles, they landed at Natal, on the east salient of Brazil. As soon as they had fueled and performed maintenance on number one engine, they were airborne again. In Trinidad, forty hours since their departure from Léopoldville and the menacing Congo River, the crew of the *Pacific Clipper* slept.

On the freezing morning of 6 January 1942, the duty officer at LaGuardia airport in New York heard the transmission: "*Pacific Clipper*, inbound from Auckland, New Zealand, Captain Ford reporting. Due arrive Pan American Marine Terminal La Guardia seven minutes."

To a flying boat had fallen the distinction of making the first round-the-world flight in a commercial airliner. Bob Ford and the *Pacific Clipper*, though they had not set out to do so, had entered history.[6]

24

In Service

Thus ended the age of elegance. With war being waged on opposite ends of the planet, an urgent need existed for long-range transport aircraft. In the United States there were no such airplanes except for a handful of army B-24 bombers, convertible to cargo use, and Pan American's fleet of oceangoing flying boats.

The newly delivered Boeing 314s, which had provided a standard of airborne luxury never seen before, entered military service. Soon after Pearl Harbor, the *Pacific Clipper* was requisitioned by the U.S. Navy. The *Anzac Clipper* went into the service of the U.S. Army Air Forces, receiving the designation C-98. The *Yankee Clipper*, *Dixie Clipper*, and *Atlantic Clipper* were also purchased by the navy, although these aircraft never actually left Pan American service. The *American Clipper*, *Capetown Clipper*, *California Clipper*, and *Dixie Clipper* followed the *Anzac Clipper* into USAAF service. The *Honolulu Clipper* stayed with Pan Am, assigned to the Hawaii–San Francisco route.

The aging Martin M-130s entered the service of the U.S. Navy. The *China Clipper* and *Philippine Clipper* were assigned to the Pacific, performing military transport duty. All the requisitioned flying boats were to be operated by the airline under military contracts.

Stripped of their civilian finery, the clippers all received coats of dull gray paint. Gone were the plush passenger amenities, gone the seats, sleeping berths, lounges, the luxurious lavatories. Gone forever were the days of silver goblets and hot meals served in real china by white-coated stewards. The stately flying boats had become military transports. They carried only cargo and priority passengers.

Within days of the Pearl Harbor attack, Captain Harold Gray was on his way to Calcutta in a B-314. His cargo was airplane tires, urgently needed for the Flying Tigers' P-40s to replace the load left on Wake by John Hamilton and the *Philippine Clipper*. Militarized flying boats were soon ranging across the Atlantic and Pacific, hauling bullets, parts, personnel, mail.

The North Atlantic, which a decade ago was a no-man's land crossed only by daredevils and pioneers, became a busy air corridor. Flying boats shuttled daily on the northern route from the United States to Britain and, on the southern route, from Natal to West Africa. One Pan Am pilot, Joe Hart, made twelve ocean crossings in thirteen days. In one twenty-four-hour period, he made two Atlantic crossings.[1] Crews flew as many as 197 hours in a three-week period.

Though still assigned to Pan American, crews had military reserve status and wore the uniform of the contracting military branch. If flying a B-314 under army command, the pilots wore khaki uniforms. When flying the M-130 on navy missions, they wore naval aviator's green uniforms with gold wings. There were inevitable conflicts between civilian and military authority. Military crews rebelled when told upon arrival at a station that they were to take their orders from the Pan American station manager. Likewise, the flying boat pilots would find their operations dictated by zealous, newly commissioned officers. A furious B-314 captain, Marius Lodeesen, found his orders countermanded by an army major. He fired a message from an outpost in the Indian Ocean: WHO IS RUNNING THIS OPERATION—YOU, THE ARMY, OR ME? From New York his chief pilot wired: YOU ARE.[2]

In Britain, BOAC had gone to a wartime footing. With their three B-314s, the *Berwick*, *Bristol*, and *Bangor*, the airline maintained a service between Poole and Baltimore, and from Poole to Lisbon, a neutral port that had now become an important diplomatic center. The Lisbon service eventually was extended to West Africa, where land planes continued to the Sudan and East Africa.

The "Horseshoe Route" was a joint BOAC and Qantas operation, flown with the C-class Empire flying boats, connecting South Africa to Australia. When the center portion, Singapore and Malaya, were overrun by the Japanese, the Short boats were forced to fly nonstop from Ceylon all the way to Perth, in Western Australia. Two Tasman Empire Airways (TEAL) S.30 Empire boats provided the only passenger service of any kind between New Zealand and Australia from 30 April 1940 until the end of the war.

Two C-class boats, the *Cabot* and *Caribou*, were lost to German attacks during the Norwegian campaign. Two other Empire boats, *Coorong* and *Cambria*, evacuated 469 British troops from Crete in April-May 1941. In the New Guinea campaign, Qantas's flying boats contributed valuable support.[3]

In the early weeks of 1942, Prime Minister Churchill journeyed to Washington for the "Arcadia" conference with President Roosevelt. Strategies were discussed, and Churchill received what he had come for—assurance from Roosevelt that the Allies would concentrate on Europe first. Hitler, then the Japanese.

Following the conference, Churchill planned to fly from Norfolk, Virginia, to Bermuda. There he was to board the battleship HMS *Duke of York*. Escorted by a destroyer screen, he would cross the Atlantic to England.

The flight to Bermuda was aboard the *Berwick*, one of the three B-314s released to BOAC. "I traveled in an enormous Boeing flying boat," Churchill wrote in his memoirs, "which made a most favorable impression on me. . . I took the controls for a bit, to feel this ponderous machine of thirty tons or more in the air. I got more and more attached to the flying boat."

So attached did he become that he asked the BOAC captain, J. C. Kelly-Rogers, whether the Boeing could fly all the way from Bermuda to England. Yes, Kelly-Rogers assured him, indeed it could. The idea provoked a stiff argument from Churchill's staff. Air Chief Marshal Sir Charles Portal and First Sea Lord, Admiral of the Fleet Sir Dudley Pound, thought it was too great a risk. "What about the U-boats you have been pointing out to me?" asked Churchill. Intelligence reports showed as many as twenty German submarines waiting along the route to England.

The two officers relented after they learned that they, too, could accompany the prime minister on the flying boat. The night before their departure, Churchill had misgivings. "I felt rather frightened," he wrote. "I thought of the ocean spaces, and that we should never be within a thousand miles of land until we approached the British Isles."

The size and luxury of the *Berwick* put him at ease. He was berthed in the "bridal suite." There were windows on either side of his cabin.

Kelly-Rogers showed the ever-curious Churchill the flight deck, the instruments and controls, and pointed out the de-icing boots on the wings and empennage. Churchill was favorably impressed with the veteran flying boat captain. "We were in sure hands," thought the prime minister as he turned in for the night.

The next morning things had changed. The skies had clouded, and celestial navigation was impossible. Rogers had intended to reach the British coastline from the southwest. They should have overflown the Scilly Islands, but the island group was nowhere to be seen. Kelly-Rogers decided to turn directly north, a track that would place them somewhere near a friendly coastline.

The decision, as it turned out, was fortuitous. Another six minutes' flying time would have taken them directly over Brest, on the French Atlantic coast, a heavily defended German submarine base. But there was danger still from the British coast. Arriving from the south, seemingly from German-occupied Europe, the lone flying boat was picked up on radar and labeled an "unidentified aircraft." Hawker Hurricane fighters were scrambled.

The fighters "were ordered to shoot us down," wrote Churchill, noting with a touch of schoolboy bravado that "they failed in their mission." Before the Hurricanes could make their intercept, Kelly-Rogers had landed the *Berwick* safely in Plymouth Harbor.[4]

A year later, on the morning of 12 January 1943, Captain Howard Cone was in Port of Spain, Trinidad, with the B-314 *Dixie Clipper*. He had been given a mysterious passenger manifest identifying his passengers only by number. Not until Passenger Number One, in his wheelchair, came aboard did Cone realize that he would be flying the president of the United States and his retinue on a secret mission.

Roosevelt was bound for Casablanca. There he would confer with his comrade-at-arms, Churchill, and meet the French general, de Gaulle. They would decide on the terms of an unconditional surrender by the Axis nations.

In 1943 flying was still considered by many to be an unacceptable risk for a head of state, particularly in time of war. No incumbent American president had flown in an airplane, nor had a president left the country in wartime. Roosevelt's top aide, Harry Hopkins, was uneasy about the flight. In his diary he wrote, "I sat with him, strapped in, as the plane rose from the water—and he acted like a sixteen-year-old, for he had done no flying since he was President. The trip was smooth, the President happy and interested."

The conference proceeded as planned. The trip home was cause for another celebration. The *Dixie Clipper*'s crew presented Roosevelt with caviar, champagne, and cake. It was the president's sixty-first birthday. The crew gave him an envelope containing eleven dollars for the Infantile Paralysis Fund, a charity close to Roosevelt's heart.[5]

The war took its toll. On the evening of 22 February 1943, the *Yankee Clipper* had crossed the Atlantic, stopping at Bermuda, and was approaching the Tagus River, near Lisbon, Portugal. Her captain was R. O. D. Sullivan, who had flown with Musick on the first transpacific flight. It was Sullivan who had made the first landing in Wake's tiny lagoon, and it was Sullivan, who from time to time outraged other airmen with his brusque manners and heavy-fisted flying. But Rod Sullivan was the world's most experienced over-ocean pilot. The previous month he had completed his one-hundredth Atlantic crossing, more than any airman in the world.

Banking low over the river, Sullivan turned onto the final leg of his approach. In light rain and semi-darkness he misjudged his altitude. At 6:47 P.M. the *Yankee Clipper*'s left wingtip caught the water. The big ship cartwheeled, smashed into the water broadside, and broke up. Within minutes she sank in the chilled waters of the Tagus River, killing twenty-four of the thirty-nine people on board.

Among the passengers were members of a USO troupe, including singers Tamara Drasin, the 1930s "First Lady of Song," and night club singer and recording star, Jane Froman. Also on board was author and war correspondent, Ben Robertson, Jr.

Drasin, who had introduced songs such as "Smoke Gets In Your Eyes," and "Love For Sale," was killed in the crash. So was Robertson, on his way to take over the London bureau of the *New York Herald Tribune*. Froman suffered severe injuries, including a smashed right leg, and would be crippled for life.[6]

Out of the disaster came a poignant love story. Froman was kept afloat for forty-five minutes in the freezing river by another survivor, Fourth Officer John Curtis Burns, who was also severely injured with a broken back and a fractured skull. Both were rescued. In 1948 they were married.[7]

In the official investigation, the accident would be blamed on Sullivan. He had turned at too low an altitude over the river, the board determined, and had inadvertently flown the clipper into the water. Sullivan, who survived the crash, denied for the rest of his life any fault, insisting that the Boeing's nose had dipped sharply downward, out of control, just prior to impact.[8]

Of the twelve Boeing 314s in wartime service, the *Yankee Clipper* was the only casualty. She had flown over a million miles and accomplished 240 Atlantic crossings, including the historic first scheduled flight across the North Atlantic.

On the morning of 21 January 1943, the *Philippine Clipper* was inbound to San Francisco from Pearl Harbor. Like her famous sister ship, the *China Clipper*, the *Philippine Clipper* was assigned to the U.S. Navy. For the past year she had performed shuttle service between the West Coast and Hawaii. In command was Captain Robert Elzay, a ten-year Pan American veteran and a former naval aviator.

Elzay had been briefed about the stationary front that lay along the northern coast of California. The front was not expected to clear for another twenty-four hours. Visibility was likely to be marginal, and strong winds were forecast to be whipping San Francisco Bay. In ordinary times Elzay might have considered delaying his departure.

This was a high-priority flight. On board the *Philippine Clipper* were Rear Admiral R. R. English, commander of the Pacific submarine force, and his staff, including two navy captains, three commanders, two lieutenant commanders, and a navy nurse. The admiral and his party were en route to a submarine warfare conference in Richmond, California.

Pan American's flying boat base was moved to Treasure Island, in San Francisco Bay, from Alameda on the eastern shore. The *Philippine Clipper*'s estimated arrival time was 10:18 A.M. local time on 21 January. Shortly before dawn Captain Elzay radioed that due to tail winds they would arrive nearly four hours sooner, at 6:35 A.M.

The coastal storm that worried Elzay appeared exactly as forecast. Treasure Island reported heavy rain, 900- to 1000-foot ceiling, visibility one to two miles. Southerly winds of forty-four to forty-eight miles per hour lashed San Francisco Bay.

The usual alternate landing site for San Francisco-bound flying boats was Clear Lake, to the north of San Francisco, but conditions there were equally bad. Because of the early arrival, Elzay had more than sufficient fuel to divert southward, all the way to San Diego. Instead, he radioed his intention to hold offshore and wait for the weather to improve. At 7:00 A.M. he reported that the *Philippine Clipper* was holding over the Farallon Islands, near the mouth of San Francisco Bay.

Elzay was mistaken. The *Philippine Clipper*'s actual position was approximately ninety miles farther north, inland from the California coast.

No further position reports were received. At about 7:30 A.M. the *Philippine Clipper* flew into a mountain near the Russian River, a few miles west of Ukiah, California.

Because the aircraft crashed so far from Elzay's last reported position, nearly two weeks elapsed before the wreckage was found. There were no survivors. Because of the military nature of the flight, little publicity was given the accident. A huge cordon was drawn around the site. There were the inevitable rumors of sabotage, particularly after the search party was unable to find Admiral English's briefcase, known to contain material pertinent to the meeting he was to attend. Not until several days later was the briefcase found near the wreck. The armed guards were relieved, and souvenir hunters eventually picked over the remains of the *Philippine Clipper*.[9]

What happened? Since the first Pacific flights, it had been a common procedure for flying boat captains, when weathered out of their destination, to drop down to sea level before reaching the coast. With surface contact established, they would continue under the cloud deck, into the bay. It was speculated by Elzay's colleagues that he did this, not realizing he was already over land when he descended through the clouds.

The CAB investigation placed the blame for the crash direcly on Captain Elzay for not having fixed his position correctly. But the most pertinent question went unanswered. *Why* had a seasoned flying boat crew been so far off in their reckoning? No satisfactory answer was ever found.

Until the crash, the *Philippine Clipper* had flown 14,628 hours without an accident. She had flown the first transpacific passenger flight, making the historic rendezvous with the SS *Lurline* in 1936. She had survived strafing by the Japanese at Wake Island in 1941, suffering some twenty bullet holes.

Of the three Martin M-130s, only the *China Clipper* remained.

25

Requiem for the Big Boats

Flying boats lived lives of hazard. Their enemies were legion. They included salt water, rough water, slick water, ice-filled water, and the darkness of night. Corrosion was a constant condition. Repair of a ruptured hull was a nightmare.

By the middle of World War II, the flying boat was in a race with the bulldozer. Across the planet military engineers were pushing aside jungle, desert, and tundra, laying concrete and Marston mat. Where once only flying boats had ventured, rubber-tired land planes were screeching down on newly surfaced runways. The great lumbering boats, with their requirements for safe harbors and their susceptibility to saltwater corrosion, had become inefficient anachronisms.

As the war progressed, the U.S. Army Air Force gradually developed its own worldwide air transport system. The mainstays of the military long-range fleet were now the Douglas C-54 (the civilian DC-4) and the Lockheed C-69 (Constellation). The army C-98s (Boeing 314s) acquired from Pan American were eventually turned over to the navy. And then when the navy was ready to release the Boeings, before the end of the war, Pan American chose not to repurchase them. Even to America's premier overseas airline, flying boats had no place in the postwar future.

The naval air station at San Diego became the boneyard for the obsolescent Pan American flying boats. BOAC's Boeing 314s went to a similar retirement in Baltimore. Put up for sale by the War Assets Administration, some of the mothballed boats were bought by start-up airlines that appeared after the war.

159

Thus did the once-mighty Boeing flying boats suffer ignominious ends. Two of them, the *Pacific Clipper* and the *Atlantic Clipper*, were cannibalized for parts. The *Capetown Clipper*, reconditioned and renamed the *Bermuda Sky Queen*, was flown to England where she was chartered to bring British delegates back to America for a United Nations meeting.

En route, the Boeing 314's inexperienced operators found the westerly headwinds stronger than forecast. Running short of fuel, they landed amid thirty-foot swells in the open Atlantic. The sixty-two passengers and seven crew bobbed on the high seas for twenty-fours while the U.S. Coast Guard cutter *Bibb* rescued them one boat load at a time.

In an attempt to take the *Bermuda Sky Queen* under tow, the bow of the aircraft smashed into the *Bibb*, staving in the flying boat's nose. The damaged aircraft was declared a derelict and the order was given to sink her. Set ablaze by gunfire, the Bermuda Sky Queen vanished in the Atlantic.

Another start-up airline, World Airways, purchased all seven remaining Boeing 314s. Two of them, the *Dixie* and *Berwick*, the historic wartime transports of Roosevelt and Churchill, were broken up for spares. Until 1949 World Airways flew the surviving Boeings on cargo and charter operations along the East Coast and to the Caribbean. History and the harsh rules of economics finally forced an end to the operation, and again the Boeing 314s went into storage.

By 1951 all but the *Bristol* had been scrapped. She had been sold to a shadowy minister, known as "Master X," who declared his intention to fly to Russia to negotiate a peace accord with Stalin. This bizarre mission came to an end before it began. A violent storm swept over Baltimore harbor, tearing the *Bristol* from her mooring and sinking her on a muddy shoal. Salvaged from the mud, she, too, went to the scrapyard. She was the last of the line.[1]

The story of the Martin clippers did not end with the M-130. Glenn Martin, perhaps naively, had gambled that Pan American would follow up its initial order of three M-130s with additional aircraft. Instead, Juan Trippe solicited proposals from other manufacturers, including Martin's competitors, Sikorsky and Boeing. Ultimately, Pan American's order went to Boeing for an advanced over-ocean flying boat. An outraged Glenn Martin was left with his unwanted M-130 derivative, a huge deficit, and no customers.

Only one model of the M-156, the advanced Martin clipper, was

constructed. She had the same distinctive lines as her M-130 predecessors, but her overall dimensions were greater. Her wings spanned
156 feet, and the maximum gross weight was increased to 62,000 pounds.
The tail was configured with dual vertical stabilizers, a design improvement intended to correct the single-finned M-130's wallowing tendency
in rough air.

Finding no buyers in the United States, the M-156 was finally sold
to the Soviet Union. Christened the *Russian Clipper*, the flying boat entered
the service of Aeroflot. In 1940 she was based in Khabarovsk, in the
Far East, replacing the shorter-ranged Savoia-Marchetti S.55.

For four years the *Russian Clipper* maintained a scheduled service. She
flew the route from Khabarovsk, along the lower reaches of the Amur
River to Nikolayevsk-na-Amure, then rounded the southern tip of the
Sea of Okhotsk to the city of Petropavlovsk on the Kamchatka Peninsula.
This 1,200-mile route suited the capabilities of the Martin boat comfortably, allowing her to transport a substantial load and still carry
sufficient fuel for diversion. Previously, Aeroflot aircraft were forced to
take the lengthy route around the perimeter of the Sea of Okhotsk, via
Magadan, using primitive coastal facilities for refueling and repair.

The *Russian Clipper*'s operations were confined to summers, the brutal
Siberian winters devoted to refurbishing the flying boat. In 1943 the
clipper was scheduled to have her Pratt and Whitney engines replaced
back in Baltimore. This plan was canceled, probably due to wartime
priorities, and Soviet-made engines, Ash-621Rs, were installed instead.

For another year the M-156 flew with her Russian power plants. In
1944, for reasons now lost in the smoke of Russian history, the M-156
Russian Clipper was sacrificed for scrap metal.

The late-arriving Sikorsky VS-44As had barely come of age before
their time was up. Flown by American Export Airlines under U.S. Navy
contract, two of the three flying boats survived the war. The *Excalibur*,
holder of numerous early speed and distance records, was lost at Botwood, Newfoundland, in a takeoff accident on 3 October 1942. At war's
end, American Export, like its competitors on the lucrative North Atlantic routes, opted for Douglas-built land planes. Both VS-44As were
sold to a charter operator and found themselves engaged in various
questionable operations in South America.

The once-proud *Exeter*, wartime transport of diplomats and flag officers, became a gunrunner. She was used to supply arms and ammunition
to rebels trying to bring down the government of Paraguay. During one

such mission on the evening of 15 August 1947, the *Exeter*'s captain failed to rendezvous with the rebel gunboats on the Paraguay River. With darkness falling, he elected to turn back to the Rio de la Plata estuary, on the South Atlantic coast. By the time he arrived over the estuary, near the Punta Brava Lighthouse, an inky darkness blanketed the water.

In a classic flying boat scenario, the *Exeter* approached too fast, too steeply, smacking the water nose first. She waterlooped, careened through the water broadside, and was destroyed.[2]

Only the *Excambian* was left. The last VS-44A was acquired by a group of Baltimore businessmen and refitted as a flying trading post for service on the Amazon River. This adventurous enterprise failed, and the *Excambian* became a derelict, mouldering in a Peruvian harbor. And then in 1957 a former navy flying boat pilot named William Probert bought the Sikorsky and ferried her home to California.

Operated by Probert's airline, Avalon Air Transport (later Catalina Air Lines), the old ocean boat carried tourists over the forty-five miles of water between Long Beach and Catalina Island, a journey that took her twelve minutes each way.

In 1969 she again changed hands. One of her earliest admirers, Charlie Blair, who had flown her as chief pilot of American Export Airlines and had set Atlantic speed records with the VS-44As, bought the old flying boat. Blair and his actress wife, Maureen O'Hara, founded Antilles Air Boats, a Caribbean-based seaplane airline. The *Excambian*, sole survivor of the great American oceangoing flying boats, became, briefly, the flagship of their airline.[3]

Based in the U.S. Virgin Islands, the VS-44 made over a thousand commercial flights. In 1971, after an accident in which her hull was run aground, it was discovered that the decades of salt water and neglect had taken too great a toll. She was no longer serviceable. Once again she was beached.

Thereafter she became a venerated relic, residing briefly in the U.S. Naval Aviation museum at Pensacola, Florida, and then returning to the place of her birth, Bridgeport, Connecticut. There, with the support of the Sikorsky Aircraft Division of the United Technologies Corporation, she underwent extensive renovation prior to her installation in the Bradley Air Museum at Windsor Locks, Connecticut.

* * *

Within the British Commonwealth still lived the remnants of a bygone, Kiplingesque era. To these outposts, many still unvisited by the engineers and bulldozers, the stately Empire-class flying boats continued to fly. For another decade beyond the war, the Empire boats and their derivatives tramped through the backwaters of Africa, the Far East, and the South Pacific.

Conceived in the middle thirties, the Empire-class flying boat had proliferated in astonishing numbers. No fewer than 792 examples were constructed, far more than any other four-engined flying boat of any nation. Most of these were S.25 Sunderlands, long-range versions delivered to the Royal Navy. Approximately forty Sunderlands were converted to civilian model Sandringhams, and a few, the Hythe class, were produced for commercial use after the war.

A slightly different variant, the S.45 Solent, was developed from the RAF's Short Seaford, much as the Sandringham evolved from the Sunderland. First launched in November 1946, the Solents were intended for use on the East Africa and Far East routes.[4]

The largest Short flying boat, the S.35 Shetland, first flew in military version on 14 December 1944. This ambitious aircraft had a 150-foot four-inch wing span and a maximum weight of 130,000 pounds. Her wings, swept back at the leading edge, mounted four 2,500-horsepower Bristol Centaurus 600 engines. The Shetland II, with accommodation for as many as seventy passengers on two decks, made her maiden flight 17 September 1947.

But by this time BOAC had cast its vision beyond the flying boat. Neither of the huge Shetlands ever entered service. The first was lost to fire and the second scrapped at Belfast in 1951.[5]

Of the famous S.26 G-class boats built at the end of the thirties, only the *Golden Hind* survived her military service. Though these most glamorous of the Empire boats were intended for the North Atlantic, their true range (with payload) never permitted such operation. Luxuriously refurbished, with accommodations for twenty-four passengers, the *Golden Hind* returned to BOAC service in September 1946 and flew the prestigious Poole-to-Cairo route. She made her last flight for BOAC in April 1948 and was finally scrapped in 1954.

The Australian airline Qantas resumed flying boat operations after the war, as did the predecessor of Air New Zealand, Tasman Empire Airways (TEAL). TEAL remained one of the staunchest flying boat adherents, keeping their Solents in operation until 1960.

BOAC's flying boat era ended on 3 November 1950 with the departure of the *Somerset*, an S.45 Solent, from Southampton to South Africa. The four-and-a-half-day flying boat journey was about to be shortened by half with the introduction of land planes. Ironically, it was on this route, formerly served by the slow but reliable flying boats, that BOAC chose to introduce the futuristic—and tragically flawed—Comet I jetliner.

In Australia, the independent airline Ansett continued to operate their two Sandringhams until 1966. Aquila Airways took BOAC's place in Southampton, operating Hythe-class and Solent boats to tourist destinations throughout coastal Europe. A string of accidents, including a grisly crash when the Solent *Sydney* crashed in a gravel pit on the Isle of Wight, hastened the end of Aquila Airways.

On 26 September 1958, the *Awateri*, a former TEAL Solent acquired by Aquila, became the last flying boat to depart on a commercial passenger flight from the historic Southampton marine terminal when she took off for Madeira, Spain. On 20 December, the last three Solents remaining at Southampton were ferried to Lisbon, where they were to commence a new airline operation. But like many such enterprises, the venture failed. For thirteen years the three flying boats lay idle on the Tagus River before being scrapped.[6]

Freed from occupation and the constraints of war, Air France resumed operations in 1946. The elegant Laté 631, ordered in 1938 and first flown in 1942, metamorphosed as a postwar production airliner, powered by American engines (six 1,600-horsepower Wright Cyclone fourteen-cylinder radials). Air France took delivery of three new Laté 631s, and on 26 July 1947 put them in service on the historic French flying boat route across the South Atlantic. One of these, F-BANU, was given the name *Guillaumet*, in honor of the pioneering Air France pilot, Henri Guillaumet, who had commanded the Laté 521, *Lieutenant de Vaisseau Paris*, during her Atlantic flights of 1938–39, and who was killed in combat during the war.

The Laté 631s thus earned the distinction of being not only the largest flying boats ever to operate a commercial passenger service, but were the last commercial boats to fly scheduled transatlantic routes. Staging from the Biscarosse base near the French Atlantic coast, the big flying boats flew to Port Etienne, in West Africa (now Mauritania), then across the Atlantic to Fort-de-France, in Martinique.

Despite their clean-lined beauty, the Laté boats proved to be too vulnerable. One was destroyed, even before entering service, during her delivery flight. And then, on 1 August 1948, one of the new boats, F-BDRC, vanished in the Atlantic with fifty-three passengers aboard.[7] Following this disaster, Air France made the decision to end its long and sentimental association with the flying boat.

A total of eight Laté 631s, including the prototype, had been produced. Following their withdrawal from Air France service, an airline called Société France-Hydro laid plans to use all seven remaining aircraft on a cargo operation between Douala and Chad, in central Africa. An experimental service was conducted for three years with one of the boats, with a large cargo door built into the port side just abaft the wing. When this aircraft was lost in an accident near Banzo, in French Equatorial Africa, the operation came to an end. Two of the Laté 631s were sold to breakers, and the others perished in hangars destroyed by a snowstorm.[8]

She was still the famous *China Clipper*. But ten years in the career of a flying boat amounted to several lifetimes. By 1945 she was obsolescent, relegated to the backwaters of Pan American's system—the route from Miami to Léopoldville on the coast of West Africa. She had just been returned from U.S. Navy custody and restored to her original colors.

Captain Marius Lodeesen was sent back to Miami to check out again in the *China Clipper* after nearly a decade of flying other aircraft. Like most of the Pan American pilots, Lodeesen loved the old flying boat. He felt at home amid the oil-and-leather cockpit smells, the old-fashioned throttles, the familiar rounded-back pilots' seats.

Not much had changed. Gone was the spiderlike candy-machine crane they had used to operate the Sperry autopilot. Gone, too, was the clothesline used to send notes from the cockpit to the engineer's station. Now there was an intercom.

On the night of 8 January 1945, Lodeesen's phone in Miami rang. It was the Pan American airport manager. "Lodi. . . there has been a crash. The *China* went in at Port of Spain. . ."

The *China Clipper* had been on final approach to Port of Spain, Trinidad. It was a clear, starlit night, the water slick as glass. The landing path was illuminated by flares. The captain, Cyril Goyette, had turned the controls over to the first officer, Leonard Cramer. As the aircraft was descending toward the flarepath at an airspeed of one hundred knots, the hull smacked into the granite-hard water and ripped apart. The

China Clipper sank like a stone in thirty feet of water. Nine of the twelve crew members and fourteen of the eighteen passengers were lost.

The official accident investigation gave the probable cause of the accident as the pilot's "failure to realize his proximity to the water and to correct his altitude for a normal landing, and lack of adequate supervision by the captain during the landing, resulting in the inadvertent flight into the water at excessive landing speed in a nose down attitude. . . ."

There were dissenting opinions. Several surviving crew members believed that the clipper had struck an object, possibly a small boat. No evidence of a foreign object was found.[9]

Marius Lodeesen had his own theory. When Lodeesen was sent to Miami to check out again in the aging *China Clipper*, his instructor was a younger man who hadn't flown the Martin boats in the Pacific.

He did not approve of Lodeesen's landing technique. "Too slow. Eighty-five knots in the approach."

"That's too fast," argued Lodeesen. "We always approached at seventy-five knots, at night even slower. She has no flap. When you come in fast, the bow is too depressed and you could waterloop."

"We want to be conservative," said the instructor. "At seventy-five knots you are only a few knots above stalling. Better do it our way and don't confuse the pilots you fly with."

Lodeesen relented. He later wished he hadn't.[10]

Until the night in Port of Spain, the *China Clipper* had led a charmed life. She had flown over fifteen thousand hours. She had covered 2,400,000 miles carrying 370,000 pounds of cargo, 380,000 pounds of mail, and 3,500 passengers. During a wartime mission to the Belgian Congo, she had brought back a cargo of uranium that would be used in the top-secret Manhattan Project—the first atomic bomb.[11]

Flying boats would soldier on for a few more years. There were still backwater outposts to visit. There were islands not yet accessible by land planes. But with the death of the *China Clipper*, the age of the great boats had come to an end.

26

Dinosaurs and
Might-Have-Beens

What was it about the flying boat that intrigued men of vision and talent like Martin and Sikorsky and Hughes? Why were they so convinced, even while history was giving its blessing to the land plane, that the great, long-range flying boat still had a place in commercial aviation?

Geniuses are often stubborn men. They can cling to outdated notions just as tenaciously as ordinary men. They can be, like Howard Hughes, driven to prove their critics wrong. They can be, like Grover Loening, simply obsessed by the mystique of a vehicle like the flying boat.

By the 1940s, certain statistics were incontrovertible. No hull-bottomed, water-based commercial airliner in the world could match the coldly efficient DC-4. The flying boat, as a viable commercial airliner for the postwar decade, had few true believers. Pan American, BOAC, and Air France, all traditional proponents of the long-range flying boat, had smelled the kerosene of the coming jet age. Speed, versatility, operating efficiency—these would be the criteria of the new generation of commercial airliners.[1]

In Britain, where the airline industry had become nationalized, a dichotomy of thinking bisected the Air Ministry. In a bold stroke to regain twenty years of lost ground, Britain was developing the futuristic De Havilland jetliner, the Comet I. In a simultaneous leap into the past, the Air Ministry had placed an order with Saunders-Roe for the largest commercial *flying boat* ever intended for airline use.

167

In May 1946, specifications were laid down for three models of the Saunders-Roe SR-45 Princess, a ten-engined transatlantic flying boat. From its inception, the project was plagued with delays. Not until 22 August 1952 did the Princess make her maiden flight. She was the first and, as it turned out, the only one of the three to fly.

Heading the list of the Princess's troubles were her engines. Turboprop engine technology was still in its infancy. The Princess was powered by Bristol Proteus turboprops, which had been advertised to produce 3,500 horsepower, but which, in fact, delivered only about 2,500 horsepower. The arrangement of engines and propellers was an engineering nightmare. The inboard and center engines were mounted in coupled pairs and drove eight-bladed, contra-rotating propellers. The outer engines were singly mounted and turned four-bladed propellers.

The Princess was a behemoth by any standard. With a wing span of 219 feet 6 inches, she had a design maximum weight of 345,000 pounds. It was intended that she have a maximum range of 6,040 miles at a cruising speed of 358 miles per hour. Her two decks and several cabins were to accommodate one hundred passengers in luxury or up to 220 in an economy configuration.

The Princess never overcame her problems, nor did she find interested buyers. After a hundred flight hours, the project was abandoned in 1954. All three aircraft were scrapped. A hugely expensive failure, the Princess was the last flying boat built for airline use.[2]

In the history of might-have-beens, one flying boat ranks as the most spectacular of them all. The Hughes H-4 *Hercules*, the largest aircraft in terms of wing span ever constructed, remains the leviathan of flying machines.

The *Hercules* had its origins in the fertile mind of an American industrialist, Henry J. Kaiser. The United States in 1942 was faced with the prospect of transporting thousands of men and millions of tons of material across the Atlantic, which had become a U-boat hunting ground. Kaiser, a man who favored direct solutions, proposed a bold idea: He would overfly the submarines. Kaiser wanted to build a fleet of giant flying boats and, moreover, he would build them with materials not listed as critical to the war effort.

Though his proposal drew a barrage of skepticism, Henry Kaiser was not a man to be taken lightly. Already he had mobilized the American shipbuilding industry into feats never thought possible. Under his direction, a new 10,000-ton Liberty ship was entering service every forty-six days.[3]

Kaiser was given his chance. But after the War Production Board gave him the go-ahead, Kaiser the shipbuilder recruited a partner who could supply the aeronautical expertise. And so did Howard Hughes's name become linked with the *Hercules*, and thus did the eccentric entrepreneur become responsible for the construction of the world's biggest aircraft.

Eventually Kaiser, who had overextended himself, dropped out. Engineering problems and the snowballing costs of the project eliminated all but one model of the giant flying boat. Despite cutbacks by the government, despite congressional accusations of misspent federal funds, and despite the end of the war and the vanished need for his giant flying boat, Hughes persevered with an obsessive tenacity.

Not until 2 November 1947 was the H-4, as it was now called, ready for testing. The events of that day have become an item of aviation legend. After demonstrating the water-handling characteristics of the big aircraft to the press, Hughes disembarked the reporters, then taxied back out to the open water. During what was supposed to be a high-speed taxi test, Hughes took off in the *Hercules*, flew for a mile at an altitude of seventy feet, then settled back into the harbor. It was the first and only flight of the Hughes H-4 *Hercules*.[4]

What was the historical significance of the Hughes flying boat? It had never been considered for commercial use, nor would it have been a suitable airliner. The big aircraft is remembered primarily as an intriguing but extravagant sinkhole for taxpayers' dollars. The grand scale of the H-4, as it turned out, represented the ultimate dimensions of the flying boat. No larger or more ambitious oceangoing aircraft was ever attempted.

How good a flying boat might she have been? Why was she never flown again? The puzzle of the Hughes flying boat remains a fascinating mystery. The answers lie sealed forever in the enigmatic mind of her builder.

One of the last true believers in the flying boat was Glenn Martin, builder of the *China Clipper*. Still seething over his treatment by Juan Trippe, Martin continued to dream of constructing a fleet of giant commercial flying boats. In the absence of airline orders, he had found a willing customer in the U.S. Navy.

The Mars XPB2M-1 was ordered by the navy in 1938. The big, four-engined flying boat, built as a patrol bomber but converted before its maiden flight to a transport, was the first of the highly successful navy Mars series. To Glenn Martin, it was to be the forerunner of a new lineage of commercial flying boats, the Martin 170 series.

Powered by four Wright Cyclone R-3350-18 engines of 2,200 horsepower each, the Mars had a 200-foot wing span, a length of 120 feet three inches, and, in her initial production model, a maximum gross weight of 145,000 pounds. In the JRM-2 version, her gross weight was increased to 165,000 pounds. The JRM-2 had an advertised cruise speed of 173 miles per hour.[5]

The prototype Mars, dubbed the "Old Lady," broke the international seaplane record in 1942, flying a closed course of 4,600 miles and staying in the air almost a day and a half.[6] By war's end the prototype Mars had delivered over three million pounds of cargo in the Pacific. In 1945 the navy contracted for twenty JRM-1s, an order subsequently cut back in the postwar budget constraints to five JRM-1s and one improved model, the JRM-2, equipped with the new Pratt and Whitney R-4360 Wasp Major engines, each delivering 3,000 horsepower. The JRM production aircraft were nearly identical in appearance to the "Old Lady," with the exception of their high, single vertical stabilizer and rudder, replacing the canted, twin fins of the prototype.

The big Mars boats enjoyed much success. Several new records were established, including a 4,738-mile nonstop flight from Honolulu to Chicago in 1948, and a flight that same year from NAS Patuxent River, Maryland, to Cleveland, Ohio, carrying a payload of 68,327 pounds. On 19 May 1949, the *Marshall Mars*, a JRM-1, carried 301 men of a carrier group plus a crew of seven from Alameda to San Diego, a flying boat passenger record.[7]

None were lost to the usual hazards of flying boat operations—waterborne accidents, night landings, submerged objects. In fifteen years of service the Mars boats logged more than 87,000 accident-free hours and carried over 200,000 passengers a total of nearly twelve million miles.[8]

These were impressive statistics—for flying boats. How successful a commercial airliner would the Mars have been? The costs of maintaining such a fleet would have bankrupted any airline. The accounting departments of the world's airlines had already closed their files on the flying boat.

Appendixes

Line Drawings

All line drawings are 1:300 scale. They are produced by J. P. Wood.

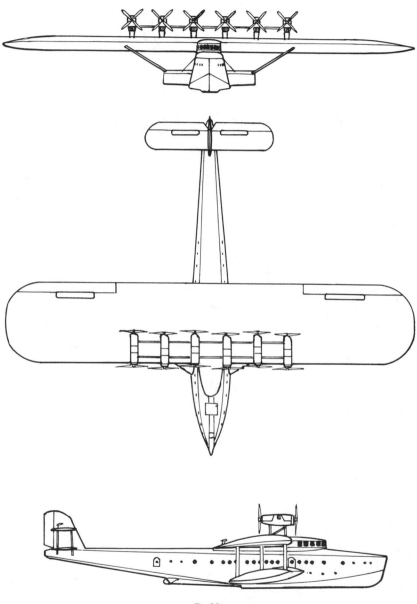

DoX

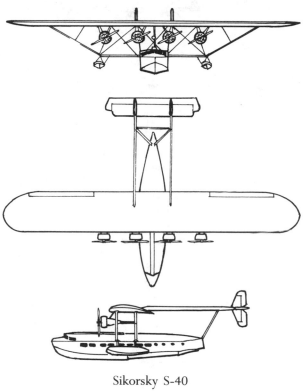

Sikorsky S-40

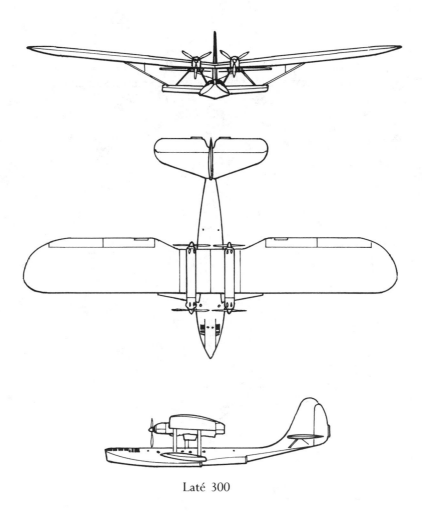

Laté 300

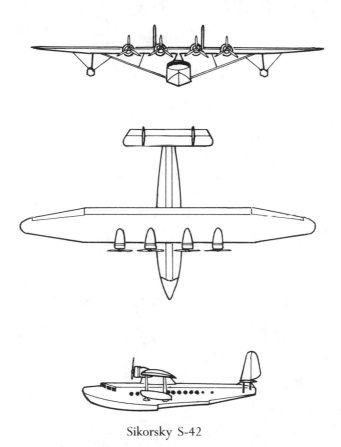

Sikorsky S-42

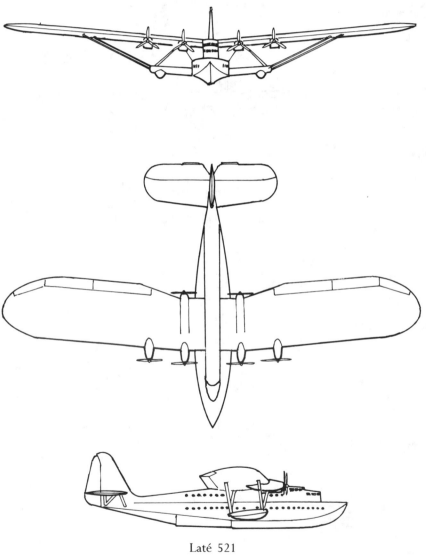

Laté 521

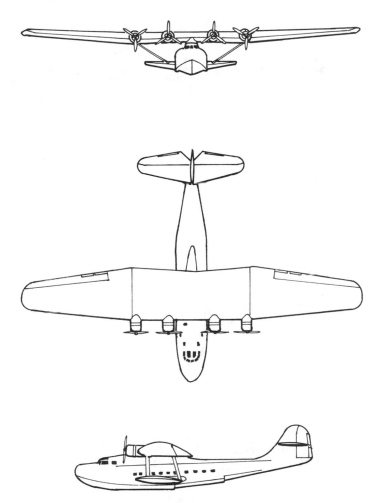

Martin M-130 *China Clipper*

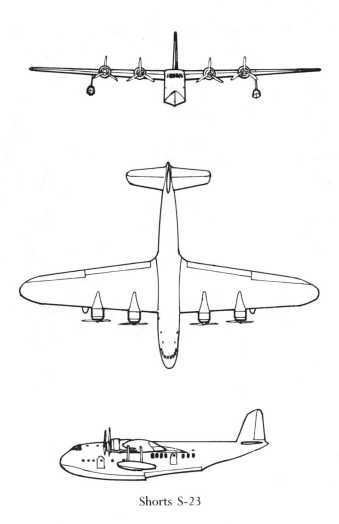

Shorts S-23

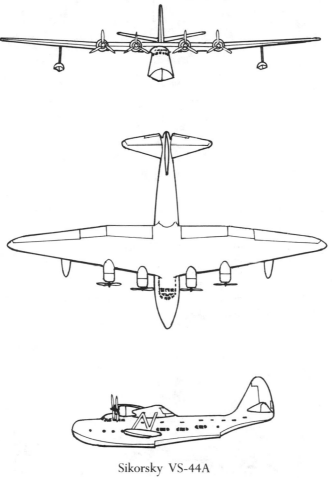

Sikorsky VS-44A

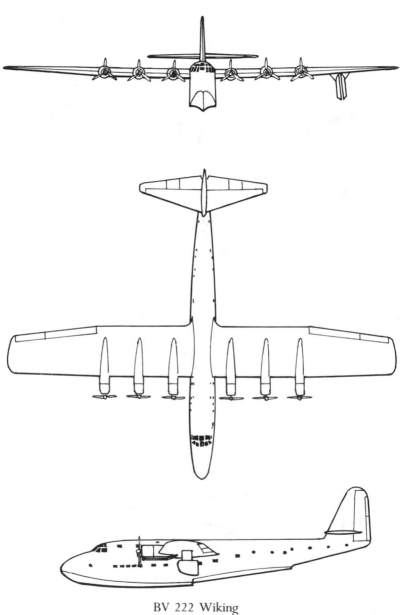

BV 222 Wiking

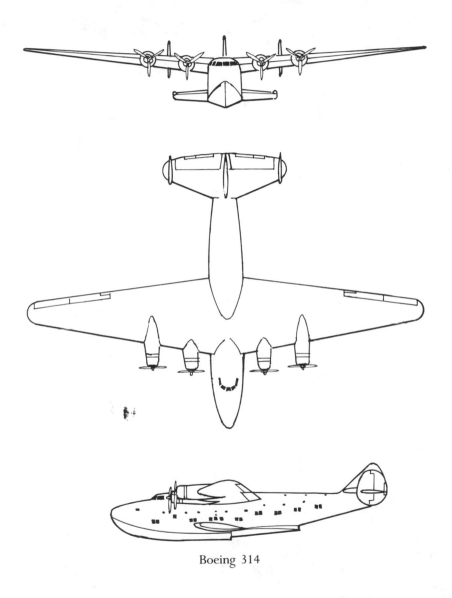

Boeing 314

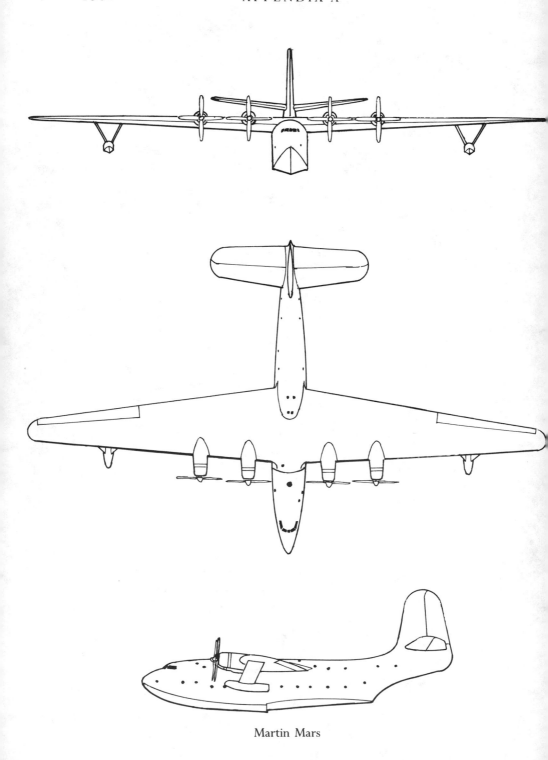

Martin Mars

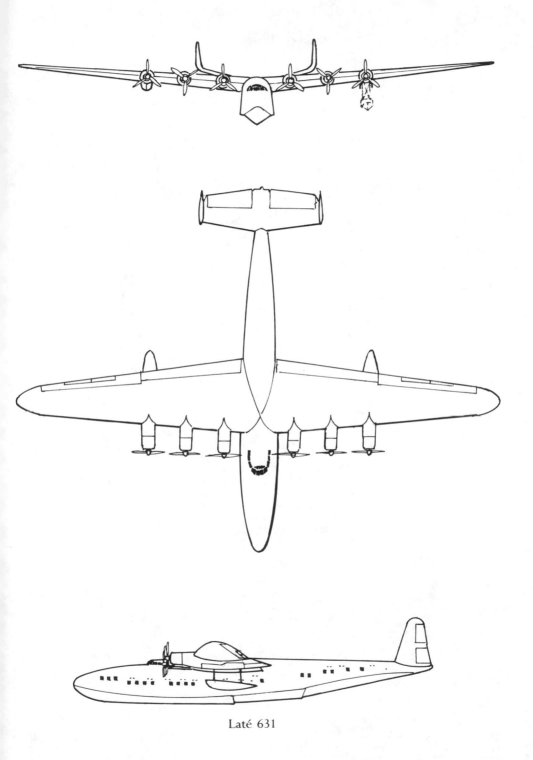

Laté 631

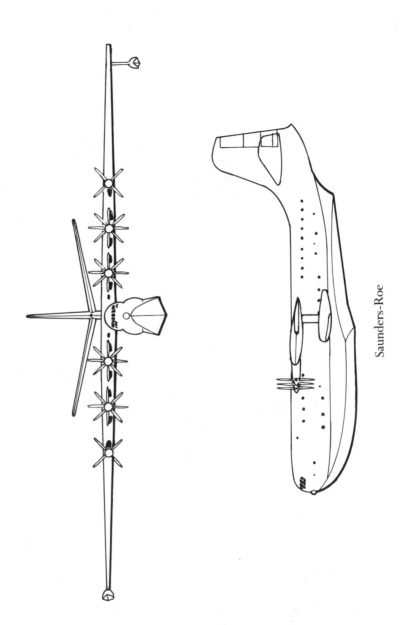

Saunders-Roe

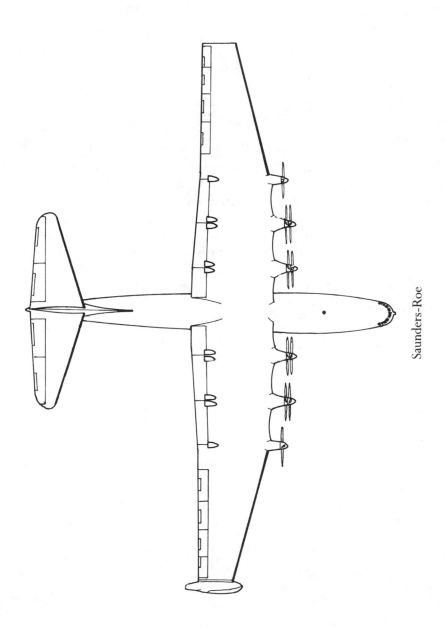

Saunders-Roe

Charts

Manufacturers' and government ministries' claims about commercial airliners' range, capacity, and speed require skeptical analysis. Advertised cruise speeds tend to reflect more optimism than reality. Seldom did actual long-range cruising airspeeds of the over-ocean boats match the advertised figures.

Statistics for range and passenger capacity can be misleading. The B-314, for example, boasted a passenger capacity of over seventy, but she could carry no more than twenty-four when fueled for an Atlantic crossing. The capacious interior of the Latécoère 631, designed for only forty-six passengers, was furnished with lounges and sleeping quarters. With more spartan furnishings, she could have accommodated eighty travelers. Though the Do X was designed with a capacity for over a hundred passengers, the big German boat never saw commercial service.

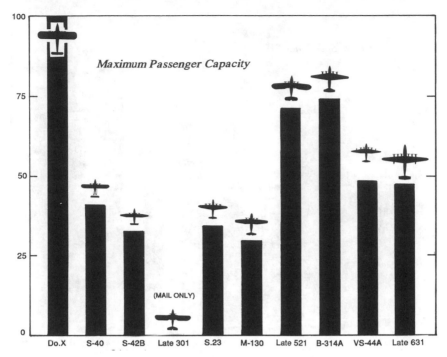

Chart A. Maximum Passenger Capacity.

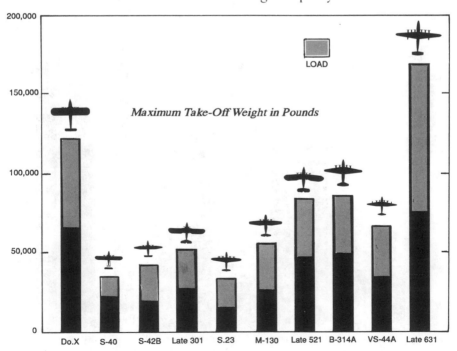

Chart B. Maximum Takeoff Weight in Pounds.

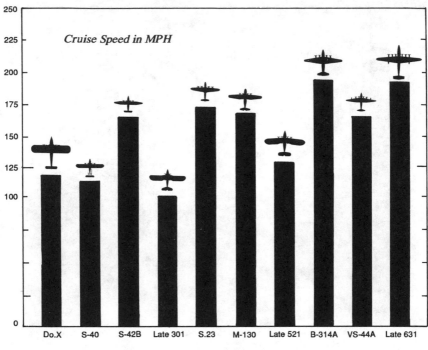

Chart C. Cruise Speed in MPH.

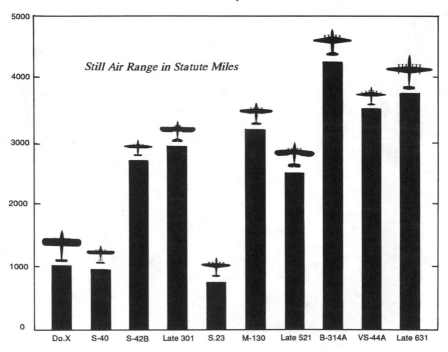

Chart D. Still-Air Range in Statute Miles.

Notes

CHAPTER ONE. MUSICK

1. Robert L. Gandt, "The China Clipper: Transpacific Pioneer," *Clipper*, November 1985.
2. The Musick profile was drawn, in part, from *Captain Lodi Speaking*, 190–94, by Marius Lodeesen, and from recollections to the author by Lodeesen and Horace Brock.

CHAPTER TWO. CURTISS AND COMPANY

1. Scharff and Taylor, *Over Land and Sea*, 19.
2. Knott, *The American Flying Boat*, 3. The five charter members of the Aerial Experiment Association were Curtiss, Dr. Alexander Graham Bell, Lt. T. Selfridge (U.S. Army), F. W. Baldwin, and J. A. D. McCurdy.
3. A cloud has surrounded Curtiss's name because of the insinuation, without basis in fact, that he pirated the Wright brothers' inventions. Many biographies of the Wrights, including the film *The Winds of Kitty Hawk* (1978), depict the brothers as heroes wronged by Curtiss and his AEA colleagues.
4. *Aerial Experiment Association Bulletin*, 19 August 1909.
5. Wragg, *Boats of the Air*, 15–16.
6. Knott, *American Flying Boat*, 10. The idea of the "step" that enabled the flying boat to "unstick" has been variously attributed to both Holden Richardson and Glenn Curtiss. Curtiss, in any case, patented the device in 1915.
7. Wragg, *Boats of the Air*, 35–36.
8. Scharff and Taylor, *Over Land and Sea*, 239.
9. Wragg, *Boats of the Air*, 47. The first downing of an enemy aircraft by a U.S.-built airplane occurred *before* the United States' entry into the war.

CHAPTER THREE. EXTENDED RANGE

1. Wragg, *Boats of the Air*, 33.
2. Beaty, *The Water Jump*, 9.
3. Knott, *American Flying Boat*, 56–57.

CHAPTER FOUR. BOATS FOR HIRE

1. "Airlines Observe 75th Anniversary," *Air Line Pilot*, January 1989, 37.
2. Stroud, *Civil Marine Aircraft*, 9.
3. Stroud, *Civil Marine Aircraft*, 14. The five known Aeromarine Type 75s in airline use were named *Columbus, Santa Maria, Pinta, Gov. Cordeux,* and *Ponce de Leon.*
4. Davies, *History of the World's Airlines*, 43.
5. The Aeromarine advertising excerpts are from brochures of Aeromarine West Indies Airways and Aeromarine Airways, Inc., preserved by Don Thomas in *Nostalgia PanAmericana* (Dunedin, Florida: 1987).
6. Jablonski, *Sea Wings*, 17.
7. Stroud, *European Transport Aircraft Since 1910*, 151.
8. Angelucci, *World Encyclopedia of Civil Aircraft*, 112–13.

CHAPTER FIVE. TRIPPE

1. Bender and Altschul, *The Chosen Instrument*, 131.
2. Ibid., 141. Trippe's unsigned piece about the NC boats was his first contribution to the *Graphic*. In the next month he was elected to the editorial board of the magazine and the following year became the editor in chief.
3. Daley, *An American Saga*, 9–10.
4. Bender and Altschul, *Chosen Instrument*, 69.
5. Ibid., 77. For the rest of his life, Trippe would look back with bitterness on the affair at Colonial. Had it gone his way, he always believed, he would have presided over the country's most powerful domestic airway system.
6. Ibid., 83. The initial investors in ACA included several former Colonial shareholders as well as various relatives and flying chums of Trippe, Whitney, and Hambleton.
7. In Pan American lore the story of the first Key West–Havana flight, including the amount of Caldwell's payment, has several versions, most of them apocryphal. Cy Caldwell, who was never on Pan Am's pilot roster, nonetheless entered company history as the man who "saved" the airline.

CHAPTER SIX. NYRBA

1. Wagner, *Reuben Fleet*, 121.
2. O'Neill, *Dream of Eagles*, 127, 131. In his book about NYRBA, O'Neill

refers to Moffett as "Admiral Bill Moffett" and cites Moffett's willingness to bend navy rules in favor of O'Neill's airline venture.

3. Ibid., 126–27. Of Moffett's roster of twenty-six navy flying boat pilots, only three were officers and the others were chief petty officers.

4. Ibid., 143–77.

5. Jablonski, Edward, *Sea Wings*, 35. Holden Richardson, veteran of the Nancy boat days and present at the conception of nearly every navy flying boat design initiative, had come to be regarded in the Bureau of Aeronautics as "elder statesman" in all matters of flying boat construction.

6. Wagner, *Reuben Fleet*, 117. While the Martin company produced their versions of the Consolidated Admiral, Consolidated's engineers, led by "Mac" Laddon, were working on a follow-up, advanced design, the XP2Y-1. On 26 May 1931 Consolidated received the navy's go-ahead to produce a prototype, and after that they were never again, as Reuben Fleet said, "sucking hind teat" on the flying boat business.

7. Jablonski, *Sea Wings*, 35.

8. Ralph O'Neill never forgot the christening incident, nor did he forgive Juan Trippe. In 1973 he wrote in *Dream of Eagles*, 203, "My stomach felt heavy as lead. I had witnessed an unbelievable masquerade that would remain engraved in my memory for the rest of my life."

9. Wragg, David, *Boats of the Air*, 117.

10. O'Neill, *Dream of Eagles*, 306. The "shameless bureaucrat" O'Neill excoriated in his speech to the NYRBA board of directors was Postmaster General Walter Brown. Brown, O'Neill believed, had colluded with Juan Trippe to force a sellout of NYRBA to Pan Am.

11. Wagner, *Reuben Fleet*, 129.

CHAPTER SEVEN. SIKORSKY

1. Sikorsky, Igor, *The Story of the Winged-S*, 90–91.

2. Ibid., 51.

3. Ibid., 1–3.

4. Ibid., 157.

5. Ibid., 169–78.

6. In an interview with Robert Daley (*An American Saga,* 93), Trippe recalled that Sikorsky pulled the airplane up into an overhead maneuver. "He looped me," Trippe said. It was the only time the startled Trippe had ever looped in an airplane.

7. Sikorsky, *Winged-S*, 185.

CHAPTER EIGHT. TEUTONIC AMBITIONS

1. Stroud, *Civil Marine Aircraft*, 31–32. The Gs I was en route to a planned demonstration tour of the Netherlands and Sweden when it caught the

attention of the Allied Control Commission. Before it reached Stockholm, it was ordered destroyed and sunk off Kiel. A larger derivative, the Gs II, was designed by Dornier but never completed.

2. Casey and Batchelor, *Seaplanes and Flying Boats*, 78. Count Locatelli's transatlantic attempt of 1924 ended short of his destination. The Wal, despite an open-sea ditching, remained seaworthy, and Locatelli was rescued by the support ships of the U.S. Army's round-the-world flight of Douglas World Cruiser floatplanes.

3. Angelucci, *Encyclopedia of Civil Aircraft*, 114.

4. Stroud, *Civil Marine Aircraft*, 34.

5. Wragg, *Boats of the Air*, 124–25.

6. Stroud, *Civil Marine Aircraft*, 39. A fourth Romar was built for the French Navy but was never completed due to an airframe corrosion problem.

CHAPTER NINE. THE LATINS

1. Bender and Altschul, *Chosen Instrument*, 140.

2. Rowe, *Under My Wing*, 118. Basil Rowe seemed to accept the takeover of his airline by Pan Am without particular bitterness. "Perhaps after all it was just as well," he wrote. "Aviation, to develop into the vast industry that it is today, needed two kinds of men: businessmen to guide and develop the growth of the industry and the men who engineered, maintained, designed and flew the planes. I belonged to the latter; I was a pilot." Rowe accepted a position as pilot with Pan Am and went on to become a senior, highly respected captain with that airline.

3. (PAWA) Though the Pan Am and Grace partnership would always be an uneasy alliance marked by boardroom fighting and clashes of powerful personalities, Panagra would last for nearly forty years. The company was sold to Braniff in 1968.

4. Turner, *Pictorial History of Pan American World Airways*, 34.

5. Bender and Altschul, *Chosen Instrument*, 156.

6. Brock, *Flying the Oceans*, 56.

7. Saint-Exupéry, *Airman's Odyssey (Night Flight)*, 234.

8. Bender and Altschul, *Chosen Instrument*, 160. In an interview with the authors, 8 June 1978, Leuteritz recalled how Trippe lured him away from his secure job at RCA. At the time Pan Am had only two airplanes and the mail route between Key West and Havana. But Trippe declared with confidence, "We'll be flying around the world." Leuteritz believed him.

9. Jablonski, *Sea Wings*, 44. Soon after the historic flight with Lindbergh, the much-respected John Hambleton lost his life in the crash of a private airplane.

10. Ibid., 46.

CHAPTER TEN. THE FLYING FOREST

1. Delear, *Igor Sikorsky*, 143. Lindbergh recalled how Sikorsky sold him on the S-40. "He argued that we had to have a larger plane quickly and that time did not permit a radical departure from the previous design. He presented his case tactfully and quietly, yet forcefully, and eventually I came to see that he was right. Priester was even quicker to see that Igor was correct, that this approach would give us a plane of proven design in a short time and that a cleaner, faster plane would have to come later as a second step."

2. Ibid., 143. Lindbergh told Frank Delear that "the S-38 was a maintenance nightmare. As far as we could tell, those Russian engineers were not much interested in maintenance problems."

3. The S-40's landing gear was "retractable" only in the sense of a water landing. Still exposed to the wind, it exacted a severe aerodynamic penalty. Eventually the gear and the railway car springs were removed from all three S-40s, and they became true flying boats.

4. Sikorsky, *Winged S.,* 190.

5. Delear, *Igor Sikorsky,* 144–45.

6. Daley, *American Saga*, 95.

7. Delear, *Igor Sikorsky,* 150.

8. Ibid., 153. Despite the readiness of both Lindbergh and Sikorsky to take the blame for the rough landing, the true cause seems to have been, quite simply, the darkness itself. Under the conditions, such a landing in a new flying boat was not at all bad.

9. Rowe, *Under My Wings*, 135.

CHAPTER ELEVEN. THE NEXT STEP

1. "I. Sikorsky's Talk to Junior Engineers," 24 October 1968, 13 (UTC).

2. Captain J. C. Kelly-Rogers, "Commercial Flying on the North Atlantic," *Aerospace*, The Royal Aeronautical Society, January 1976, 20. Though the *Graf Zeppelin*'s passenger capacity and regularity of schedule were impressive, the trip across the Atlantic took three and sometimes four days, a scarce improvement over the fast transatlantic steamers.

3. In an article, "The Superiority of the American Transoceanic Airliner 1932–1939," *American Aviation Historical Society Journal*, Summer 1984, Richard K. Smith praises the achievements of the S-42. He supports his case with statistical evidence comparing, among other things, the S-42B's ultimate wing loading (33.5 pounds/square foot) with that of contemporary aircraft such as the DC-2 (19.4), the Boeing 247 (15.1), and the Boeing P-26A fighter (19.5).

4. For his development of the variable-pitch propeller, Hamilton Standard's Frank Caldwell received the Collier Trophy, aviation's highest award, in 1934.

5. Ralph B. Lightfoot, "Sikorsky Flying Boats," *American Aviation Historical Society Journal*, Winter 1979.
6. Smith, "Superiority of the American Airliner," 86.
7. The S-42's record-gathering flight of 1 August 1934 has been documented by many sources, but is best described by Sikorsky himself in *Winged-S*, 205–9. On the day of the record attempt, shortly before the flight, Sikorsky received a letter from the president of the National Aeronautic Association urging him to attempt to establish world records. After the flight, Sikorsky was able to reply that "on August 1st we returned to the United States eight world records to be added to the two already obtained by the S-42. By so doing, the United States now holds first place in the tenure of world records—exclusive of light planes—holding seventeen to France's sixteen."
8. In 1932 the British Air Ministry had abandoned the development of a Vickers six-engine flying boat, which was intended for Imperial Airways' transatlantic service. Not until the appearance in 1936 of the Short S.23 did Imperial Airways have any airplane that even approached the capability of the S-42.

CHAPTER TWELVE. PACIFIC

1. In *North to the Orient*, Anne Morrow Lindbergh wrote of the journey she and her husband made in a Lockheed Sirius, surveying the northern route to Asia. Their findings contributed to Trippe's decision to take the mid-ocean route across the Pacific.
2. Ibid., 231.
3. Ibid., 233.
4. In three books written during his Pan American years, William Grooch chronicled his career and the rise of Pan American. Leaving the navy to join Ralph O'Neill's NYRBA, he then went to Pan Am where he participated in the China operation, then headed the expedition to Wake. His life was clouded by bizarre tragedy. While on assignment for Pan Am in China, his wife and two young sons leapt to their deaths from a Shanghai apartment building. After the Wake expedition, Grooch left Pan Am to found an airline of his own in Mexico. He was killed soon thereafter in an aircraft accident.
5. Daley, *American Saga*, 153. The official who opposed the Pacific flight was Dr. George Lewis. As chairman of the National Committee on Aeronautics, Lewis's thoughts, if made public, would have been devastating to Trippe's plans. Trippe, apparently, was able to persuade the well-intentioned scientist that Pan Am did indeed possess the technology to make the flight to Hawaii with a great margin of safety.
6. Because of a peculiar provision of the Nine-Power Treaty of 1922, Pan American's subsidiary, CNAC, had landing rights inside China, but Pan

Am's aircraft *not based* inside the country were still denied landing privileges there.

7. Turner, *Pictorial History of Pan American World Airways*, 56–57. The S-42B was capable of carrying a 7,000-pound maximum load over 900-mile stages. A similarly modified version, but with a 40,000-pound maximum gross weight, was designated the S-42A. All other S-42s were eventually modified to either S-42A or S-42B standards in 1936.
8. Daley, *American Saga*, 147.
9. Bender and Altschul, *Chosen Instrument*, 139.
10. The portrait of Captain R. O. D. Sullivan was drawn from correspondence and accounts given the author by veteran Pan Am flying boat captains Marius Lodeesen, Horace Brock, and Al Terweleger.
11. Daley, *American Saga*, 163–64.

CHAPTER THIRTEEN. WINGS OF EMPIRE

1. Richard K. Smith, "The Superiority of the American Airliner 1932–1939," *American Aviation Historical Society Journal*, Summer 1984, 88. The 1934 MacRobertson race sent a tremor through London. The *Times* commented, "Thus it has been held by implication that if the United States can produce a Douglas airliner and Sikorsky flying boat then Great Britain should be able to produce something better than the airliners and seaplanes which cruise at speeds between 105 and 125 miles an hour."
2. Stroud, *Civil Marine Aircraft*, 66.
3. Norris, Geoffrey, *Shorts*, 3–7.
4. Smith, "Superiority of the American Airliner," 94.
5. Davies, *History of the World's Airlines*, 182–86.

CHAPTER FOURTEEN. THE FRENCH FLAIR

1. Stroud, *European Transport Aircraft Since 1910*, 142.
2. Vie-Klaze, Marie-Paul, *Les grands Latécoère sur l'Atlantique*, 87.
3. Davies, *The World's Airlines*, 93. Aéropostale had run into severe financial difficulties, and its management became involved in a much-publicized scandal.
4. Saint-Exupéry, *Wind, Sand and Stars*, 33.
5. Stroud, *European Transport Aircraft*, 57–58.
6. Ibid., 160–62.
7. Stroud, *Civil Marine Aircraft*, 84.
8. Stroud, *European Transport Aircraft*, 146.
9. Ibid., 146.
10. Ibid., 149–50.

CHAPTER FIFTEEN. MARTIN

1. *Who's Who in America*, Vol. 24, 1946–1947.
2. Bender and Altschul, *Chosen Instrument*, 244.
3. *Time*, 5 June 1935. "Builder Martin's engineering staff is always of the best, but he is not a good mixer, has had numerous bitter quarrels with business associates and employees. One such is his onetime chief engineer, Donald Douglas, now a famed airplane builder of bombers, amphibians, transports, in his own right."
4. Jablonski, *Sea Wings*, 115. Martin's optimism about the future of the flying boat was told to his friend and one-time employee, James "Dutch" Kindleberger, who later joined North American Aviation.
5. Ibid., 114–15. The Martin Company was in financial trouble because of large sums spent on the development of a bomber for the army. No return had yet been realized on this investment. The project would eventually be accepted and become the B-10, an army staple that would win for Martin the Collier Trophy in 1933.
6. Daley, *American Saga*, 165–66.

CHAPTER SIXTEEN. CHINA CLIPPER

1. *Time*, 2 December 1935, profiled Musick in its cover story. Additional information comes from *Chosen Instrument* by Bender and Altschul, and *From Crate to Clipper* by Grooch.
2. Pan American Archives. The transcript of the *China Clipper* inaugural ceremony was printed by Pan American's publicity department and distributed as a handout.
3. In *Pan American Air Ways*, November–December 1935, Pacific Supplement No. 2, and in *Flight Ops*, a Pan Am company publication, No. 6, Feb. 1975, Vic Wright remembered, "It had been our intention to fly over the bridge, but Musick quickly saw that with the engine cowl flaps open he wouldn't be able to get up enough speed to clear the wires, so he nosed the Clipper down at the last moment and went under the bridge cables, threading his way through the dangling construction wire. We all ducked and held our breath until we were in the clear. I think the little planes must have been as surprised as we were, but they all followed us right through."
4. Captains Horace Brock and Marius Lodeesen described the difficulties and techniques of navigation aboard the *China Clipper*. The problem was compounded by the flying boat's tendency to wallow, even in smooth air. According to Brock, the *China Clipper* "was unstable in all three axes."
5. "Aim off" was described by Australian navigator Harold Gatty, who flew round the world with Wiley Post in 1931.

CHAPTER SEVENTEEN. ORIENT EXPRESS

1. Marius Lodeesen, early flying boat pilot, was recruited as "technical advisor" for the *China Clipper* film. "Of that picture," he recalled, "the less said, the better." Bogart remembered the movie as a mistake for him. "But at least I did not have to go on location," he told Lodeesen. "You fellows did that for me."
2. Bender and Altschul, *Chosen Instrument*, 254–56.
3. Wake's rats vanished during the WW II Japanese occupation. Presumably, the Japanese garrison, isolated from resupply ships for nearly four years, hunted them for food until they became extinct.
4. *Pan Am Clipper*, November 1985, Vol. 25, No. 11., 40.

CHAPTER EIGHTEEN. LOSSES

1. Wright, Victor, *Early Bird*. In his unpublished manuscript, retired Pan Am pilot Vic Wright refers to the "flying gas tank" (*Samoan Clipper*) and Musick's string of curse words when he first saw Pago Pago harbor.
2. Bender and Altschul, *Chosen Instrument*, 272.
3. Flight engineer Wright (later a Pan Am captain) who had been with Musick on the first survey flight and had experienced the fuel mist inside the cabin, theorized that the explosion came from vapor being ignited *inside* the wing by the actuation of the flap motor. The debris from the crash was found in a proximity to Pago Pago where Musick would probably have begun flap extension prior to his approach.
4. The Terletsky profile, including Terletsky's fear of flying, is a composite of descriptions by captains Horace Brock, Marius Lodeesen, Robert Ford, and others.
5. Noonan had been dismissed by Pan American because of his chronic drinking problem.
6. Bender and Altschul, *Chosen Instrument*, 269. The intelligence-gathering theory is supported, at least in part, by evidence of official government sponsorship. The construction of the runway at Howland Island for Earhart's flight was authorized directly by President Roosevelt, who drew funds from the WPA (Works Progress Administration) to finance the project.
7. Horace Brock, then a junior flight officer, was assigned as navigator aboard the M-130 when its fuel line became plugged by a cork. (*Flying the Oceans*, Brock). Though the FBI investigated the incident, there was no evidence of sabotage.
8. The sabotage theory continued to attract believers. *China Clipper*, by Ronald Jackson (New York: Everest House, 1980) presented circumstantial evidence to support the idea that two Japanese hijackers stowed away on the *Hawaii Clipper* during its transit of Guam, then forcibly diverted the flying boat to

a Japanese base. However, every veteran Pan Am pilot interviewed in the course of writing this book believed that Leo Terletsky inadvertently flew the *Hawaii Clipper* into a violent Pacific storm.

CHAPTER NINETEEN. THE RIGHT VEHICLE

1. Richard K. Smith, "The Superiority of the American Airliner 1932–1939," *The American Aviation Historical Society Journal,* Summer 1984, 90–91.
2. *Imperial Airways Gazette*, August 1937, No. 8, Vol.9.
3. Smith, JAAHS, Summer 1984, 90.
4. Norris, *Shorts.* The composite scheme reappeared a few years later during WW II when fighter cover was needed to protect Allied convoys across the Atlantic. A composite of a B-24 Liberator bomber mated to a Hurricane fighter was being developed at Hawker, but the project was dropped when other means of protection became available.
5. Lindbergh, *Autobiography of Values*, 116.
6. Beaty, *The Water Jump*, 136–37.
7. Hannah, *Shorts*, 37.

CHAPTER TWENTY. BOATS OF THE REICH

1. Casey and Batchelor, *Seaplanes and Flying Boats*, 108.
2. Beaty, *Water Jump*, 99–100. Following Aéropostale's bankruptcy and non-use of the Azores facility, the Portuguese government had granted landing authority to both Pan American and Imperial Airways. By way of the many bilateral discussions regarding North Atlantic facilities, Germany, too, was permitted to stage their catapult ships from the Azores.
3. Stroud, *Civil Marine Aircraft*, 36–37.
4. Beaty, *Water Jump*, 118–20.
5. Stroud, *European Transport Aircraft*, 258–59.

CHAPTER TWENTY-ONE. AMERICAN EXPORT AIRLINES

1. "Trans-Atlantic Air Line," *Intavia World*, September 1945, No. 6, Vol. 5.
2. Peter Berry, "The Excalibur," *American Aviation Historical Society Journal* (Winter 1975), 236–38.
3. Delear, *Igor Sikorsky*, 170–71. The problem of the unbreakable champagne bottle was solved by Jack Hospers, Vought-Sikorsky's service manager.
4. Blair, *Red Ball in the Sky*, 42. *Excalibur*'s fuel tanks still had ninety-five gallons remaining, enough for almost another hundred miles of flight.
5. Delear, *Igor Sikorsky*, 171.
6. The *Excalibur*'s pilot, Captain Joe Wilson, had chosen to ferry the aircraft from Botwood to a nearby military facility to obtain fuel. Darkness was near and a hurried, unprepared takeoff was made. Because the flap switch

was in a vulnerable spot in the cockpit, it is conjectured that the first officer, still scrambling to position himself, inadvertently tripped the electric flap switch with his knee, lowering the flaps to the full landing position. The nose-down pitch of the aircraft could not be overridden by the captain. (F. L. Wallace to author, 1 November 1989)

7. Juptner, *U. S. Civil Aircraft*, 185.
8. The dimensions of the VS-44A are from a brochure written by Harvey Lippincott, "Sikorsky VS-44A Flying Boat," contained in *Factsheet*, printed by United Technologies, Sikorsky Aircraft.
9. Davies, *History of the World's Airlines*, 326.

CHAPTER TWENTY-TWO. BOEING

1. Bender and Altschul, *Chosen Instrument*, 264.
2. Peter Bowers, "The Great Clippers," *Wings*, January–March 1974, 28.
3. Ibid., 32. The XB-15 had been designed to use the Allison V-3240 engines, then ultimately handicapped with the undersized Pratt and Whitney R-1830s. Pan American and Boeing were taking a gamble that the Wright R-2600 would provide the advertised performance for the 314.
4. Juptner, *U. S. Civil Aircraft*, 23. The 314's airfoil was NACA-23018 at the root and NACA-23010 at the tip.
5. Jablonski, *Sea Wings*, 179–80.
6. Juptner, *U. S. Civil Aircraft*, 23.
7. Bender and Altschul, *Chosen Instrument*, 291. The British Air Ministry's dismissal of Clause H came as the result of a blunt inquiry via the American embassy in London. Were the British ready to begin service to the U.S.? If not, would they object if Pan American went ahead? In a rare display of realism, the Air Ministry gave the go ahead.
8. Ibid., 293. Ironically, on the day of Trippe's transatlantic victory, Pan American's board of directors had deposed him as chief executive and appointed Sonny Whitney in his place. Trippe would not return to power until January 1940 after Whitney proved unequal to the job.
9. Ibid., 299.

CHAPTER TWENTY-THREE. WAR DAY

1. *New Horizons*, January 1942, the Pan American in- house newsletter, describes the adventures of all four clippers caught in the Pacific on Pearl Harbor day.
2. *New Horizons*, January 1942. Also left behind on Wake were the stewards at the Pan American hotel. These were Chamorros—natives of Guam. Another Pan Am employee, Waldo Raugust, had been working on another part of the island and missed the departure of the *Philippine Clipper*. Like

other survivors of Wake, he spent the next three-and-a-half years as a prisoner of the Japanese.

3. Ibid., 21.

4. Ibid. 22. The circumstances of the attack on the *Hong Kong Clipper* and Fred Ralph's refuge in an open sewer were described in correspondence from Ralph to the author, May 1977.

5. Ford to author 3 November 1989.

6. Ford to author 19 September 1989.

CHAPTER TWENTY-FOUR. IN SERVICE

1. Bender and Altschul, *Chosen Instrument*, 364–65.

2. In *Back Doors of the World* and *Captain Lodi Speaking*, Captains Masland and Lodeesen each related the incident with a supercilious army major in the Seychelles.

3. Stroud, *Civil Marine Aircraft*, 68.

4. Churchill, *The Grand Alliance*, 707–11. Kelly-Rogers was a renowned BOAC flying boat captain. During the flight aboard the *Berwick*, he made a favorable impression on Churchill, who thought he "seemed a man of high quality and experience."

5. Bender and Altschul, *Chosen Instrument*, 365.

6. "Tamara Reported Missing In Lisbon Clipper Crackup," *New York Times*, 24 February 1943.

7. Jane Froman's story was made into a popular movie, *With A Song In My Heart*, starring Susan Hayward.

8. M. D. Klaas, "Yankee Vs. Dixie," *Air Classics*, Vol. 23, No. 4, April 1987, 74. Rod Sullivan continued to deny any fault in the crash of the *Yankee Clipper*. His spirit broken, he died in 1955.

9. Jablonski, *Sea Wings*, 143–44. It was not believed that the *Philippine Clipper* could have been so far off course. A Mrs. Wallach, who lived in a farmhouse near Ukiah, California, heard the roar of aircraft engines that morning and saw a large plane flying north at low altitude. Worried, she tried to telephone, but the storm had washed out the lines. She then reported the incident in a letter to the district attorney. The information was ignored, however, while search planes combed the wrong area.

CHAPTER TWENTY-FIVE. REQUIEM FOR THE BIG BOATS

1. Jablonski, *Sea Wings*, 188–90.

2. To westerners, the fate of the *Russian Clipper* remained for many years an intriguing mystery. During a 1990 visit to the museum of the Aeroflot Far Eastern Regional Center at Khabarovsk, Mr. R. E. G. Davies, Curator of Air Transport at the Smithsonian National Air and Space Museum, obtained the information about the missing M-156. The account is based

in part from the translation of a report by A. P. Bajkov, an Aeroflot technician who had serviced the clipper.

3. Marijane Nelson, "Twilight for the Sikorsky Giants," *Air Classics* (March 1973), 51–58. The captain of the wrecked *Exeter* had been checked out by Charlie Blair for daylight operations only when the flying boat was ferried from Baltimore to Montevideo.

4. Delear, *Igor Sikorsky*, 172.

5. Rance, *Seaplanes and Flying Boats of the Solent*, 51–58.

6. Stroud, *Civil Marine Aircraft*, 73.

7. Rance, *Seaplanes and Flying Boats of the Solent*, 58.

8. "Another Laté 631 Flying Boat is Lost," *Aviation Week* (19 June 1950), 50–51.

9. Stroud, *European Transport Aircraft Since 1910*, 149–50.

10. Brock, *Flying the Oceans*, 232. Horace Brock was the Pan American chief pilot in Miami. "The type of accident was not unusual," he wrote, "and not understood then. It was always over water, either with boats or landplanes. . . . There were many such crashes until it came to be understood they were due to an optical illusion. In most cases, the experienced pilot who survived swore on a stack of bibles that he was at least 200 feet in the air when the plane was seen to hit the water in normal descending flight."

11. Lodeesen, *Captain Lodi Speaking*, 159.

12. Ibid., 158. The story of the uranium from the Congo was corroborated by Lodeesen's chief pilot, Horace Brock, to the author, 17 May 1980.

CHAPTER TWENTY-SIX. DINOSAURS AND MIGHT-HAVE-BEENS

1. Pan Am's chief engineer, Andre Priester, according to an anecdote by Captain James O'Neal, a former Pan Am chief pilot, arranged a conference call in 1949 with the engineering departments of Boeing, Lockheed, and Douglas. Before him on his desk was the stunning report of the maiden flight of the De Havilland Comet I in England. When he had all his audience on the line, he said into the phone, "The British are coming." Then he hung up.

2. Stroud, *Civil Marine Aircraft*, 81–84. The Princess's advertised passenger configuration was only 105, which, considering her great size, double decks, and various cabins, implied a standard of comfort to match the prewar days of the Empire boats and the Pan Am ocean clippers.

3. "Is Kaiser Crazy?" was the title of an article in *Air News* (October 1942). The article reached the same conclusion, however, as the War Production Board, who thought a man with Kaiser's record should be given the chance to make good his claim. Kaiser was authorized to proceed with the project.

4. Knott, *The American Flying Boat*, 193–98.

5. An experienced American Export Airlines flying boat captain, C. T. Robertson, was "loaned" to Martin to do much of the flight testing on the prototype Mars. (F. L. Wallace to author, 16 October 1989).

6. Knott, *The American Flying Boat*, 183.

7. Ibid., 186. The 1948 records were set by the newly delivered JRM-2, christened *Caroline Mars*.

8. Ibid., 187.

Sources

PRIMARY SOURCES:

Beyer, Captain Harry. Interview/correspondence July 1989: M-130, B-314.

Blackburn, E. F. Correspondence March–August 1989: aerial navigation, anecdotal material.

Blair, Maureen O'Hara. Interview June 1987: career of Captain Charles Blair.

Brock, Captain Horace. Interviews/correspondence January–December 1980: *China Clipper* and B-314.

Ford, Captain Robert. Telephone interviews/correspondence January–November 1989: B-314 and round-the-world wartime flight, 1941.

Lodeesen, Captain Marius. Interviews/correspondence January–September 1980: *China Clipper* and Pacific operations.

Martin Marietta Corp. Corporate archives: M-130, Glenn L. Martin.

Musée de l'Air. (Stephane Nicolaou), archival material, French flying boats and airmen.

National Air and Space Museum. (NASM) Archival material.

O'Neal, Captain J. D. Correspondence May–November 1989: B-314, anecdotal material.

Pan American World Airways. (PAWA) Corporate archives.

Ralph, Captain Fred. Correspondence Sept. 1977: *Hong Kong Clipper*, 8 December 1941.

Roberts, Captain Thomas. Correspondence March 1989: survey flights, B-314.

Sikorsky, Sergei. Sikorsky company archives/correspondence 1986–1989: Igor Sikorsky and Sikorsky flying boats.

United Technologies Corporation. Corporate archives.

Wallace, Captain F. L. Interviews/correspondence August–December 1989: VS-44A, American Export Airlines.

SECONDARY SOURCES:

Angelucci, Enzo. *World Encyclopedia of Civil Aircraft*. New York: Crown Publishers, 1981.

Beaty, David. *The Water Jump*. New York: Harper & Row, 1976.

Bender, Marylin and Selig Altschul. *The Chosen Instrument*. New York: Simon & Schuster, 1982.

Blair, Charles F. *Red Ball in the Sky*. New York: Random House, 1960.

Bowers, Peter M. *Curtiss Aircraft 1907–1947*. London: Putnam & Co. Ltd., 1979.

Brock, Horace. *Flying the Oceans*. Lunenberg, VT: Stinehour Press, 1978.

Casey, Louis, & John Batchelor. *Seaplanes and Flying Boats*. New York: Exeter Books, 1980.

Churchill, Winston S. *The Grand Alliance*. Boston: Houghton Mifflin, 1950.

Daley, Robert. *An American Saga*. New York: Random House, 1980.

Davies, R. E. G. *A History of the World's Airlines*. London: Oxford University Press, 1964.

Delear, Frank. *Igor Sikorsky*. New York: Dodd, Mead & Co., 1969.

Duval, G. R. *American Flying Boats*. Cornwall, U.K.: D. Bradford Barton Ltd., 1966.

Grooch, William S. *Skyway to Asia*. New York: Longmans, Green & Co., 1936.

Grooch, William S. *Winged Highway*. New York: Longmans, Green & Co., 1938.

Grooch, William S. *From Crate to Clipper*. New York: Longmans, Green & Co., 1939.

Gütschow, Fred. *Die deutschen Flugboote*. Stuttgart: Motorbuch Verlag, 1978.

Hannah, Donald. *Shorts*. Stamford, England: Key Publishing Ltd., 1983.

Jablonski, Edward. *Sea Wings*. Garden City, NY: Doubleday, 1972.

Jackson, Ronald. *China Clipper*. Saddle Brook, NJ: Everest House, 1980.

Josephson, Matthew. *The Empire of the Air: Juan Trippe and the Struggle for World Airways*. New York: Harcourt, Brace, 1943.

Juptner, Joseph P. *U.S. Civil Aircraft, Vol. 8*. Fallbrook, CA: Aero Publishers, 1980.

Kaucher, Dorothy. *Wings Over Wake*. San Francisco: John Howell, 1947.

King, H. F. *Aeromarine Origins*. London: Putnam, 1976.

Kipling, Rudyard. "With the Night Mail." *Actions and Reactions*. London: Macmillan, 1951 (1909).

Knott, Richard C. *The American Flying Boat*. Annapolis, MD: Naval Institute Press, 1979.

Lindbergh, Anne Morrow. *North to the Orient*. New York: Harcourt, Brace and World, 1935.

Lindbergh, Charles A. *Autobiography of Values*. New York: Harcourt Brace Jovanovich, 1976.

Lodeesen, Marius. *Captain Lodi Speaking*. Minneapolis: Argonaut Press, 1984.

Loening, Grover. *Our Wings Grow Faster*. Garden City, NY: Doubleday, 1935.

Loening, Grover. *Amphibian: The Story of the Loening Biplane*. Greenwich, CT: New York Graphic Society, 1973.

Masland, William M. *Through the Back Doors of the World in a Ship That Had Wings*. New York: Vantage, 1984.

Messimer, Dwight R. *No Margin for Error*. Annapolis, MD: Naval Institute Press, 1981.

Munsen, Kenneth. *Flying Boats and Seaplanes Since 1910*. New York: Macmillan, 1971.

Norris, Geoffrey. *Shorts*. London: Profile Publications Ltd.

O'Neill, Ralph. *A Dream of Eagles*. Boston: Houghton Mifflin Co., 1973.

Rance, Adrian B. *Sea Planes and Flying Boats of the Solent*. Southampton: Southampton University Industrial Group, 1981.

Rowe, Basil L. *Under My Wings*. New York: Bobbs, Merrill, 1956.

Saint-Exupéry, Antoine. *Airman's Odyssey (Wind, Sand and Stars, Night Flight, Flight to Arras)*. New York: Harcourt Brace Jovanovich, 1984.

Scharff, R. and W. S. Taylor. *Over Land and Sea: A Biography of Glenn Curtiss*. New York: McKay, 1968.

Sikorsky, Igor. *The Story of the Winged S*. New York: Dodd Mead and Co., 1938.

Smith, Richard K. *First Across!* Annapolis, MD: Naval Institute Press, 1973.

Stroud, John. *European Transport Aircraft Since 1910*. London: Putnam, 1966.

Stroud, John. *The World's Civil Marine Aircraft*. London: The Bodley Head, 1975.

Studer, C. *Sky Storming Yankee: The Life of Glenn Curtiss*. New York: Stackpole Sons, 1937.

Turner, P. St. John. *Pictorial History of Pan American World Airways*. London: Ian Allen, 1973.

Vie-Klaze, Marie-Paul. *Les Grands Latécoère sur l'Atlantique*. Paris: Editions Denoel, 1981.

Wagner, William. *Reuben Fleet and the Story of Consolidated Aircraft*. Fallbrook, CA: Aero Publishers, 1976.

Wragg, David. *Boats of the Air*. London: Robert Hale, 1984.

Index

Ad Astra Aero, 46
Adcock direction finder, 76, 104,
    145–46
Aerial Experiment Association, 4–5
Aeroflot, 161
Aeromarine aircraft, 19, 20, 24
Aeromarine Airways, 20, 21, 100
Aéropostale, 67, 86, 88, 124
Aim off (navigational technique), 104
Air France, 85, 87–89, 92–93, 122
Airmail, 35; FAM contracts, 27, 36–37,
    52–54, 98, 101
Alameda, 77, 79, 100, 103, 106, 157
Alcock, John, 16
Alexander, Wallace, 108
Allen, Edmond, 130, 138
American Export Airlines, 128–33, 161
American Overseas Airlines, 133
Amundsen, Roald, 48
Antilles Air Boats, 162
Anzani engines, 4
Apollo mission, 17
Argus engines, 41
Arnold, Henry H. "Hap", 26
Ash-621R engines, 161
Aspect ratio, 68, 87, 93
Avalon Air Transport, 162
Aviation Corporation of America, 26–27
Avocet, USS, 115

Bahama Airways, Ltd., 38
Barnett, T. E., 144–45
Bauer, Peter Paul von, 51

Beall, Wellwood, 135–36, 138
Bell, Alexander Graham, 4
Bell, W. H., 142
Bellinger, Patrick, 8, 12, 14
Benoist Airboat Co., 18
Bermuda Sky Queen, 160
Bibb, USS, 160
Blair, Captain Charles, 131, 162
Blériot aircraft, 87, 89
Blohm und Voss aircraft, 127
BMW engines, 47, 51, 125, 127
BOAC, 141, 153–54, 159, 163–64
Boeing aircraft, 135, 137; 314 develop-
    ment, 111–12, 120, 133, 135–41;
    World War II, 143, 148–57; 314
    final disposition, 159–60
Boeing Aircraft Co., 29
Bogart, Humphrey, 106
Bond, William Langhorne, 148
Bradley Air Museum, 162
Bristol engines, 122–23, 163, 168
Brock, Horace, 56
Brown, Arthur Whitten, 16
Brown, Walter (postmaster general),
    36–37
Burns, John Curtis, 156
Byrd, Richard E., 13

Caldwell, Cy,28, 52–53
Caldwell, Frank, 68
Canaday, Harry, 79, 113
Caproni Ca 60, 22
Carimare, SS, 125

209

Carter, Amon, 108
Chennault, Claire, 110
China Clipper, 3, 91, 96–107, 115, 147, 158, 169; crash, 165–66. *See also* Martin M-130
Churchill, Winston, 154–55, 160
Clause H, 113, 128, 139–40
Clippers, Pan American
  American Clipper (Boeing 314), 139, 152
  American Clipper (Sikorsky S-40), 40, 63, 65, 67
  Anzac Clipper, 141–42, 152
  Atlantic Clipper, 139, 152, 160
  California Clipper, 111, 139, 141, 152
  Capetown Clipper, 141, 152, 160
  Caribbean Clipper, 65
  China Clipper. *See China Clipper* and Martin M-130
  Clipper III, 119–20
  Dixie Clipper, 139, 152, 155–56
  Hawaii Clipper, 96, 107, 117–18
  Hong Kong Clipper, 109–10, 142, 147–48
  Honolulu Clipper, 139, 141, 152
  Pacific Clipper, 141–42, 148–52, 160
  Pan American Clipper, 77–80
  Philippine Clipper, 96, 107–8, 142, 144–47, 152–53, 157–58
  Russian Clipper, 161. *See also* Martin M-156
  Southern Clipper, 65
  Yankee Clipper, 139–41, 152, 156–57
CMA (Compañía Mexicana de Aviación), 53
CMASA (Construzioni Meccaniche Aeronautiche), 47
CNAC (China National Aviation Corp.), 38, 77, 107, 147–48
Collier Trophy, 7
Colonial Air Transport, 25–27, 43
Cone, Captain Howard, 155
Consolidated Aircaft Corp., 30, 32
Consolidated aircraft:
  Admiral, 32–33, 37
  B-24 Liberator, 152
  Catalina, 129
  Commodore, 30, 35, 52
  PB2Y, 130, 136

Cooke, John, 144–45
Courtney, Captain Frank, 48
Cram, Ralph, 135
Cramer, Leonard, 165
Cunningham, Admiral, 131
Cunningham, Commander W. S., 144
Curtiss, Glenn Hammond, 4–12, 23
Curtiss aircraft
  America, 8–9, 10; Small America (H-4) and Large America (H-12, H-16), 9, 10
  A-1 and A-2, 7
  F boats, 7, 10, 18
  Golden Flier, 6
  HS-2L, 19
  June Bug, 5
  Loon, 5
  NC boats, 12–17, 33
  Triad, 7
Curtiss engines, 5, 7–8, 24, 49

Dabry, Jean, 86
Daurat, Didier, 56
De Gaulle, General Charles, 155
Deutsche Luft Hansa, 47, 50–51, 86, 121, 124–27
Deutsche Luft Reederei, 21
Devereaux, Major James, 144
Dewoitine aircraft, 85
Dornier, Claudius, 46–51, 126
Dornier aircraft:
  Delphin, 47
  Do X, 45–46, 49–51, 137
  Do 18, 124–25
  Do 24, 125–26
  Do 26, 126
  Do 214, 127
  Gs I, 46–47
  Wal series, 47–48
Douglas, Donald, 95
Douglas aircraft, 82, 93, 133, 137, 148, 159
Doyle, Mike, 132
Drasin, Tamara, 156

Earhart, Amelia, 118
Eastern Air Transport, 25
Ebel, W. K. ("Ken"), 96

Egtvedt, Clair, 135
Electrolysis, problem of, 61, 97
Ellyson, Lieutenant T. G. ("Spuds"), 6
Ely, Eugene, 6
Elzay, Captain Robert, 157–58
Empire-class flying boats, 83–85. *See*
    Shorts
English, Rear Admiral R. R., 157–58

Fabre, Henri, 5–6
Fairchild, Sherman, 26, 53
Fairchild aircraft, 28, 52–53
Farley, James, 100–101
Felixstowe flying boats, 10, 19
Felixstowe Seaplane Experimental Estab-
    lishment, 10
Fiat engines, 50
Fleet, Reuben, 30, 32, 37
Flossenstummel, 46, 49, 135
Focke-Wulf Condor, 121
Fokker, Tony, 54
Fokker aircraft, 28, 57, 76
Fonck, René, 43
Ford, Captain Robert, 142–43, 148–51
Ford trimotor, 32
Franco, Major, 48
Froman, Jane, 156

Gatty, Harold, 114
Gimie, Léopold, 86
Glover, W. Irving, 34
Gluhareff, Michael and Serge, 69
Gnome engines, 90, 92
Gooney birds, 108–9
Gouge, Arthur, 82–85
Goyette, Cyril, 165
Grace, W. R., Corp., 53
Graf Zeppelin, 67, 124
Gray, Harold, 119, 141, 153
Grieve, Mackenzie, 16
Grooch, William, 35, 75
Guillaumet, Henri, 91, 164
Gulf Caribbean Airways, 27

Hallett, George, 8
Hambleton, John, 25, 26, 58
Hamilton, John, 142–47, 153
Hamilton Standard, 68–69, 78, 135–36

Hammondsport, N. Y., 5, 9
Handley Page Harrow, 122
Harmon Trophy, 105, 115
Hart, Joe, 153
Hauptmann, Bruno, 97
Hawker, Harry, 16
Hemingway, Ernest, 110
Hindenburg, 124
Hinton, Walter, 13
Hispano-Suiza engines, 24, 47, 87, 89–91
Hong Kong, 107, 109–10, 142, 147–48
Hoover, Mrs. Herbert, 33–34, 63
Hopkins, Harry, 155
Horta, 9
Howard, Roy, 108
Hoyt, Richard F., 27
Hughes, Howard, 167, 169
Hughes H-4, 168–69
Hurtsky, J. A., 146
Hydravion, 5–6

Imperial Airways, 72, 82–85, 113–14,
    123, 139–41
Ionia, SS, 14

Jannus, Tony, 18
Jarboe, Wilson, Jr., 79, 103
Johnson, Osa and Martin, 44
Junkers Jumo engines, 124, 126

Kaiser, Henry, 168–69
Kawanishi flying boat, 125
Kelly Act, 25
Kelly-Rogers, J. C., 154–55
Keuka, Lake, 5
Keys, Clement, 57
Key West, 26–28
Kido butai, 111, 146
King, George, 103
Kingman Reef, 112–14
KLM (Dutch airline), 85
Kurusu, Saburo, 110–11

Lame Duck, 15, 16
LaPorte, Captain Arthur, 140
LARA (Ligne Aérienne du Roi Albert), 21
Latécoère aircraft, 67:
    Laté 28, 86

Latécoère aircraft cont.
  Laté 520–21, 90–92
  Laté 631, 92–93, 164–65
Leuteritz, Hugo, 57, 76–77, 79, 145
Levy-Lepen flying boat, 21
Liberty engines, 13
Lindbergh, Charles, 26, 43, 57–66, 97,
  105, 140
Lindbergh, Anne Morrow, 58
Lioré et Olivier aircraft, 89–90
Litvinoff, Maxim, 110
Load-to-tare, 66, 85, 93, 97, 126, 133, 139
Locatelli, Count, 48
Lockheed aircraft, 159
Lodeesen, Captain Marius, 153, 165–66
Loening, Grover, 26, 167
London Daily Mail prize, 8, 11, 12, 16
Lorber, Charles, 64
Lurline, SS, 108, 158

McAdoo, Senator William, 107
MacArthur, General Douglas, 110
McCarty (radio officer), 117
Machado, Gerardo, 25–27
Manhattan Project, 166
Marine Corps, U.S., 100, 144, 146
Marston mat, 159
Martin, Clarence and Araminta, 94
Martin, Glenn L., 7, 33, 37, 70–71,
  94–96, 134–35, 160, 167, 169–70
Martin aircraft
  during World War II, 142, 144–47,
    152, 157–58
  M-130, 70–71, 73, 85, 96–98, 106–11,
    116, 120, 126, 134, 141, 160. See
    China Clipper
  M-156, 161
  Mars, 170
Masland, Captain William, 55
Master X, 160
Matson Steamship Line, 108
Maybach engines, 46
Mayo, Major R. H., 83, 120
Meigs, USS, 117
Mercury-Maia composite, 120–21, 139
Mermoz, Jean, 86, 88–89, 91
Midway, 1, 74–75, 80, 103–4, 108; dur-
  ing World War II, 144–46

Milburn, Lassiter, 96
Mitchell, Billy, 26, 95
Mitscher, Marc A., 12
Moffett, Admiral William, 30–33
Monsun, 48
Montgomery, John K., 26–27
Morgan, C. W. P., 16
Morton, Norma, 106
Mullahey, Bud, 80
Musick, Captain Edwin, 1–3, 21, 69

Naval Aircraft Factory, 19
Naval Air Transport Service, 131
Navigation, aerial, 11, 78, 102–4
Navy, French, 21, 87–88, 92
Navy, Royal, 9–10, 131, 163, 165
Navy, Russian, 42
Navy, U.S.: cooperation with Curtiss, 6–8;
  Consolidated aircraft, 30, 32–33, 37,
  130; during World War I, 10–11;
  during World War II, 131, 144, 146,
  152–53, 157, 159, 161; Martin air-
  craft, 33, 37, 95, 169–70; Moffett
  helps NYRBA, 30–33; NC boats,
  11–17; P2Y Pacific crossing, 73, 79;
  Pan American ocean bases, 73–75,
  77, 109; search for missing clippers,
  115, 117; Sikorsky aircraft, 30–31,
  44, 66, 130–31; Trippe, 23–24
Night Flight, 56
Noonan, Fred, 78–79, 102–4, 118
North Haven, SS, 75, 77, 108, 144
North Wind, SS, 113
NYRBA (New York, Rio & Buenos Aires
  Line), 29–38, 44, 52, 75

O'Brien, Pat, 106
O'Hara, Maureen, 162
O'Neill, Ralph, 29–38, 75
Ostrich theory, 39

Pago Pago, 112–16
Panagra (Pan American-Grace Airways,
  Inc.), 44, 54
Panair Do Brazil, 38
Pan American, 27, 40; takeovers, 30,
  34–38; aircraft orders, 44–45, 167;

Atlantic expansion, 139, 167. *See also*
    Trippe
Parish, Jocko, 150
Patterson, Paul, 108
Pennsylvania, USS, 6, 7
Pheil, A. C., 18
Philadelphia Rapid Transit, 54, 100
Piaggio Co., 47
Plesman, Dr. Albert, 54
Portal, Air Chief Marshal Sir Charles, 154
Porte, John Cyril, 8, 9
Port Washington, 91, 141
Post, Wiley, 105
Post Office, U.S. *See* airmail
Pound, Sir Dudley, 154
Powell, Ethel, 106
Pratt and Whitney engines, 44, 48, 61,
    66, 68, 77, 97, 102, 130, 132, 149
Priester, Andre, 54–57, 60–61, 67, 97,
    100, 138
Probert, William, 162

Qantas, 72, 114, 153–54, 163
Quezon (governor of Philippines), 105

Rachmaninoff, Sergei, 43
Ralph, Captain Fred, 142, 147–48
Rand, James, 30–31
Raynham, Freddie, 16
Read, Albert C., 13, 15
Richardson, Holden, 7, 13, 33
Rickenbacker, Eddie, 27
Rihl, George, 53
Robertson, Ben, Jr., 156
Rockaway Beach, N. Y., 12
Rockefeller, William A., 25
Rohrbach, Adolf, 51
Rohrbach aircraft, 50–51
Rolls-Royce engines, 47
Roosevelt, Eleanor, 139
Roosevelt, Franklin D., 100, 105, 110
Roth, William, 108
Rothe, Swede, 150
Rowe, Basil, 52, 63–65
Russian Clipper. See Martin M-156

Saint-Exupéry, Antoine de, 56, 88
St. Petersburg-Tampa Airboat Line, 18, 21

Saunders-Rowe Princess, 167–68
SCADTA (Sociedad Colombo-Alemana de
    Transportes Aéreos), 26, 51–52
Schildhauer, C. H. "Dutch", 73
Schwabenland, 48, 125
Sergievsky, Boris, 62, 69
Short, Oswald, 83, 85
Short's flying boats, 82, 85, 119–23, 126;
    during World War II, 153–54; final
    disposition, 163–64
Siemens engines, 49
Sikorsky, Igor, 30, 39–45, 60–65, 67–69,
    135, 167
Sikorsky aircraft
    Grand, 39, 40–41
    Ilia Mourmetz, 41–42
    S-1 through S-6, 41
    S-29A, 43
    S-34, 43
    S-35, 43
    S-36, 44
    S-38, 30–31, 44, 52, 58–59, 60
    S-40, 40, 60–67
    S-42, 67–71, 77, 85, 112–13, 116,
        119–20, 126. *See also Hong Kong
        Clipper*
    S-44, 129–33, 161–62
SNETA, 21
Société France Hydro, 165
Spaatz, Carl, 26
Sperry, Lawrence, 9
Sperry autopilot, 103, 165
Standardization, 55
Stone, Lieutenant Elmer, 13
Sullivan, R. O. D., 79–81, 103, 141, 156–
    57
Swanson, Claude, 74

Taylor, Rear Admiral David W., 11, 12
TEAL, 153, 163–64
Terletsky, Leo, 116–18
Tilton, Captain John, 108
Towers, John, 8, 12–15
Treasure Island, 157
Trepassey Bay, Newfoundland, 13
Trippe, Elizabeth, 58, 108
Trippe, Juan, 2, 22, 124, 129; AEA fight,
    128–29; aircraft orders, 45, 60–61,

Trippe, Juan *cont.*
  96–98, 169; Atlantic, 139–41; early
  career, 23–28; Latin America, 52–
  59; NYRBA takeover, 34, 37; Pacific,
  72–74, 106–8, 113, 162; World
  War II, 143. *See also* Pan American
Turner, H. Lanier, 142–43
TWA, 57

U-boats, 11, 168
United Aircraft Corp., later United Tech-
  nologies Corp., 129–30
United Nations, 160
Uppercu, Inglis M., 20

Vanderbilt, William H., 26
Van Dusen, C. A., 96
Van Dusen, William, 101, 103
Vought-Sikorsky. *See* Sikorsky aircraft

Wake, William, 73

Wake Island, 1, 73, 75, 80–81, 108–9,
  141; during World War II, 142,
  144–47, 158
Walker, "Tex", 117
Wallace, Mrs. Henry, 130
Wanamaker, Rod, 8, 11
Warner, Edward, 33
Wead, Frank, 106
Westfalen, 48, 125
West Indian Aerial Express, 52–53
Whitney, Cornelius "Sonny", 25–26, 108
Wilcockson, A. S., 119
Wing loading, 68, 97, 126, 132, 136–37
Woods, Clarence, 35
Wright, Vic, 79, 113
Wright, Wilbur and Orville, 4, 23
Wright engines, 93, 95, 135–36, 164, 170

Yale Aero Club, 24, 25
Yamamoto, Admiral Isoroku, 111

Zeppelin, 10, 46

ABOUT THE AUTHOR

Robert Gandt is a former naval officer and aviator. An international airline captain, airshow pilot, and aviation journalist, he has written extensively on military and aeronautical subjects. His 1982 book, *Season of Storms*, documents the World War II battle for Hong Kong. He lives in Crescent City, Florida.

THE NAVAL INSTITUTE PRESS is the book-publishing arm of the U.S. Naval Institute, a private, nonprofit, membership society for sea service professionals and others who share an interest in naval and maritime affairs. Established in 1873 at the U.S. Naval Academy in Annapolis, Maryland, where its offices remain today, the Naval Institute has members worldwide.

Members of the Naval Institute support the education programs of the society and receive the influential monthly magazine *Proceedings* and discounts on fine nautical prints and on ship and aircraft photos. They also have access to the transcripts of the Institute's Oral History Program and get discounted admission to any of the Institute-sponsored seminars offered around the country.

The Naval Institute also publishes *Naval History* magazine. This colorful bimonthly is filled with entertaining and thought-provoking articles, first-person reminiscences, and dramatic art and photography. Members receive a discount on *Naval History* subscriptions.

The Naval Institute's book-publishing program, begun in 1898 with basic guides to naval practices, has broadened its scope in recent years to include books of more general interest. Now the Naval Institute Press publishes about 100 titles each year, ranging from how-to books on boating and navigation to battle histories, biographies, ship and aircraft guides, and novels. Institute members receive discounts of 20 to 50 percent on the Press's nearly 600 books in print.

Full-time students are eligible for special half-price membership rates. Life memberships are also available.

For a free catalog describing Naval Institute Press books currently available, and for further information about subscribing to *Naval History* magazine or about joining the U.S. Naval Institute, please write to:

Membership Department
U.S. NAVAL INSTITUTE
291 Wood Road
Annapolis, MD 21402-5035
Telephone: (800) 233-8764
Fax: (410) 269-7940
Web address: www.usni.org